PROVENCE

FOOD, WINE, CULTURE
AND LANDSCAPE

PROVENCE

FOOD, WINE, CULTURE AND LANDSCAPE

Lars Boesgaard

CLEARVIEW

CONTENTS

PART 3: PROVENÇAL WINES AND VINEYARDS 351

PREFACE

My love of Provence goes right back to a summer in my child-hood, when my parents rented a wonderful old stone cottage in the mountains behind Nice with a fabulous view of the Mediterranean. My brothers and I would play beneath the palm trees in the huge garden. We ate figs and plums, caught scorpions, fireflies and pray-ing mantises, and we were given the freedom to roam the narrow, pungent streets of the nearby village, an unheard of liberty for three small boys.

Years later, I managed to buy a house of my own in Provence. It clings to the side of the mountains to the south of a small village with wide views of olive groves and huge, dark-green pine forests. Our terrace is so high up that we can actually watch the swallows' elegant and acrobatic flight from above. In the evenings, we can just catch a glimpse of the lights twinkling in the villages further down towards the coast. Wind, rustling through the trees down in the valley, almost convinces you that there is still water in the dried out riverbed. You can stare for hours at the starry night sky or watch the geckos as they sprint up and down the steep stone walls, hunting for insects under the street lamps' yellow glow.

The first time we saw the house, the real estate agent gave us a worried look as he asked, 'Why on earth do you want a place like this? There's nothing and nobody here.' Our point exactly – and for the record, the real estate agent could not have been more wrong. Much goes on in these small villages.

My love affair with Provence increases day by day. We have, finally, finished renovating our old, ramshackle house and we've started up our own olive production. And yet, I'm still discovering new places where I would love to settle down.

The Provençal countryside provides one with a very special sense of inspiration and well-being. Its appeal lies in the combination of culture and nature. You are close to nature but never far from where a superb glass of local wine and excellent Provençal food can be enjoyed.

The first part of this book focuses on what and how to eat in Provence: a modest, sun-drenched cuisine based on exquisite yet simple produce from the surrounding sea and mountains. I've collected a number of classic recipes; my favourites, easy to source and prepare whether or not you are actually in Provence. The recipes are, first and foremost, meant to inspire and remind us of how easy it is to produce our own delicious Provençal dishes. *Faites simple*, 'keep it simple', as they say there.

I was introduced to genuine Provençal cuisine one summer when I worked as a handyman for a Parisian family, who had a house right on the coast in Ramatuelle. When we got up in the mornings, the housekeeper, Marie-Thérèse, was already busy in the kitchen. Pots were on the boil and a divine smell would spread through the house and onto the terrace beneath the bougainvillea. She was a superlative cook, who understood that the ingredients had to speak for themselves. And she carefully coached me before sending me off to the markets in Saint-Tropez and Ramatuelle, so I knew exactly which mongers had the best fish and which stalls had the best vegetables. I'll never forget my surprise when I first tasted her fish soup made from the small, ugly fish her husband caught off the rocks at night (it was years before I realised that he was in fact catching one of the most desirable fish along the coastline, *la rascasse*). Or the roughly minced olive tapenade, which she always served as an appetiser. It was a tour de force.

The middle part of the book examines topics particular to Provence, which would enhance anyone's knowledge of the region if they found themselves travelling though it. The last part of the book focuses on wine producing areas. My intention was always to present a basic introduction to the different areas, as a sort of preparation for the traveller, enabling him or her to explore this wonderful part of Provence in greater depth. Following each presentation, there is a list of the best vineyards in that area. Use it as a guideline and then make up your own mind. I have undoubtedly not managed to cover them all.

I hope this book will prove a useful introduction to rural Provence, which is only a short distance from the celebrity hurly-burly of the fashionable Riviera. And I hope you will enjoy the read, whether at home in your own kitchen or on your journey through Provence.

Lars Boesgaard

COMPOSITION
THYM
ROMARIN
SARRIETTE
ORIGAN
MARJOLAINE
DE
DE
DE
DE

SUN-DRENCHED CUISINE

Provençal cuisine is not elegant and refined – it's the exact opposite. The inhabitants of rural Provence produce simple and uncomplicated food. However, their talent for combining the best of their raw produce is what has made Provençal cuisine so famous.

They adhere to the old tradition of using whatever resources are at hand to the fullest capacity. Nothing is wasted. Fishermen, who work along the coast, have found use for practically anything and everything they might catch in their nets, even small, poisonous fish and lean crabs as well as prickly black sea urchins.

In the surrounding countryside, vegetables sweetened by the strong sun have always proliferated, and farmers are able to harvest crops several times a year, as long as their water supplies are sufficient.

There was hardly any meat, and most families would only enjoy meat on very special occasions. Of course, they went hunting, and if lucky, they could provide a little extra for the dinner table by shooting a partridge, a boar or by catching little birds in traps. Hunting continues to be an important aspect of life in the mountains, even though venison is no longer a necessary addition to the menu. However, the tradition of procuring food directly from the mountainside and forests has survived. Following an elderly Provençal woman as she gathers thyme, rosemary, wild asparagus, snails, shoots of young dandelions and mushrooms from the dry slopes, where you would never expect to find anything edible, is an education. Life in the mountains has always been hard and rather isolated, but, as a result, the need for inventiveness and a respect for raw produce created the magnificent cuisine we know today.

The four cornerstones of Provençal cuisine are garlic, olive oil, thyme and tomatoes; they form part of practically every dish and are often enhanced by adding anchovies or capers.

Dried herbs are frequently used, as they produce the most elegant result, the point being that herbs should enhance and not obscure other ingredients. There is one exception, though, fresh basil, which is used for *pistou*, a Provençal version of the Italian pesto.

The journey from field to kitchen is short. Most vegetables are produced locally and then sold at the markets that practically all villages have twice a week. The markets are fascinating and they always reflect the local traditions as well as the different seasons, although you can of course buy imported produce as well.

The market is also the place to experience the genuine foundations of Provençal gastronomy, because this is where to see, taste and touch the goods. It's not just acceptable to pinch and prod; it's practically a requirement. Traders are proud of their produce and they're happy to let you in on the best way to prepare whatever you put in your shopping basket.

The market atmosphere is always cheerful, even when it's freezing cold and stall-keepers have been up since dawn, meticulously arranging their stalls to best advantage. Perhaps it's because they know they can look forward to a hearty lunch and a pastis at the end of it. Working up an appetite is not at all difficult when you walk among the tempting stalls offering grilled garlic-chickens, air-dried sausages or freshly baked olive loaves.

OLIVES AND OLIVE OIL

Originally, the Greeks introduced the olive tree to France. The cultivation of olives quickly spread and alongside grain, salt and wine, olive oil rapidly became one of the most important commodities in the South of France. The Romans later systematised the trade in their usual energetic manner.

There are olive trees practically everywhere in Provence, though never beyond 2,000 feet above sea level, where it is too cold. And, although the olive tree is renowned for its hardiness, it does not cope very well when frost sets in, so if you are looking for a house in Provence, it is a good idea to look in areas with olive trees – because then you know that the winters will not be too harsh.

The olive tree, with its silver-green leaves and gnarled branches has inspired numerous painters with van Gogh and Cézanne as two of the more persistent admirers. In 1889, van Gogh described his enthusiasm thus, 'Ah, if only you could see the olive trees now ...the silvery leaves, as they turn green against the blue. And the orange-brown arable soil ... there is something intimate about the wind whispering through an olive grove, something immensely old. It is too beautiful to paint, or even fathom.' Which after all he did, and he probably grasped it better than most.

Olives are harvested in winter, from November to February, and visiting one of the old olive mills, where they will gladly fill your container with freshly pressed virgin oil, is a wonderful treat.

Olives are practically only harvested by hand. The fastest olive pickers can harvest approximately 10 kg in an hour. When it is time to harvest the olives, they spread huge nets underneath the olive trees, ensuring that the olives do not get dirty or perish. Olive farmers expect to get 1 litre of olive oil for every 5–6 kg of olives.

At the mill, the olives, including stones, skin and everything, are ground into a thick paste, which is then spread onto mats and when pressed, the oil separates from the paste and is gathered in containers underneath. Then it's ready for consumption – and is the purest, most flavoursome oil you can find.

In Nyons, located in the *Drôme Provençale* region, you can visit a museum that traces the cultivation of olives in the South of France. The town itself and its surrounding areas have been recognised as a central area for olive cultivation since olden times, and some of France's finest – and most expensive – olive products come from this area. The oil is of such great value that it has obtained its own *Appellation Contrôlée*.

Pickled edible olives are a classic speciality anywhere in Provence. There are lots of different varieties, each with its own characteristics. Some are ready for picking when still green, in the early autumn, while others benefit from maturing in full after the first couple of frosty nights. Around Nyons, you find *Tanches*, a large and fleshy black olive. Salon-de-Provence is renowned for its exquisite *Salonenques*, often seasoned with a bit of fennel. *Cailletier* are the small, delicate olives from Nice, and you find the green, egg-shaped *Picholines* almost everywhere in Provence.

Les Alpilles at Les Baux in Bouches-du-Rhône is a particularly important olive area. It's breathtakingly beautiful and you only get first rate olives and olive oil from here.

The quality of olive oil does not just vary from area to area, but also from year to year. As with wine, it is a question of variety, climate and maturity – and of course, it is also a question of how prudent the individual miller is when it comes to the craft of pressing oil. Apart from Nyons, you will find good olive mills in Maussane, Fontvieille, Buis-les-Barronies, Callas, Flayosquet, Aups, Manosque and Opio.

In Provençal cooking, olive oil is crucial and can't be replaced by any other kind of oil. It's used in just about everything: salads, dressings, *aïoli* (the wonderfully strong garlic mayonnaise), and it's used for frying as well as for preserving fresh goat's cheese. And perhaps best of all, it's also used on bread to which you just add some freshly crushed garlic, salt and thyme before grilling. It is, however, vital that you use good quality olive oil, or your Provençal dishes will never be at their best. Your oil should be as young as possible, and you should keep it somewhere dark and cool. Most importantly, it must never be rancid; that will spoil everything. Unfortunately, you'll often come across oil that is too old, so you need to keep an eye open for that. Provençal cooking may be simple, but it demands the finest quality olive oil.

Olive Tapenade

TAPENADE

The small, climbing caper shrub is well suited to the Mediterranean climate and is cultivated in the areas surrounding Nice, Menton and Toulon. It does, however, also grow in the wild. The capers you buy in salt and vinegar brine are buds from this bush. In Provençal, the caper is called tapénié *and hence you have the name of one of the greatest delicacies in Provence, tapenade. Please note that it is simply not possible to get a really good result if you do not stone the olives yourself. The pre-stoned olives you buy in a jar will never make anything as delicious.*

250 g black olives
100 g capers
75 g fillets of anchovy in oil
5 tbsp extra virgin olive oil
Freshly ground black pepper
2 tsp of cognac or marc (can be left out)

Halve the olives and take out the stones. Rinse the anchovy fillets thoroughly under running water to get rid of the salt. Add all ingredients, except for the olive oil, to a food processor and purée until it becomes a paste. While stirring on low speed, add the olive oil in a steady flow. Pour the finished paste into a bowl and place somewhere cool.

Serve as an appetiser on little pieces of toasted country bread, in the whites of hardboiled eggs with chopped yolks on top, in a tomato salad or with fresh pasta.

BASIL SAUCE

PISTOU

1 bunch of basil
5 garlic gloves
30 g pine nuts
100 g grated Parmesan
50 ml pure virgin olive oil
Salt and freshly ground pepper

Add all ingredients to a blender, except for the olive oil, and purée until smooth. Add the olive oil in a steady flow while stirring. Season with salt and pepper.

Pistou is used in vegetable soups or in pasta dishes, such as *pâtes fraîches au pistou* (fresh pasta with basil sauce) which is one of the most popular dishes. To make this, you simply add pasta and a finely chopped tomato to the *pistou*.

Carefully mix in the finely chopped tomato with the *pistou* and then add the pasta, boiled *al dente*, just before serving.

TOAST WITH OLIVE OIL AND ANCHOVIES

ROUSTIDOU

When the olive mills are in action from December until mid-January, you are surrounded by the wonderful smell of freshly pressed olive oil, and it is this oil that the workers at the mill will use for their roustidou – a piece of bread soaked in fresh oil, with crushed garlic and anchovy on top. When the roustidou *is grilled in the oven, it's transformed into a wonderful snack that will keep you warm on a cold winter's day.*

4 slices of country bread
2 cloves of garlic
Olive oil
4 anchovies
Salt and freshly ground pepper

Dip the slices of bread in olive oil, coating them well. Crush the cloves of garlic onto the bread. Mash the anchovies and spread them across the bread slices. Place them under a hot grill until crispy.

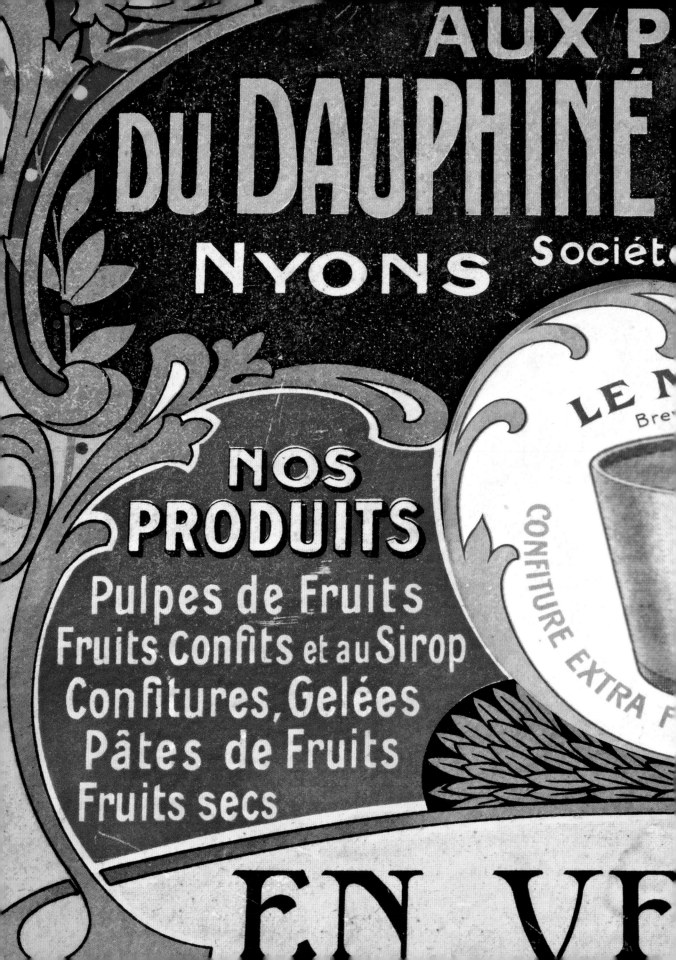

GARLIC MAYONNAISE

AÏOLI

Aïoli is a strong garlic mayonnaise, which is often served with fish dishes and boiled vegetables. It is an important part of the grand aïoli, *where it is served with boiled, salted and dried cod.*

6 cloves of garlic
1 cold, boiled potato
300–400 ml olive oil
2 egg yolks
Lemon juice
Salt and freshly ground pepper

Traditionally, *aïoli* is made in a mortar, but you can also use a food processor. Add garlic cloves to the food processor and blitz until finely chopped.

Then add the cold potato, salt and pepper and blitz again in the mixer. Leave the food processor running while you add 1 tbsp of olive oil, some lemon juice and the egg yolks.

Then add the remaining olive oil in a steady stream while the mixer continues running on a slow speed, in exactly the same way you would when making mayonnaise. The *aïoli* should be quite firm.

SALT – THE WHITE GOLD

The Provençal vehemently maintain that simplicity is always best. This also holds true for their use of salt from Camargue, which partners wonderfully with olive oil and a warm climate. The author Jean Giono, who wrote about the simple life in the highlands of Provence, around Manosque, paid homage to oil and salt with these words: 'My mother would slice a loaf of bread. Then she sprinkled salt on a slice and doused it in olive oil as she said, "eat" ... Oh, mother! You fed me oil and salt, oil and bread from these hills.'

Today it's difficult to imagine just how important salt was to the Provençal. For centuries, fishermen along the coast would salt sardines and anchovies and send them up into the mountains as an important protein supplement for the poorer families who lived there. Salt came from the marshes around the Camargue, where seawater has been contained and salt extracted ever since the Greeks first settled here 2,000 years ago. The Greeks knew that salt was a vital ingredient as well as a highly valuable commodity. The low, flat areas around the estuary of the river Rhône proved excellent for extracting salt, and it is said that it was the Greeks from Rhodes after whom the Rhône was named.

Today the company *Les Salins du Midi* is in charge of salt production. It collects the salt from Aigues-Mortes and Salins-de-Giraud, enormous areas that cover 21,000 hectares in total. The concentrated sea salt is harvested in late summer, by which time it's accumulated into huge mountains, the so-called *camelles* that are up to 20 metres high. It's then washed and rinsed before being sold as table salt. In one single day, it's possible to produce up to 15,000 tonnes of salt.

The finest salt consists of the little crystals that form on the water's surface called *fleur de sel*. It is carefully harvested by hand and sold at a high price, in little containers with cork lids, signed by *le saunier*, the salt harvester, as a guarantee of its high quality. The name *fleur de sel* is said to derive from the scent of flowers, violets in particular, that the salt yields while drying.

SALT-FRIED AUBERGINES

AUBERGINES AU GROS SEL

1 large aubergine
½ tsp coarse salt
3 tbsp olive oil
4 tbsp basil leaves
Freshly ground pepper

Cut the aubergine lengthways into slices of approximately 3 mm in thickness. Heat the salt in a frying pan. Place the aubergine slices on top and fry them for about 3–4 minutes on both sides, until golden. Then place in a dish and sprinkle chopped basil and olive oil on top. Leave the dish to cool in the fridge. Serve as a light starter.

Cueillie par
Luc Vernhes
SAUNIER
à AIGUES-MORTES

LE SAUNIER DE
CAMARGUE
Savoir-Faire Ancestral

Fleur de Sel

Sud de France

GRILLED BREAD WITH SALT AND OLIVE OIL

PAIN GRILLÉ AU SEL

½ baguette
Olive oil
Salt
Dried thyme

Cut the bread into slices of roughly ½ cm and place them under the grill until they start turning brown. Take out the bread, turn over and sprinkle olive oil on top. Then sprinkle with salt and dried thyme and place back under the grill until golden and crispy. Serve as a snack with a glass of chilled rosé wine.

SALTED ALMONDS

AMANDES AU SEL

400 g almonds
4–5 tbsp fine salt from Camargue

Blanch the almonds and pour them into a bowl, sprinkle with salt and add approximately 400 ml water. Mix until the salt is completely dissolved.

Drain the almonds into a sieve and allow the water to drip off. Heat the oven to 140°C and spread the almonds onto a baking sheet.

Place the sheet in the oven and roast the almonds for 25–35 minutes or until they are nice and crispy. Turn them over every now and again. They must not turn dark brown.

Enjoy the salted almonds with a glass of wine or pastis.

Roasted Chestnuts

CHÂTAIGNES GRILLÉES

Harvesting chestnuts begins in mid-October and the results can be found in the markets throughout winter, where there will always be a barrel of fragrant, roasting chestnuts. The inhabitants from Collobrières and other villages surrounding the mountain range Les Maures, behind Saint-Tropez, have specialised in harvesting and preparing chestnuts for centuries. But don't make the mistake of thinking that you can just enter a forest and pick them at your leisure; chestnut forests are strictly divided into harvest areas and the locals are not lenient when it comes to thieving visitors.

Chestnuts are used in many different recipes, but they are at their best when freshly picked and roasted. They're also brilliant at keeping your hands warm on a chilly autumn afternoon. Enjoy a bag of them while still at the market – or roast them at home and serve with salt, butter and red wine. Throughout their history, the Provençal have placed clay pots directly in an open fire when roasting chestnuts.

500 g chestnuts
300 g salt

Make a little cross at the chestnuts' pointy end, which ensures that they don't explode when placed in the oven. Pour salt into an oven-proof dish and place the chestnuts with their pointy ends upwards. Bake in the oven at 200°C until they open and are easy to peel – approximately 20 minutes. You can also roast the chestnuts, without salt, on a frying pan, but remember to stir them from time to time.

BREAD

Bread is one of the cornerstones of daily Provençal cuisine and will often be served instead of potatoes or rice, which is why you need to buy plenty of it (not least to replace the one you started nibbling on your way home from the baker's shop).

The Provençal hardly ever make their own bread, and the smallest villages in the mountains will often have two or three bakeries. The selection will not be wide, but each bakery has its very own specialities.

Provençal bakers usually adhere to the traditional way of baking bread in old-fashioned stone ovens, heated with charcoal. It gives the bread a unique flavour and a very crisp crust. Just adding olive oil and a little salt to the newly baked bread makes for a most delicious treat. If your bread goes stale, which it quickly does, it's still fine to toast it, to make crispy bread croutons to use in salads or as an important supplement to various soups.

If you take a particular interest in bread baking, the Bread Museum in Bonnieux is well worth a visit. It is housed in the town's old bakery and they take you through bread making, right from when the grain is poured into the old vaulted cellar to when the freshly baked loaves come out of the oven.

OLIVE LOAF

FOUGASSE

350 ml tepid water
40 g yeast
650 g flour
1 tsp coarse salt
100 g black olives
1 tsp *herbes de Provence*
4–6 tbsp olive oil

Stone the olives and chop the flesh coarsely. Mix the yeast and tepid water, slowly adding flour. You can either use a dough hook on an electric mixer or you can do it by hand, kneading the dough for approximately 5 minutes. Then place the dough somewhere warm for 1–1½ hours.

Sprinkle a little flour on your tabletop and roll out the dough into a square of approximately 30 x 40 cm thick. Spread olives and herbs on top. You can also use fresh herbs and whatever else you might pick up at the local market, like artichokes or sundried tomatoes.

Sprinkle with olive oil and close the loaf from left to right. Dip tepid water around the edges and press down on the sides.

Brush olive oil on top and place angular cuts every 2 cm, which will reveal the olive filling.

Bake in a preheated oven for approximately 30 minutes at 200°C, or until the loaf is nicely brown and crisp on top.

COUNTRY BREAD

PAIN DE CAMPAGNE

15 g yeast
2 tbsp coarse salt
900 ml cold water
100 ml olive oil
300 g organic durum flour
1 kg organic wheat flour

Dissolve the yeast and salt in a little bit of water before adding the remaining water and olive oil. Then add the durum flour and stir. Add the wheat flour in two batches. Knead the dough well and then leave it to prove in the fridge until the following day, or at least for 8 hours.

The following day, knead the dough again and halve it. Then shape the two halves into round shapes or flat long ones. Place the loaves on a baking sheet covered with baking paper. Place a roasting tray at the bottom of the oven, which you then set at 250°C, and leave the loaves to prove for as long as it takes to heat the oven.

Sprinkle the loaves with water and place them in the middle of the oven. Pour a glass of cold water into the roasting tray and quickly close the oven door, so as not to let out steam. Bake for 20 minutes at 250°C after which turn the oven down to 200°C and bake for approximately another 25 minutes. The loaves should sound hollow when you tap them on the bottom. Leave to cool on a rack.

You can also use this recipe for baguettes or other kinds of bread, including *fougasse*, but then, of course, you also have to adjust baking time.

CHICKPEA PANCAKE

SOCCA

Socca isn't really bread; it's more like a pancake made with chickpea flour. It is best when cooked over a wooden fire, but you can also bake it under the grill in your oven. It's an ancient speciality, still sold by street vendors in Nice and Menton, where they bake them on huge, flat pans.

250 g chickpea flour
500 ml water
2 tbsp olive oil
Salt and freshly ground pepper

Mix the chickpea flour with water, oil, salt and pepper and whisk thoroughly, making sure there are no lumps in the dough. Grease a baking sheet and pour the dough onto it in a layer of 2–3 mm. Heat the oven to 225°C and light the grill. Bake the *socca* until it is golden (make sure it does not burn under the grill), then take it out of the oven and serve while hot.

FRENCH STICKS

BAGUETTES

20 g yeast
500 ml water
1 tsp fine salt
700 g wheat flour

Dissolve the yeast in water. Add the salt and flour, little by little. Knead thoroughly and leave to prove in the fridge overnight.

Gently shape the dough into three long French sticks and make 3–4 angular cuts down each. Leave them to prove for 30 minutes on a baking sheet.

Sprinkle with water and bake in a very hot oven – 250°C – for 10 minutes. Then turn the oven down to 200°C and bake until golden and crisp – approximately 15 minutes.

VEGETABLES

Vegetables are by far the most important ingredients in Provençal cuisine. The sun gives them a wonderful taste and sweetness and this can actually prove the greatest challenge when trying to cook Provençal dishes outside Provence. Finding properly ripened vegetables is difficult, and sometimes you may have to cheat and add a little sugar to your dishes if you want to obtain that sun-ripened flavour. When you walk around local markets, you can't help being excited over the vegetables on offer. You simply want to buy everything: the fully ripened and deeply red tomatoes; huge bundles of garlic; small, purple artichokes; green asparagus; beans; glossy aubergines, and courgettes. You have to be quite a seasoned shopper not to overdo it.

You'll find some of the biggest vegetable markets in the towns of Cavaillon and Carpentras, renowned by people all over France to whom they export their fruit and vegetables. The Friday market in Carpentras is spread over most of the inner city. The market in Arles is another great attraction.

Classic Provençal vegetable dishes include *ratatouille*, a vegetable ragout, as well as stuffed tomatoes, courgettes and peppers. *Pissaladière* is a kind of pizza made with onions and anchovies, originating in Nice, where they have specialised in a unique, Italian-inspired cuisine.

Salads are popular, and you will often begin a meal with a bowl of *mesclun*, a mixture of different sorts of lettuce including dandelion and other wild leaves. *Mesclun* can be bought at the markets, if you don't relish picking your own in the local ditches.

ARTICHOKES WITH BUTTER AND SALT

ARTICHAUTS AU BEURRE ET SEL

The artichoke is really a thistle. You eat the not yet fully-blown flower. In France, there is a significant distinction between the large and rather rough artichokes from Brittany and the delicate, small violet ones from Provence. Both taste absolutely wonderful but the Provençal artichokes are more delicate and need less cooking time. Furthermore you can eat the stalk as it often becomes as supple as the heart. The Provençal also like to prepare raw baby artichokes. Make sure you always buy fresh, closed and crunchy artichokes – on no account must they be dry and semi-withered.

4 artichokes
Salt
Olive oil
Juice of ½ a lemon or
 white wine vinegar
Butter or olive oil
Salt and freshly ground pepper

Cut off the roughest part of the stem and boil the artichokes in salty water with lemon juice or white wine vinegar, which will prevent them from discolouring. Boiling time naturally depends on how big the artichokes are, but 15–30 minutes should be sufficient. The artichokes are ready when their leaves come off easily.

Eat the fleshy lower part of the leaves as well as the heart of the artichoke with butter and salt, or you can use olive oil instead of butter. Enjoy with a glass of rosé wine.

ARTICHOKE PURÉE

ARTICHAUNADE

4 artichoke hearts (can be bought in a jar)
Juice of ½ a lemon
Olive oil
Salt and freshly ground pepper

Purée the artichoke hearts with the lemon juice and carefully add olive oil until the purée is smooth but firm. Season with salt and pepper and serve on toast.

ARTICHOKE SALAD

SALADE AU COEUR D'ARTICHAUTS

8 artichoke hearts
100 g pine nuts
200 g mixed lettuce

Mustard Dressing
1 tsp mustard
3 tbsp olive oil
1 tbsp wine vinegar
Salt and freshly ground pepper

Tear the lettuce into shreds before you rinse and carefully dry it off. Place on a flat dish. Boil the artichokes and quarter the hearts before you spread them over the lettuce. Roast the pine nuts and sprinkle them on top. Mix the ingredients for the dressing in a small bowl or glass and pour over the salad.

PROVENÇAL VEGETABLE SOUP WITH BASIL SAUCE

SOUPE AU PISTOU

250 g fresh, shelled white beans
  (if you use dried beans they must soak in water
  for approximately 24 hours)
250 g potatoes
2 leeks
3 tomatoes
2 mild onions
200 g carrots
2 small courgettes
100 g green beans
50 g pasta or short spaghetti
Salt and freshly ground pepper
A little *pistou* (p. 24)

Peel the potatoes and cut them into chunks. Finely chop the onions and leeks. Skin the tomatoes, remove pips, and dice. Slice the carrots thickly and dice the courgettes. Cut the green beans into pieces of approximately 1 cm.

Pour 2 litres of water into a huge pot and add the white beans. Bring the water to a boil and turn the heat down low. Skim any foam off the top and leave the beans to boil for 30 minutes.

Add the potatoes, leeks, onions, tomatoes and carrots and bring the soup to a boil again. Season with salt and pepper. Put the lid back on and let it simmer for another 30 minutes. Then add green beans, courgettes and pasta and let it simmer for yet another 15 minutes.

Gently stir in a little *pistou*, or serve in a dish on the side, enabling guests to help themselves.

ONION SOUP

SOUPE À L'OIGNON

1 kg onions
2 cloves of garlic
5 tbsp olive oil
300 ml white wine
1 tsp sugar
1 litre chicken or beef stock
4 twigs of thyme
1 bay leaf
Country bread
100 g freshly grated Gruyère
50 g freshly grated Parmesan

Peel the onions, halve them and finely slice them. Add the onions to a pot and sauté lightly in olive oil for 10 minutes. Add the garlic and sauté for another couple of minutes. Do not fry the garlic too harshly.

Once the onions turn light brown, add the wine and sugar and leave it all to simmer for 5 minutes.

Then add the stock, thyme and bay leaf and leave to simmer for approximately 20 minutes. Heat the oven to 250°C and toast the bread slices. Pour the soup into ovenproof bowls. Place one slice of bread on top of the soup in each bowl, sprinkle cheese over the bread and cook *au gratin* until the cheese turns a lovely light-brown colour. Serve with country bread and a glass of chilled rosé or white wine.

GARLIC SOUP

L'AIGO BOULIDO

L'aigo boulido *actually means boiled water, but once you have tasted this soup, you'll realise that it's pretty strong and far from watery.*

1 litre of water
5 cloves of garlic
1 bay leaf
1 tbsp olive oil
1 small sage twig
2 egg yolks
Salt and freshly ground pepper
4 slices of one-day-old country bread
100 g Gruyère

Boil the water, crushed garlic, olive oil, bay leaf and sage for 15 minutes. Strain the soup. Add the two egg yolks to a small bowl and whisk with 100 ml of the soup.

Pour this mixture back into the soup, which you must ensure doesn't reach boiling point, and season with salt and pepper.

Place a slice of country bread in each soup dish, sprinkle Gruyère on top of the bread and pour soup over both.

62

SNAILS IN GARLIC BUTTER

PETIT GRIS À LA PROVENÇALE

The Provençal are very fond of gathering the small, striped snails that break out in abundance when a rare but heavy rain shower has drenched the parched mountainside. A perfectly acceptable substitute would be to use escargots, *which after all are easier to get hold of; you can even buy them tinned with clean shells on the side.*

This dish is often served in Burgundy, a region that lays claim to its invention and where it is named Escargots à la Bourguignonne. *And indeed it holds true that snails taste delicious when accompanied by a bottle of Burgundy, however, when you study the recipe, it becomes quite obvious that this is in fact a classic Provençal dish.*

1 bunch of parsley
4 cloves of garlic
Salt and freshly ground pepper
200 g butter
1 thyme twig
24 snails
300 g salt

Heat the oven to 250°C. Chop the parsley and crush the garlic and mix in with butter, salt and pepper. Put a little of the seasoned butter and a snail into each snail shell and fill it up with the rest of the seasoned butter. Place the shells in a thick layer of salt and bake in the oven until the butter sizzles – this should take about 10 minutes. Serve with a glass of chilled white wine and a freshly baked baguette.

CAULIFLOWER AU GRATIN

GRATIN DE CHOU-FLEUR

1 cauliflower

3 eggs (separate the whites from the yolks)

1 clove of garlic

A pinch of grated nutmeg

100 g grated Gruyère

75 g flour

50 g butter

500 ml milk

Salt and freshly ground pepper

Breadcrumbs

Cut the cauliflower into chunks and boil until tender – this should take approximately 5 minutes. Divide into smaller florets with a fork and place in an ovenproof dish.

Melt the butter and add the flour. Then add the milk little by little, before adding the finely chopped garlic and nutmeg. Add almost all of the Gruyère and stir thoroughly. Leave the sauce to cool for a while and then whisk in the egg yolks one at a time. Whisk the egg whites until stiff and gently fold them in.

Spread the sauce over the cauliflower and sprinkle the remaining cheese and breadcrumbs on top. Add little knobs of butter. Bake in the oven for approximately 45 minutes at 175°C, or until the gratin is beautifully golden.

TOMATOES ON GRILLED BREAD

BRUSCHETTA

These days the tomato is the bedrock of modern Provençal cuisine. However, it was not always so. It wasn't until about 100 years ago that the tomato achieved proper recognition in the South of France. Now, the Provençal have access to lots of sun-ripened tomatoes, which they poetically call pommes d'amour.

This is a very simple dish, but it only really tastes good if the tomatoes are perfectly ripe and sweet. Please note that you can use basil instead of thyme, as both herbs go incredibly well with tomatoes.

4 slices of country bread
1 clove of garlic
4 tbsp olive oil
4 ripe tomatoes
Salt and freshly ground pepper
Fresh basil or thyme

Toast the bread slices and rub with garlic. Place the slices on a dish and drizzle olive oil over them. Halve the tomatoes and remove pips before chopping coarsely. Then gently mix in salt and pepper and leave it all to drain in a sieve.

Spread the tomatoes over the bread slices. Then sprinkle a bit of olive oil and some fresh basil or thyme on top.

You can also place the tomato-topped slices in an ovenproof dish and add a little more oil and then place them under the grill for a couple of minutes.

TOMATO SOUP

SOUPE DE TOMATES

1 kg tomatoes

2 onions

4 cloves of garlic

4 large tbsp olive oil

1 glass of white wine

1 litre water

A pinch of sugar

8 slices of baguette

100 g freshly grated Parmesan

1 bunch of potherbs made from small
 sprigs of parsley, fresh thyme and
 a bay leaf

Fresh basil or thyme as garnish

Make a cross at the top of the tomatoes with a sharp knife and blanch
in boiling water before skinning them. Fry the coarsely chopped
onions in olive oil until golden, add the tomatoes and boil for 10
minutes. Add wine and boil for another 5 minutes. Add water and
potherbs and season with sugar, salt and pepper. Boil for another
10 minutes. Remove the potherbs and blend the soup until smooth.

   Grill the bread slices and rub them with garlic. Serve with a bowl
of Parmesan on the side. Garnish the bowls with fresh basil or thyme.
You can serve the soup warm as well as chilled.

JERUSALEM ARTICHOKE SOUP

SOUPE DE TOPINAMBOURS

500 g Jerusalem artichokes
200 g potatoes
4 shallots
3 tbsp olive oil
1 litre chicken or beef stock

50 ml sour cream or crème fraiche
 (38% fat)
1 glass of white wine
Salt and freshly ground pepper
Chopped chives or parsley

Peel the Jerusalem artichokes and potatoes and dice them. Chop the onions finely.

Sauté all the vegetables gently in olive oil for approximately 10 minutes. Add ²/₃ of the stock and boil until the Jerusalem artichokes become soft. Blend to a fine purée. Put the purée back in the pot and add the remaining stock, white wine and sour cream. Bring to the boil and season with salt and pepper. Garnish with chives or parsley.

JERUSALEM ARTICHOKE SALAD

SALADE DE TOPINAMBOURS

250 g Jerusalem artichokes
2–3 carrots
50 g almonds

Dressing
3 tbsp olive oil
1 tsp lemon juice
Salt and freshly ground pepper

Rinse and scrub the Jerusalem artichokes and peel the carrots. Grate both coarsely and mix in a dish. Mix the ingredients for the dressing in a bowl and pour on top.

Chop the almonds coarsely and roast on a dry frying pan. Season with salt while still warm and sprinkle on top.

Asperges Blanches

7€
80 le kilo

Asparagus

ASPERGES

In March and April, you'll be able to find wild asparagus plants growing in ditches and olive groves. They're fragile green sprouts, which just need to boil for a moment before serving with scrambled egg. You can also use them raw in salads.

Fields are also abundant with farmed asparagus from Carpentras and Cavaillon at this time of year. Both white and green asparagus is grown and it comes in all sizes. Both are delicate, but the green is a little less bitter than the white.

You should never use the stringy, bottom part of either though. You peel the white asparagus with a potato peeler, from the head down. You boil the white asparagus for 4–6 minutes and the green asparagus for 1–3 minutes. Keep an eye on them though; it is important not to overcook them. Asparagus features in numerous dishes and salads; however, the Provençal will often enjoy the spears on their own, with just a drizzle of vinaigrette.

Vinaigrette
200 ml olive oil
50 ml wine vinegar
Salt and freshly ground pepper

Dissolve the salt in the vinegar and add the other ingredients before whisking. Alternatively, you can add a pinch of Dijon mustard or some finely chopped tarragon.

OMELETTE WITH ASPARAGUS

OMELETTE AUX ASPERGES

6 eggs
20 spears of green asparagus
4 tbsp olive oil
Salt and freshly ground pepper

Rinse the asparagus and break off the lower part. Cut into pieces of 2–3 cm and boil lightly in salted water for 2 minutes. Drain and cool the asparagus in a bowl with ice cold water. Dry in a tea towel.

Heat 3 tbsp of olive oil in a frying pan over medium heat. Carefully fry the asparagus for 3 minutes. Leave in the pan.

Whisk the eggs in a bowl. Add salt and pepper and 1 tbsp of olive oil. Whisk vigorously. Heat the frying pan again and pour the eggs over the asparagus. Mix with a spatula and bake the omelette for 4–5 minutes.

FARMER'S OMELETTE

OMELETTE PAYSANNE

2 onions
4 tbsp olive oil
100 g air-dried ham or lean bacon
2 boiled potatoes
5 eggs
2–4 tbsp milk
Parsley or chives

Chop the onions and fry until golden. Dice the ham (or bacon) and potatoes. Add the ham and potatoes to the frying pan and sauté lightly.

Whisk the eggs and milk lightly using a fork. Pour the eggs over the onions, ham and potatoes and bake the omelette.

Prick the mixture with a fork to allow the liquid middle to run down to the bottom. Bake until the eggs are set. Sprinkle with parsley or chives and serve immediately.

Mesclum de Villefranche/su
cultivé sans aucun Produit
chimique de synthese

1 € les 100g

Mixed Salad with Garlic Croutons

MESCLUN AUX CROUTONS À L'AIL

Mesclun consists of different kinds of lettuce and fresh herbs. The name is derived from the Provençal word mescal, *which simply means to mix. There is no set rule for which lettuces to use, but you should always include mild and bitter as well as soft and crunchy leaves. Typically, the salad will include fresh dandelion leaves, chervil, rocket, red salad bowl, romaine, as well as red endive. The leaves should be small and fresh.*

1 tbsp white wine vinegar
5 tbsp olive oil
4 spring onions
300 g *mesclun* salad
2 cloves of garlic (halved)
Croutons from three large slices of
  country bread
2 hardboiled eggs
Salt and freshly ground pepper

Rub the halved cloves of garlic on the bread and grill lightly before cutting into cubes.

Mix the white wine vinegar, oil, salt and pepper for the dressing. Use a hand blender to mix the ingredients and pour into a salad bowl. Chop the spring onions and mix them in with the dressing before adding the *mesclun*. Sprinkle the croutons and chopped hardboiled eggs on top. Season with salt and pepper. Toss carefully and serve immediately.

Sunflower Salad

SALADE DE TOURNESOL

1 head of curly endive lettuce
150 g sunflower seeds
3 avocados
1 tsp lemon juice

Mustard Dressing
1 tsp mustard
3 tbsp olive oil
1 tbsp wine vinegar

Roast the sunflower seeds lightly on a dry frying pan. Tear the lettuce into medium sized shreds. Rinse the lettuce thoroughly and dry off before spreading it across a flat dish.

Cut the avocados into small pieces and squeeze a little lemon juice on top to prevent discolouring. Spread the avocados over the lettuce and sprinkle sunflower seeds on top. Mix the ingredients for the dressing and pour on top.

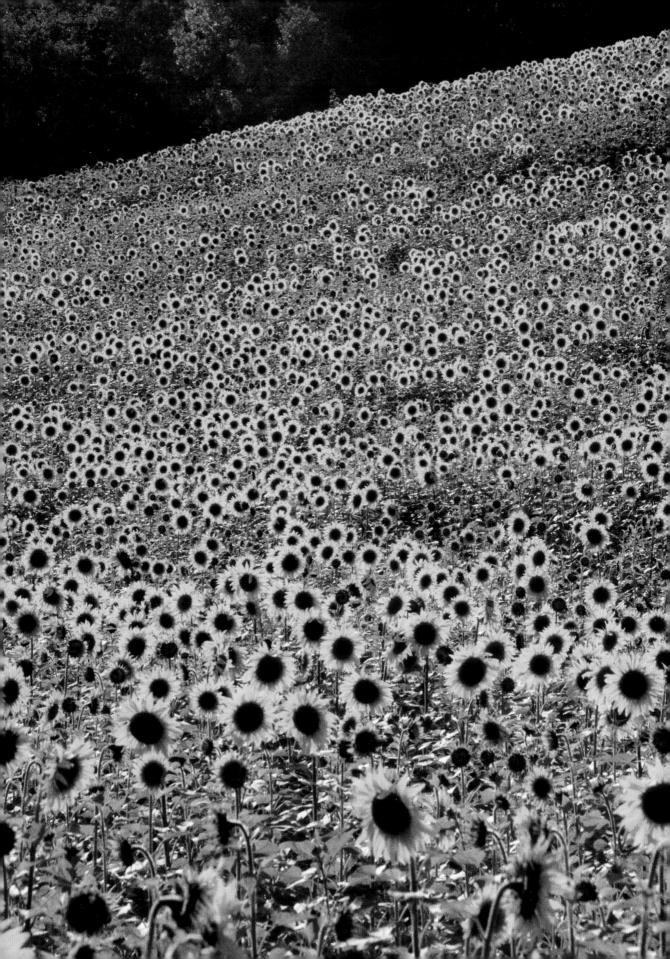

SALAD WITH PINE NUTS, GOAT'S CHEESE AND BAKED TOMATOES

SALADE DE PIGNONS

200 g *mesclun* salad
20 cherry tomatoes
200 g creamy goat's cheese
100 g pine nuts

Mustard Dressing
1 tsp mustard
3 tbsp olive oil
1 tbsp wine vinegar

Halve the tomatoes and place on a baking sheet, open side up. Bake
for 45 minutes at 150° C, and then put aside to cool down.
Roast the pine nuts lightly on a dry frying pan. Cut the cheese into
small chunks. Mix all the salad ingredients. Then mix all ingredients
for the dressing and pour over the salad.

ROASTED PEPPERS

SALADE DE POIVRONS GRILLÉS

4 large red or yellow peppers
18–20 black olives
5 tbsp olive oil
2 cloves of garlic
1 tsp balsamic vinegar
Salt and freshly ground pepper
Capers to garnish

Roast the peppers under a hot grill. Turn them over as their skin bubbles and turns black. Take the peppers out of the oven and wrap them in aluminium foil. Leave for 30 minutes before peeling off the skin with a paring knife.

Quarter the peppers and remove ribs and pips and then cut them into strips and place in a dish. Garnish with olives and capers.

Mix olive oil, finely chopped onions, balsamic vinegar, salt and pepper in a small bowl and pour over the peppers. Leave the dish to marinate for at least an hour before serving.

It is also possible to make this dish a day in advance. Anchovies can be used instead of capers, and you can also choose to use just olive oil for marinating the peppers.

PURÉED PEPPERS

POIVRONADE

2 red peppers
1 tbsp mild mustard
Olive oil
Salt and freshly ground pepper

Grill the peppers in the oven until they turn black. Take them out of the oven and wrap in aluminium foil for 15 minutes. Remove the skin, ribs and pips. Purée the peppers with the mustard and oil. The purée should be fairly thick. Serve on toast.

You can also slice the peppers and place them on a dish, which you sprinkle with olive oil, a little salt and possibly a squirt of lemon juice. Leave the dish to set before serving. It is possible to prepare this dish a day in advance as long as you keep it in the fridge until approximately 1 hour before serving.

STUFFED RED PEPPERS

POIVRONS ROUGES FARCIS

4 red peppers
3 onions
2 cloves of garlic
1 large bunch of parsley

6 rusks
Olive oil
Salt and freshly ground pepper

Chop the onions and parsley finely. Cut off the top of the peppers and remove ribs and pips. Crush the rusks. Place the peppers in a greased ovenproof dish and sprinkle a little olive oil over them. Mix the onions, parsley, garlic, rusks and fill the peppers with this mixture.

Sprinkle olive oil, salt and pepper on top and bake in the oven for 35 minutes at 200°C. If necessary, add extra olive oil while baking. The peppers should be soft when served.

ROQUEFORT SALAD

SALADE DE ROQUEFORT

6 ripe tomatoes   *Mustard Dressing*
150 g Roquefort   1 tsp mustard
100 g walnuts   3 tbsp olive oil
                         1 tbsp wine vinegar

Slice the tomatoes. Chop the cheese and walnuts coarsely and arrange carefully on a dish with the tomatoes. Mix the ingredients for the dressing and pour on top.

THE WINE GROWER'S SALAD

SALADE DU VIGNERON

200 g green and   *Mustard Dressing*
  red lettuce   1 tsp mustard
100 g Roquefort   3 tbsp olive oil
200 g seedless   1 tbsp wine vinegar
  black grapes

Tear the lettuce into small shreds. Rinse and dry thoroughly. Chop the cheese and walnuts coarsely and halve the grapes. Arrange all the ingredients beautifully on a flat dish. Mix the ingredients for the dressing and pour on top.

CHICKEN LIVER SALAD

SALADE DE FOIES DE VOLAILLE

1 head of curly
  endive lettuce
250 g chicken liver
2 slices of country
  bread
Olive oil
4 slices of smoked bacon
Salt and freshly ground pepper

Mustard Dressing
1 tsp mustard
3 tbsp olive oil
1 tbsp wine vinegar

Fry the chicken liver in a bit of olive oil in a hot frying pan for approximately 5 minutes. Dice the bread and bacon and fry separately in a frying pan. Tear the lettuce into smaller shreds and mix everything. Mix the ingredients for the dressing and pour on top before serving.

SALAD WITH AIR-DRIED HAM AND PARMESAN

SALADE DE MONTAGNE

200 g green and
  red lettuce
1 spring onion
200 g air-dried ham
100 g Parmesan

Mustard Dressing
1 tsp mustard
3 tbsp olive oil
1 tbsp wine vinegar

Tear the lettuce into medium sized shreds, then rinse and dry thoroughly. Spread the lettuce over a flat dish and place the slices of ham on top. Chop the spring onion finely and flake the Parmesan before sprinkling both on top of the salad. Mix the ingredients for the dressing and pour on top before serving.

ONION PIZZA WITH ANCHOVIES

PISSALADIÈRE

This is a great speciality from Nice. It gets its name from pissala, *which is a strong purée of little anchovies in salt brine, which the fishermen sell from their market stalls in the old town. For this version however, regular salted anchovies are used instead of* pissala.

Dough	*Filling*
15 g yeast	5 tbsp olive oil
125 ml tepid water	1.5 kg onions (preferably mild ones)
150 g durum flour	3 cloves of garlic
250 ml tepid water	1 bay leaf
2 tbsp milk	Thyme
4 tbsp olive oil	8 salted, rinsed and filleted anchovies
1 tsp fine salt	125 g black olives (preferably the
500 g wheat four	small ones from Nice)
	Salt and freshly ground pepper

Dissolve the yeast in the tepid water. Add flour and leave to prove somewhere nice and warm for 30 minutes. Then mix in more water, milk, olive oil and salt with the remaining flour. Leave to prove for another hour.

Heat the olive oil in a pot at very low heat. Add the finely chopped onions, crushed garlic, herbs and salt. Leave to simmer at a very low heat for 1 hour, but don't forget to stir regularly. The onions must not turn brown. Take the pot off the heat, remove the bay leaf and thyme twigs and mix in the mashed anchovies.

Grease a baking sheet with oil and roll out the pizza dough to fit the baking sheet. Gently press the dough onto the sheet and make the edge a little thicker. Leave to prove for 15 minutes. Prick with a fork except along the edge and spread the onions on top. Sprinkle the black olives on top and press them down into the onion mixture. Brush some oil on the edge and drizzle some over the onion mixture as well.

Place the *pissaladière* in the oven and bake for 30 minutes at 220°C, until golden and crisp. Grind some fresh pepper on top before serving.

PROVENÇAL PIZZA

PIZZA PROVENÇALE

The Italian influence on Provençal cuisine is extensive. Pizza is so common in Provence that you could be fooled into thinking it was a French invention, stolen by the Italians.

Dough	*Filling*
15 g yeast	1 clove of garlic
125 ml tepid water	2 tins of cherry tomatoes
150 g durum flour	2–3 shallots
	3 slices of boiled ham
250 ml tepid water	3 artichoke hearts
2 tbsp milk	100 g mushrooms
4 tbsp olive oil	1 tsp dried thyme
1 tsp fine salt	1 tsp dried marjoram
500 g wheat flour	200 g grated cheese
	Salt and ground pepper
	100 ml olive oil

Dissolve the yeast in the tepid water. Add the durum flour and leave to prove somewhere nice and warm for 30 minutes. Then mix in water, milk, olive oil and salt with the remaining flour. Leave to prove for another hour.

Chop the garlic, onions and tomatoes finely. Fry the onions and garlic in a little olive oil and then add the tomatoes. Season with herbs as well as salt and pepper.

Chop the slices of ham coarsely, quarter the artichoke hearts and slice the mushrooms.

Roll out the dough onto a baking sheet covered in baking paper. Spread the tomato sauce on top before adding ham and vegetables. Sprinkle with cheese and brush the edge with a little olive oil. Bake in the oven for approximately 30 minutes at 200°C.

AUBERGINE PURÉE

CAVIAR D'AUBERGINE

3 aubergines
2 cloves of garlic
5 tbsp olive oil
A pinch of coarse salt
Freshly ground pepper
4 anchovy fillets

Slice the aubergines lengthways and place in an ovenproof dish, sprinkle olive oil and a little salt on top. Bake in the oven for 45 minutes at 180°C, or until they become very soft.

Take the aubergines out of the oven and leave to cool. Scoop out the flesh and mash with a fork or chop coarsely with a big kitchen knife. Add chopped garlic, salt and fillets of anchovy to a food processor. Purée until very smooth and then add the aubergine flesh. Slowly pour in the olive oil, until the mixture is quite light. Season with salt and pepper.

This can be served hot or cold on toasted country bread. It is especially nice when accompanied by a glass of chilled rosé wine.

Potatoes with Herbes de Provence

POMMES DE TERRE AUX HERBES

Potatoes are mostly cultivated in the Provençal highlands, around Manosque for example. This rather simple dish is wonderful and a great way to make use of dried herbs.

8–12 baking potatoes
1–2 tbsp *herbes de Provence*
200 ml olive oil
Salt and freshly ground pepper

Scrub the potatoes thoroughly and cut into wedges leaving the skin on. Then toss the wedges in a bowl with olive oil, dried herbs, salt and pepper. Pour into an ovenproof dish and bake for 30–35 minutes at 220°C or until they become crisp and beautifully golden.

These potato-wedges are particularly complementary with lamb or grilled fish. As an alternative, you can boil the potatoes slightly first, before cutting them into wedges. Sprinkle with salt and pepper and perhaps a little thyme. Bake in the oven for approximately 30 minutes at 200°C. Sprinkle a little lemon juice on top before serving.

POTATO GRATIN

GRATIN DE POMMES DE TERRE

1 kg potatoes

Approximately 500 ml of
  stock

2 eggs

150 ml whipping cream

100 g freshly grated Gruyère

A pinch of grated nutmeg

Salt and freshly ground
  pepper

Peel the potatoes and cut them into fairly thick slices. Boil the potatoes in a pot, only just covered by stock, until they are almost soft. Strain, but save the stock. Place the potatoes in a dish greased with olive oil and leave to cool.

Whisk half the cheese with cream and eggs in a bowl. Add the nutmeg and whisk thoroughly.

Add a little of the stock (used to boil the potatoes) to the cheese, cream and eggs and pour over the potatoes. Sprinkle salt and pepper on top as well as the remaining cheese. Bake in oven for approximately 25 minutes at 180°C, or until the liquid has been reduced and the potatoes are beautifully golden.

POTATO SOUP WITH FRESH GOAT'S CHEESE

SOUPE DE POMMES DE TERRE

1 kg potatoes

1 litre of chicken stock

4 onions

2 cloves of garlic

3 twigs of thyme

Salt and freshly ground
  pepper

4 tbsp olive oil

2 small courgettes

100 g bacon

200 g fresh goat's cheese

Parsley

Chop the onions finely and peel the potatoes. Dice the potatoes and courgettes. Add oil to a deep pot and sauté the onions. Add the potatoes, courgettes, crushed garlic and thyme, and mix thoroughly. Add the chicken stock and leave to simmer on a low heat until the potatoes are completely cooked. In the meantime, you can fry the bacon until crispy. Blend the soup and leave to simmer for another 10 minutes. Pour the soup into individual bowls. Add a couple of scoops of goat's cheese and garnish with bacon and parsley.

POTATO GNOCCHI

GNOCCHIS À LA PROVENÇALE

1 kg potatoes
3 eggs
50 g butter
100 g flour
Salt

Boil the unpeeled potatoes in salty water. Then peel them and mash thoroughly with a fork. Whisk the eggs lightly using a fork, and then mix in with butter and mashed potatoes. Add flour and salt, little by little, and mix thoroughly. You can also use an electric mixer until the dough is supple yet firm and easy to roll out.

Quarter the dough. Sprinkle flour over a chopping board and make 4 rolls of dough, approximately 2 cm in width. Cut each roll of dough into pieces of 2 cm. Squeeze each little *gnocchi* gently with a fork, leaving little grooves on one side, and then press your thumb gently down on the opposite side.

Boil the *gnocchi* in plenty of salty water. They are ready, when they rise to the surface, after 3–4 minutes. Use a skimmer or slotted spoon to take them out and sprinkle a little olive oil over them, to keep them from sticking together, and keep them warm while you boil the rest. Serve immediately with tomato sauce, meat sauce, sour cream or butter.

You can also mix in blanched, chopped spinach or Swiss chard with the potatoes, which makes the *gnocchi* beautifully green.

STUFFED TOMATOES

TOMATES PROVENÇALES

1 kg ripe tomatoes
1 bunch of parsley
3 cloves of garlic
50 g breadcrumbs
4 tbsp olive oil
Salt and freshly ground pepper

Rinse and halve the tomatoes, then remove the pips with a spoon. Place the halves in a greased ovenproof dish and squeeze them close together. Sprinkle with salt and pepper. If the tomatoes are not quite ripe, you can also sprinkle a little sugar on top.

Chop parsley and garlic and stuff the tomatoes. Sprinkle breadcrumbs on top and then a little olive oil.

Bake for 45 minutes at 190°C. The dish can be enjoyed hot or cold, as a starter or as a side dish with meat or fish.

Tomato Salad

SALADE DE TOMATES

4–5 ripe tomatoes
1 mild onion
1 clove of garlic
Fresh basil

Dressing
1 part white wine vinegar
5 parts olive oil
Salt and freshly ground pepper

Slice the tomatoes thinly. Squeeze out some of the pips and place the tomatoes in a dish. Slice the onion finely and chop the garlic clove. Spread onion-rings, chopped garlic and fresh basil leaves over the tomatoes.

Drizzle the oil-vinegar dressing on top and sprinkle with salt and pepper. Leave to set before serving.

You can also garnish the salad with chopped walnuts and small chunks of Roquefort.

Tomato Tart with Mustard

TARTE À LA TOMATE ET À LA MOUTARDE

Pastry
250 g flour
120 g butter
A pinch of salt
1 whole egg
1 egg yolk
1–2 tbsp water

Filling
6 tbsp Dijon mustard
5 tomatoes
300 g Gruyère
Thyme
1 tbsp olive oil
Salt and freshly ground pepper

Add the butter and flour to a bowl and rub the butter into the flour, then add salt and the whole egg. Knead together with a little water until the pastry is shiny and firm. Leave to set in the fridge for half an hour. Sprinkle a little flour on your worktop and roll out the pastry before you place it in a greased tart mould. Place it somewhere cool for 1 hour prior to baking or the dough will shrink.

Prick the dough with a fork allowing hot air to escape without lifting up the bottom, which will result in an uneven tart shell.

Smear a decent layer of Dijon mustard over the pastry and place the cheese slices on top. Quarter the tomatoes and squeeze out the juice. Spread them on top of the cheese. Sprinkle with thyme, salt and pepper. Then drizzle olive oil on top and bake for 35 minutes at 180–190°C. Serve while hot with a green salad on the side.

FRIED COURGETTE FLOWERS

FLEURS DE COURGETTES FRITES

15 courgette flowers   ½ tsp salt
125 g flour   25 g butter
1½ eggs   Olive oil
125 ml milk

Pinch the stalk off the flowers and remove any calyx or style.

Mix the flour, eggs, milk and salt. Melt the butter and mix in with the batter. Leave to set for approximately half an hour.

Gently dip each flower in the batter and let them drip off before frying them in olive oil until golden and crispy.

STUFFED COURGETTE FLOWERS

FLEURS DE COURGETTES FARCIES

15 courgette flowers   1 jar of anchovy fillets
50 g mozzarella   4 tbsp olive oil
  or mild goat's cheese   1 glass of white wine

Pinch the stalk off the flowers and remove any calyx or style.

Stuff each flower with cheese and 1 fillet of anchovy. Close the flowers and place next to one another in an ovenproof dish.

Pour the wine into the dish and drizzle with olive oil. Bake in the oven for 15 minutes at 200–225°C.

OVEN-BAKED COURGETTES

TIAN DE COURGETTES

1 large onion
500 g small courgettes
5 tbsp olive oil
500 ml milk
100 g fresh breadcrumbs
3 eggs
100 g boiled long grain rice
100 g grated Parmesan
Salt and freshly ground pepper

Warm a little oil in a frying pan and sauté the finely chopped onions for about 10 minutes, until soft but not brown. Add the sliced courgettes and simmer for approximately 5 minutes. Sprinkle salt and pepper on top.

Add the fresh breadcrumbs to a dish along with 250 ml milk, the three eggs, the remaining oil and ¾ of the cheese. Whisk thoroughly.

Add the onion-courgette mixture and the boiled rice and then mix thoroughly before pouring the mixture into a greased ovenproof dish. Place the nicest looking slices of courgettes on top. Pour the remaining milk into the dish and sprinkle the remaining cheese on top. Bake in the oven until golden – approximately 45 minutes – at 180°C and serve while hot.

Fleurs de Courgette
de St Laurent du Var
2,00 € "le
... "bouquet"

COURGETTES AU GRATIN

GRATIN DE COURGETTES

10 small courgettes

2 shallots

2 cloves of garlic

250 g sour cream or crème fraiche
  (18% fat)

100 ml water

Salt and freshly ground pepper

4 tbsp olive oil

1 twig of thyme

Slice the courgettes and chop the onions finely. Heat the oil in a cast iron pot and add the thyme and shallots. Sauté the onions until soft but not brown. Add the courgettes and fry over a medium heat. Add the water, turn the heat down and leave to simmer for approximately 2 hours. Make sure they do not burn; you may have to add more water. Then remove the lid and reduce as much as possible, before taking the pot off the heat. There should not be much sauce left. Mix crushed garlic, sour cream, salt and pepper and add to the courgettes before pouring the entire mixture into a greased ovenproof dish and bake for approximately 40 minutes at 190°C, covering with baking paper for the first 30 minutes.

COURGETTE SOUP

SOUPE DE COURGETTES

500 g firm courgettes

500 g potatoes

3 cloves of garlic

1 twig of thyme

1½ litres of chicken stock

Salt and freshly ground pepper

3 tbsp olive oil

Peel the potatoes, then dice both potatoes and courgettes. Add the oil to a pot and sauté the courgettes and thyme. Then add the stock, potatoes, crushed garlic, salt and pepper. Leave to boil over high heat for 20 minutes. Blend the soup and leave to simmer for another 10 minutes.

RATATOUILLE

RATATOUILLE

You can enjoy ratatouille as a side dish or as a main course and you can serve it hot or cold. You can easily make it a day in advance and you can also use any leftovers in an omelette.

The traditional way to ensure that your ratatouille is really superb is, allegedly, by preparing the different vegetables individually and only mixing them at the very end.

1 kg tomatoes	1 bay leaf
3 peppers	1 twig of fresh thyme
500 g courgettes	100 ml olive oil
2 aubergines	A pinch of sugar
3 onions	Salt and freshly ground pepper
3 cloves of garlic	

Scald the tomatoes and dice them (you can also skin them and remove the pips, but this is not strictly necessary). Chop the onions and garlic coarsely. Chop the peppers into small pieces and dice the courgettes and aubergines.

Heat the oil in a thick-bottomed pot before adding the courgettes and sauté until golden, for approximately 3–4 minutes. Then remove them and place in a colander to get rid of excess oil. Add a little more oil to the pot and sauté the aubergines. Then remove them and place in a colander. Then add the onions, garlic and peppers to the pot and sauté for 5 minutes before adding the tomatoes. Put a lid on the pot and leave this mixture to simmer for 10 minutes, while stirring at regular intervals, before adding the courgettes and aubergines. Sprinkle with salt, pepper and a little sugar. Then add the bay leaf and thyme. Leave to simmer over low heat for half an hour.

P. ROUGES
3.€kg

RATATOUILLE

ONION TART

TARTE À L'OIGNON

Pastry	*Filling*
250 g flour	1 kg onions
120 g butter	2 tbsp olive oil
A pinch of salt	A pinch of ground nutmeg
1 whole egg	1 egg
1 egg yolk	6 tbsp milk
1–2 tbsp water	100 g grated Gruyère
	Salt and freshly ground pepper

Add the butter and flour to a bowl and rub the butter into the flour, then add salt and the whole egg. Knead together with a little water until the pastry is shiny and firm. Leave to set in the fridge for half an hour. Sprinkle a little flour on your worktop and roll out the dough before placing it in a greased tart mould. Place somewhere cool for 1 hour prior to baking or the pastry will shrink.

Prick the pastry with a fork allowing hot air to escape without lifting up the bottom, which would result in an uneven tart shell.

Slice the onions finely and sauté in a little oil for approximately 20 minutes over low heat. Whisk the egg, milk, cheese, nutmeg, salt and pepper. Add this mixture to the onions and pour everything into the tart mould. Bake in the oven for approximately 30 minutes at 180–190°C.

SPINACH TART WITH WALNUTS AND ROQUEFORT

TARTE AUX ÉPINARDS AUX NOIX ET AU ROQUEFORT

Pastry	Filling
250 g flour	1 kg fresh spinach
120 g butter	120 g Roquefort
A pinch of salt	3 whole eggs
1 whole egg	1 egg yolk
1 egg yolk	30 g walnuts
1–2 tbsp water	100 ml sour cream or crème fraiche (38% fat)
	20 g butter
	Salt and freshly ground pepper

Add the butter and flour to a bowl and rub the butter into the flour, then add salt and the whole egg. Knead together with a little water until the pastry is shiny and firm. Leave to set in the fridge for half an hour. Sprinkle a little flour on your worktop and roll out the pastry before placing it in a greased tart mould. Place somewhere cool for 1 hour prior to baking or the pastry will shrink.

Prick the pastry with a fork allowing hot air to escape without lifting up the bottom, which would result in an uneven tart shell.

Rinse the spinach thoroughly and then dry the leaves. You can pinch off some of the coarser stalks. Heat the butter in a pan and sauté the spinach.

Whisk the 3 eggs with a fork. Add sour cream and whisk some more. Add the coarsely chopped walnuts and chunks of Roquefort to the egg mixture. Add a little salt and pepper and then mix thoroughly.

Glaze the rim of the tart with the whisked egg yolk and a little water. Squeeze the spinach leaves dry and place them on the base of the tart. Add the egg mixture.

Bake in the oven for approximately 30 minutes at 210°C, until the crust is golden. Leave to set in the oven for 5 minutes before serving.

QUICHE PROVENÇAL

QUICHE À LA PROVENÇALE

Pastry	Filling
250 g flour	3 tomatoes
120 g butter	3 cloves of garlic
A pinch of salt	3 large onions
1 whole egg	2 tbsp olive oil
1 egg yolk	3 eggs
1–2 tbsp water	125 g sour cream or crème fraiche (38% fat)
	Salt and freshly ground pepper

Add the butter and flour to a bowl and rub the butter into the flour, then add salt and the whole egg. Knead together with a little water until the pastry is shiny and firm. Leave to set in the fridge for half an hour. Sprinkle a little flour on your worktop and roll out the pastry before you place it in a greased tart mould. Place somewhere cool for 1 hour prior to baking or the pastry will shrink.

Prick the pastry with a fork allowing hot air to escape without lifting up the bottom, which would result in an uneven tart shell.

Dip the tomatoes in boiling water and peel off their skins. Then quarter them and remove pips. Chop the garlic cloves finely and slice the onions. Add the tomatoes, garlic and onions to a pan with the olive oil and leave to simmer over a low heat for 30 minutes. Season with salt and pepper. Take the pan off the heat and leave to cool for a while. Whisk the eggs and sour cream and add to the slightly chilled tomato mixture. Pour the tomato mixture into the pastry and bake the quiche for approximately 35 minutes at 180–190°C.

BRAISED FENNEL

FENOUILS BRAISÉS

4 fennel roots
4 tbsp olive oil
250 ml white wine
6 cloves of garlic
  (unpeeled)
1 twig of thyme
2–3 bay leaves
1 tsp coriander seeds
A little flour
Salt and freshly ground
  pepper

Rinse the fennel roots and remove the outer layers. Cut in half and add to a heavy-bottomed saucepan. Add the wine and cover with water. Then add the thyme, bay leaves and coriander seeds and boil for 20 minutes. Drain and dry off the roots.

Heat the oil in a frying pan and roll the fennel roots in a little flour before placing them in the pan along with the garlic cloves. Add salt and pepper and braise over medium heat for approximately 10 minutes until golden, then turn them over and braise on other side. This dish can be enjoyed both hot and cold.

FENNEL AU GRATIN WITH PARMESAN

GRATIN DE FENOUIL AU PARMESAN

4 fennel roots
50 g butter or olive oil
250 ml white wine
6 cloves of garlic (unpeeled)
1 twig of thyme
2–3 bay leaves
1 tsp coriander seeds
40 g freshly grated
  Parmesan
Butter
Salt and freshly ground
  pepper

Rinse the fennel roots and remove the outer layers. Cut in half and add to a heavy-bottomed saucepan. Add the wine and cover with water. Then add the thyme, bay leaves and coriander seeds and boil for 20 minutes. They must not become too soft. Drain and dry off the roots.

Cut the fennel roots lengthways and place in a greased ovenproof dish. Add little knobs of butter and sprinkle with Parmesan, salt and pepper. Bake in the oven for approximately 20 minutes at 200°C until the cheese is nicely golden. Serve at once.

mole
3€

Poulet

Nouveau
Melange
Tajines

Curry Maison
extra €
9.50

Melange
s

Mélange Maison
Paela

Melange
s

OVEN-BAKED POTATOES

TIAN DE POMMES DE TERRE

1 kg potatoes

2 large onions

500 g tomatoes

2 cloves of garlic

Thyme

A few fresh basil leaves

100 g Gruyère or Parmesan

1 small cup of water

6 tbsp olive oil

Salt and freshly ground pepper

Peel and thinly slice the potatoes. Slice the tomatoes and onions. Chop the garlic cloves finely. Grease a gratin dish with olive oil. Add a layer of onions, then a layer of potatoes and then a layer of tomatoes. Sprinkle with 2 tbsp of olive oil, some grated cheese, and salt and pepper. Repeat this procedure and finish with a layer of both tomato and potato slices.

Chop the basil leaves coarsely and sprinkle on top. Add a little more salt and pepper. Sprinkle the rest of the cheese and olive oil on top.

Drain any excess water and bake in the oven for approximately 1 hour at 180°C until the potatoes are soft and nicely golden.

SALAD NICOISE

SALADE NIÇOISE

There are many variations on this speciality from Nice, considered to be one of the more exclusive Provençal dishes. Enjoy it with a Bellet-rosé from the mountains behind Nice.

100 g green beans
1 clove of garlic
4 tbsp extra virgin olive oil
5 basil leaves
1 small head of lettuce
200 g tinned tuna in oil
10 anchovy fillets
1 green pepper
5 ripe tomatoes
3 hardboiled eggs
100 g small, black olives from Nice
5–6 tbsp olive oil

Blanch the green beans in boiling water for approximately 5 minutes; do not let them get too soft. Then rinse in cold water using a sieve. Halve the garlic clove and rub around the inside of a large salad bowl. Mix olive oil, torn basil leaves, salt and pepper in a little bowl, to use as dressing.

Slice the anchovies. Remove the ribs and pips from the green pepper before slicing it. Cut the tomatoes and eggs into wedges.

Rinse and dry the lettuce leaves before tossing them gently in the dressing, then place them in the bottom of the salad bowl, spreading the tomatoes, green pepper, green beans and tuna across the leaves. Garnish with anchovies, olives and hardboiled eggs. Pour the remainder of the dressing over the salad.

SANDWICH WITH OLIVE OIL

PAN BAGNAT

This is another popular speciality from Nice. Pan bagnat *is Provençal for 'bathed bread', referring to the generous use of olive oil. Some choose to use tuna instead of anchovies – which also makes for a brilliant sandwich. Leftovers from a salad Niçoise can also be used in a* pan bagnat.

For each sandwich
1 sandwich roll or ½ baguette
½ onion
1 clove of garlic
1–2 sliced tomatoes
2–3 basil leaves
2 anchovies
5 tbsp olive oil
5 olives
1 tsp vinegar
Salt and freshly ground pepper

Cut the roll or baguette in half and take out a little of the soft middle. Rub the inside with garlic and drizzle with olive oil. Make a salad with onions, sliced tomatoes, anchovies, garlic, coarsely chopped olives and basil. Douse in a dressing of olive oil and vinegar, with an emphasis on olive oil. Sprinkle salt and pepper on top. Fill the bread with salad and squeeze tight. Wrap in aluminium foil and leave to set, until the bread has become slightly moist.

Fresh Peas with Lettuce and Thyme

PETITS POIS À LA MÉNAGÈRE

1 small head of lettuce	1½ kg fresh peas
3 twigs of thyme	50 g butter
1 small bunch of	3 tbsp water
flat leaf parsley	A pinch of salt
150 g peeled and	A sprinkling of sugar
parboiled pearl onions	

Add the head of lettuce to a heavy-bottomed saucepan along with the thyme, parsley, onions and water. Shell the peas and dice the butter. Mix the peas and butter before pouring them over the lettuce. Sprinkle with salt and sugar. Leave to simmer under a lid for approximately 5 minutes. Remove the thyme twigs and parsley before serving.

Oven-baked Vegetables

TIAN DE LÉGUMES

400 g onions	6 tbsp olive oil
800 g tomatoes	Thyme
800 g courgettes	Salt and freshly ground pepper
2 cloves of garlic	

Peel and thinly slice the onions before leaving them to simmer in a heavy-bottomed saucepan in 3 tbsp olive oil. Do not let them brown. Sprinkle with salt and freshly ground pepper. Rinse the tomatoes and courgettes. Cut the tomatoes into slices of approximately ½ cm. Use a potato peeler to make little grooves along the courgettes before cutting them into slices of approximately ½ cm. Rub an ovenproof dish with the halved garlic cloves. Add the onions and place the sliced vegetables on top, adding one red layer followed by a green one. Sprinkle with the remaining oil, thyme, salt and pepper. Bake in the oven for approximately 40 minutes at 180°C, until the vegetables are soft and nicely golden.

STUFFED VEGETABLES

LÉGUMES FARCIS AUX HERBES DE PROVENCE

4 tomatoes	150 g breadcrumbs
4 onions	200 g minced beef, venison
4 red peppers	or pork
	150 g Parmesan
Stuffing	75 g fresh basil
200 g mushrooms	50 g parsley
3 courgettes	2 twigs of tarragon
4 cloves of garlic	Salt and freshly ground pepper

Cut off the top of the tomatoes and remove the pips and juice, but save both as well as the top. Salt the tomatoes on the inside before turning them upside-down to drip dry. Place the onions and peppers on a baking sheet and bake in the oven for 20 minutes. Cut the tops off the onions and carefully remove the insides. Cut the peppers lengthways and remove the ribs and pips.

Rinse the mushrooms and slice them. Rinse the courgettes and dice them. Heat some olive oil in a sauté pan and brown the meat. Add the mushrooms, courgettes and the insides of the onions. Brown everything. Turn the heat down low and add the tomato juice. Leave to simmer for approximately 25 minutes. Remove from the heat and leave to cool.

Grate the cheese and chop the garlic and herbs finely. Mix together with the meat and add the breadcrumbs. Season with salt and pepper.

Grease an ovenproof dish with some olive oil. Stuff the tomatoes, onions and peppers with the meat stuffing and put the 'lids' back on. Drizzle a little olive oil on top before baking in the oven for approximately 30 minutes at 190°C, until tender.

Pumpkin Soup

SOUPE DE POTIRON

500 g pumpkin flesh	250 ml milk
2 onions	A sprinkling of grated nutmeg
50 g butter or olive oil	Salt and freshly ground pepper
500 ml chicken stock	8 tbsp grated Parmesan

Dice the pumpkin flesh. Chop the onions finely. Melt the butter in a saucepan and leave the onions to simmer for 6–8 minutes over a low heat. Add the pumpkin to the saucepan and leave to simmer for another 3 minutes. Then add the stock and boil for 15 minutes, until the pumpkin flesh turns soft. Take the saucepan off the heat. Purée the soup with a hand blender or use a food processor and then pour it back into the pot before adding the milk, nutmeg, salt and pepper.

Bring the soup back to the boil, then add the Parmesan and serve at once.

Pumpkin au Gratin with Olives

GRATIN DE COURGE AUX OLIVES

1 kg yellow pumpkin flesh	100 g black olives
4 cloves of garlic	100 ml olive oil
1 tbsp flour	Salt and freshly ground pepper
A small cup of sour cream or crème fraiche (38% fat)	

Dice the pumpkin flesh. Heat the oil in a heavy-bottomed saucepan before adding the pumpkin and leave to simmer for 20 minutes over a low heat. Add salt and pepper as well as the whole, peeled garlic cloves. Take the pan off the heat when the pumpkin is soft and mash with a fork. Add flour and sour cream and mix thoroughly. Remove the stones from the olives and chop coarsely before adding to the pumpkin mixture. Pour everything into a greased gratin dish and drizzle a little olive oil on top. Bake in the oven for approximately 20 minutes at 190°C.

FRIED CHANTERELLES WITH OLIVE OIL AND GARLIC

GIROLLES

500 g chanterelles
1 clove of garlic
Olive oil
Salt and freshly ground
  pepper
4 slices of country bread

In late summer, the markets will start to display an abundance of wild mushrooms. The common chanterelle grows beneath the pine forests, tastes lovely and doesn't cost much at all.

Clean the mushrooms with a small brush and knife. Try not to rinse them during this process. Fry the cleaned mushrooms in a frying pan with olive oil. Add crushed garlic and season with salt and pepper. Serve on a thick slice of toasted country bread.

FRIED CHANTERELLES WITH GOAT'S CHEESE

GIROLLES AU CHÈVRE

12 slices of country bread
2 red peppers
Olive oil
250 g chanterelles
Salt and freshly ground
  pepper
6 small round goat's cheeses
½ bunch of rocket
Olive oil
Balsamic vinegar

Toast the slices of bread in the oven until golden. Remove the ribs and pips from the peppers and cut into small pieces. Fry gently in a pan with some olive oil without letting them gain too much colour. Add the mushrooms and season with salt and pepper and leave to fry for another 2–3 minutes. Lay the mushrooms and peppers on the slices of toast. Halve the little round goat's cheeses and place them on top, squeezing them just enough to stay put. Place the slices of toast in an ovenproof dish before baking them in a pre-heated oven for 8–10 minutes at 200°C. Toss the rocket in olive oil and balsamic vinegar and use to garnish.

SALAD WITH CEPS

SALAD AUX CÈPES

2 slices of country bread

2 cloves of garlic

Olive oil

4 tbsp pine nuts

Dressing

50 ml olive oil

50 ml balsamic vinegar

1 tbsp lavender honey

½ tsp mustard

Salt and freshly ground pepper

10 *boletus edulis* (ceps)

Olive oil

Salt and freshly ground pepper

1 bunch of mixed lettuce

1 bunch of rocket

Cut the bread into strips and fry them gently until golden in olive oil along with the two garlic cloves. Dry on a paper towel and use the same frying pan to toast the pine nuts.

Mix the olive oil, balsamic vinegar, honey and mustard and season with salt and pepper. Halve the mushrooms and fry them in olive oil in a hot pan until golden and crisp. Season with salt and pepper. Tear the lettuce into small shreds and toss in a bowl with the dressing.

Serve the salad in a soup plate and place the mushrooms and bread sticks on top. Garnish with the roasted pine nuts.

FRIED CEPS WITH THYME

CÈPES

In October, it's easy to buy fresh ceps and other sorts of boletus. For the rest of the year, you'll have to settle for the dried versions, but autumn is the season for enjoying them straight from the wild, and the best way to do this is to prepare them as simply as possible.

500 g *boletus edulis* or any other kind of *boletus*
3 tbsp olive oil
Thyme

Clean the mushrooms thoroughly and slice thinly. Fry them in olive oil and sprinkle with thyme. Serve as a starter on their own, or with freshly baked bread.

TRUFFLES – THE BLACK GOLD

There is no ingredient as shrouded in mystery and secrecy as the truffle. It is the jewel in the crown of *haute cuisine* and the black gold of Provence. This is due to the fact that no one has yet succeeded in taming or cultivating it, so to track a truffle down in the wild requires enormous skill and local knowledge.

The truffle has had a fascinating and unpredictable history. In the *The Physiology of Taste*, Brillat-Savarin described its existence thus almost two hundred years ago: 'you simply find it where it is, and the large oak forest of Provence is one such place.'

Along with Périgord in the South West of France, Provence prides itself on producing some of the world's finest truffles. Even though you may find truffles in many areas, there is an immense difference in quality. In Provence, people are mainly interested in the black truffle: *Tuber melanosporum*.

These are found mostly in the forested mountains of the Provençal hinterland, away from the Mediterranean Sea. A truffle grows symbiotically with the roots of the oak tree, providing it with many important nutrients, while the oak delivers vital nutrients back to the truffle, without which it would not be able to survive.

In autumn, the mushroom begins to sprout subterranean fruits, and it is these black roots we call truffles. They grow an inch or so below ground and develop a strong smell, attracting both squirrels and boars. The animals will quickly locate the mushroom, dig it out and eat it. This is how the truffle spreads its spores, and they happen to sprout much more successfully when passed through the intestines of an animal.

The hunt for truffles in Provence is at its most intense from November until March. However, in contrast with boar hunting, which takes place at the same time, the Provençal do not make a song and dance about hunting for truffles; the last thing they want is to reveal where their treasure is buried.

As with other hunts, the truffle hunt is strictly organised. There are signs on the oak trees informing you of who has the right to gather truffles from the different plots; and I wouldn't recommend that you challenge the rights of a truffle-hunter. Stealing truffles is a serious matter and if you trespass, you are literally at risk of being shot. In any case, hunting for truffles is not for tourists. You have to be in the know to find the right spots. The truffle-hunters, *les rabassiers*, often look for small patches of bare ground or singed areas around the oak trees. Another tell tale sign is clouds of *mouches aux truffes*, tiny flies that are drawn in by the truffles' odour, and whose larva mature in the mushroom.

In the old days, truffle-hunters would train pigs to go hunting for truffles, but it's now more common to use dogs. The main reason for this being that pigs find the smell of truffles irresistible and it takes several men to hold back a pig that has got wind of truffles. Keeping a dog in check is definitely easier. When the dog starts digging, the truffle-hunter will take over and finish the digging with his hands. The dog will have to settle for a piece of cheese as a reward.

It may seem odd that these muddy roots with coarse, deformed bulges on them, really are extremely delicate. However, once you've smelled a black truffle, you're in no doubt that you're in the presence of something very special. It is a delicate scent, best described as sharp, almost bitter, with a light touch of sweet forest floor. It is this unique aroma that chefs and gourmets all over the world can't get enough of. In Provence, truffles are most often served with scrambled eggs. You get the best result by using a generous amount of fresh truffles, grated onto the eggs while still in the pan, but you can also simply leave your truffle in a closed bag along with the fresh eggs. Within 24 hours, your eggs will have absorbed the truffle's flavour. This is actually how most people in Provence use their truffles. It's the most economical way to make a truffle last, and always yields an impressive result.

The most important truffle towns in Provence are Carpentras in the Vaucluse and Aups in Var. The oak forests in the mountains surrounding the little village of Aups, which lies at an altitude of 500 m to the high north of Draguignan, produce a particularly rich supply of truffles. The red clay soil gives the truffles taste and density, and the climate is ideal. Aups itself is a charming village with mossy fountains and narrow lanes, where primitive stone buildings lean against each other for support. Traditionally the village was well known for producing olives, honey and wine. But today, it's the truffle that has put Aups firmly on the gastronomic map.

Aups is also one of the few places where you can buy fresh truffles in winter. From November until the middle of March, there is a truffle-market in town every Thursday. It's a peaceful, quiet market that infuses the entire village with a magical scent of truffles.

Café du Grand Cours, on the corner of the market square with its speckled plane trees, is the unofficial trading centre. On cold winter mornings, the café fills up with an insistent, pungent smell of smoke, coffee and alcohol. Customers at the zinc-bar are an odd mixture of tourists, farmers and hopeful buyers. It is here, at the café, that truffle-hunters meet and sniff out a little information about everyone else's success as well as the price of the day. The atmosphere is tense before the actual bargaining begins. Everyone is waiting for the market to open. It happens suddenly, indicated by a sign, which to the uninitiated can seem utterly insignificant, but once given, everybody rushes into the market square. Outside the café, people gather around those selling truffles, and they all look rather uncomfortable. It's all very secretive. Most of the truffle-hunters are not registered, and nobody seems overly enthusiastic about paying VAT or taxes.

Those who sell the sought-after truffles are withdrawn farmers dressed in hunting gear. They stand by their battered old cars and discreetly pull the goods from scrunched up bags while the cacophony of hunting dogs, barking and jumping around on car seats, drowns out any attempt at normal conversation.

The market in Aups is far from sophisticated. On the contrary, everything appears incredibly primitive, and it's immediately clear that overheads for this particular industry are kept very low. However, as soon as money changes hands and wallets are opened, huge wads of bank notes fall out. Business is conducted in a hurry, and the spoils of the day are quickly distributed. And this is regardless of whether the day's harvest is no more than 50 kg or if the numbers reach several hundred kg, as is often than case in January and February. Tourists can also buy truffles. Expect to pay £20–£30 for a small truffle. It might only be enough for a portion of scrambled eggs, but the fun had acquiring it will be far greater.

POTATO SALAD WITH TRUFFLES

SALADE DE POMMES DE TERRE ET DES TRUFFES

500 g small, firm potatoes
1 fresh truffle (approximately 50 g)

Dressing
3 tsp white wine vinegar
4 tbsp olive oil
1 tbsp white truffle oil
Salt and freshly ground pepper

Whisk the truffle oil, olive oil and vinegar in a little bowl and add salt and pepper. Brush and scrub the truffle very carefully and dry it off with a damp cloth. Then peel the truffle and chop the peel before adding it to the dressing. Leave the dressing to stand for an hour.

Boil the potatoes with their skins on, then peel them and leave them to cool down. Then slice them and place in a dish. Pour the dressing over the potatoes and leave to marinate for approximately 1 hour. Then finely slice the peeled truffle and sprinkle it over the potatoes. Season with salt and pepper.

Toast with Truffles

LA TARTINE DU RABASSIER

4 slices of country bread
1 fresh truffle (approximately 50 g)
Olive oil
Salt and freshly ground pepper

Drizzle the bread with olive oil before toasting it in the oven. Add the finely sliced truffle and grill until beautifully golden.

Sautéed Truffle with Garlic and Olive Oil

TRUFFES SAUTÉES À L'AIL

1 fresh truffle (approximately 50 g)
3 tbsp olive oil
3 cloves of garlic
Salt and freshly ground pepper

Chop the garlic coarsely. Warm the olive oil on a pan and just allow the garlic to turn brown, but not burnt. Then throw away the garlic. Add the finely sliced truffle to the pan and leave until heated. Season with salt and pepper and serve with pasta or on toast.

Scrambled Egg with Truffle

BROUILLADE AUX TRUFFES

5 fresh eggs
1 fresh truffle (approximately 50 g)
1 tbsp olive oil
50 g butter
Salt and freshly ground pepper

Put the fresh eggs and the scrubbed truffle together in an airtight bag overnight – or at least 5 hours – prior to using. The truffle aroma will permeate the porous eggshell and add flavour to the raw egg.

Grate half the truffle and slice the remaining half finely. Heat the olive oil in a pan and add the beaten eggs, salt and pepper as well as the grated truffle. Mix carefully.

Just before the eggs set completely, add the butter and gently mix it in. Sprinkle the sliced truffle on top and serve immediately with toast.

SEAFOOD

Some of the most famous Provençal dishes are based on the seafood caught off its rocky coastline, such as *bouillabaisse, bourride* and *anchoïade*. Fishing has been a part of coastal life for centuries, but in the last 25 years, it has diminished greatly. There are not enough fish left and no living to be made. Even so, nearly every harbour has a few active fishermen, who try to supply local demand.

They fish for mackerel, John Dory, octopus, sea bass, red mullet, mullet, sardine, anchovy, and the small fish they sell as *poissons de roche* – which include different kinds of wrasse, gurnard and of course, *la rascasse*, also known as the scorpionfish in English. They also harvest mussels along the coast as well as oysters and the small *tellines* from the Camargue.

Most of the fishing is done off small wooden boats, which are called *pointus*. They're colourful dinghies that are highly seaworthy and they cope very well with the short, sharp Mediterranean waves. The name *pointus* is derived from their shape: the ends are pointy while the body itself is curvy. Formerly, they only carried lateen sails and oars, but these days, most of them also use a motor. They're also characterised by not having a cabin or anything else to provide shelter for the fishermen.

You'll often find this type of boat in the western part of the Mediterranean. Some of the best boat builders came from Sicily, Naples or Catalonia and they settled along the coast of Provence, where they built boats for the local fishermen. A typical trait of a *pointu* is *le capien*, which is the part of the sternpost that stretches forward like a small figurehead and is used to keep the moorings in place. The keel does not have a deep draught, which makes it easy to sail close to the rocky coastline, and furthermore, the boats are easy to pull up on land, which is why you'll often see them in the inner harbour, where the water is shallow. This is most certainly true of the harbour in Saint-Tropez, where you can see quite a few well-preserved and lovely examples. The dinghies will often be white on the outside, while the deck and railing will be bright blue, green or red.

It's now the exception, rather than the rule, to see big fishing boats in the harbours, probably because fishing is not a highly profitable business; it has always been a rather tough and primitive way of making a living.

Moreover, the salted and dried cod used for *brandade* and *grand aïoli* is not from the Mediterranean, but from the North Atlantic Sea – often all the way from the north of Norway. In earlier days, when olive oil was carried to Norway by ship, merchant vessels would stock up on salted and dried cod before returning to Provence, and this is what led to the invention of dishes containing Norwegian fish. Distributing the salted and dried cod to markets in little mountain villages would have been easy, and *grand aïoli* has become a very popular festive dish.

The fish markets in Nice, Saint-Raphaël, Saint-Tropez and especially Marseilles don't offer a particularly varied selection and the fish will often be small in size: so small that fishermen further north would think twice before reeling them in. However, the Provençal know exactly what to do with them. The fish soups served along the coast are made from the little, ugly, prickly fish and they are often nothing short of sublime.

There are numerous versions of fish soups and all along the coast, they argue about the right way to prepare a real *bouillabaisse* or *bourride*. There is no definitive answer, but visiting the small seafood restaurants along the coast of Cassis and Marseilles is highly recommended, so then at least the visitor can make up his or her own mind.

ANCHOVY PASTE

ANCHOÏADE

It's important to use proper anchovies, and not salted sprats, which often masquerade as the real thing...

25 anchovy fillets in oil
3 cloves of garlic
25ml olive oil
1 tsp mustard

1 tbsp white wine vinegar
1 egg yolk
Freshly ground pepper

Chop the garlic and anchovies finely in a blender. Add 1 tbsp of olive oil, and the mustard, vinegar and egg yolk while the blender is still running. Then turn the blender down to a low speed and add the remaining oil slowly. Serve at once, or place somewhere cool. *Anchoïade* is used as a side dish with raw vegetables, hard-boiled eggs or on small pieces of toasted country bread.

ANCHOVY BREAD

PAIN AUX ANCHOIS

A jar of anchovies in brine
2–3 cloves of garlic
Olive oil
Country bread or baguettes

This recipe is a light version of the *anchoïade*. Soak the anchovies in water and remove their spines. Then pound the anchovies, garlic and olive oil in a mortar until they become a paste. Spread this paste on small pieces of bread and roast in the oven for 5 minutes.

SEA URCHINS

OURSINS

From late October until the end of March, you might get lucky and find fresh sea urchins at the markets. Divers, who look for them along the coastline and carefully pry them off the rocks with a knife, gather these.

Sea urchins are so popular that the authorities have had to ban harvesting all together in the summer season, and quotas for how many each diver is allowed to take per day outside the summer season have been introduced. The Provençal eat them without any kind of preparation; they just rinse them in a little lemon juice and enjoy them with a glass of chilled rosé wine. It doesn't get much simpler or fresher than that.

You open a sea urchin at the bottom using a special tool called a *coupe oursin*. In fact, you're only supposed to eat the star-shaped orange ovaries, also known as corals. However, enthusiasts eat the entire creature raw or use it in soups, sauces or dressings.

In January and February, you will find special markets with sea urchins in Carry-le-Rouet and Sausset-les-Pins, west of Marseilles.

Oysters au Gratin

HUÎTRES FARCIES

24 large oysters
3 shallots
1 clove of garlic
2 tbsp butter
1 bunch of parsley
Salt and freshly ground pepper
500 g coarse salt, for putting the shells in

Heat your oven to 240°C. Chop the onions and parsley finely and mix with the crushed garlic, butter, salt and pepper.

Place the salt in the bottom of an ovenproof dish and place the whole oysters on top.

Bake in the oven until the oysters open and then pull off the top shell.

Place a knob of the herb butter on each oyster and return the dish to the oven for another 1–2 minutes, until the butter is sizzling. Serve at once.

Botargo

POUTARGUE

If you are really lucky, you can find *poutargue*, the pressed and salted *botargo* (roe) from mullet caught at Martigues.

The mullet are caught when passing between the salt lake *Étang de Berre* and the Mediterranean. Locally the *botargo* is called *caviar martégal*.

You can also get *botargo* from Italy or North Africa, however, the Provençal aren't interested, claiming that their produce is far superior to all others, both in terms of quality and taste.

The production is very limited and so it's quite rare, but it is an exquisite delicacy that should be enjoyed thinly sliced and drizzled with lemon juice, accompanied by a cool glass of white wine from Cassis.

If the *botargo* is sold in a wax coating, you'd be correct in thinking that it's not the genuine article, but rather *botargo* imported from North Africa, which is often called Mediterranean caviar.

BOILED LANGOUSTINE

LANGOUSTE BOUILLIE

2 langoustines, approximately 500 g

Stock
Thyme
1 carrot
2 onions
4 litres of water
3 tbsp salt
1 tsp sugar

Slice the onions and the carrot. Bring the water, herbs and vegetables to a boil. Then add the langoustines to the boiling stock. Put a lid on the pot and leave to boil for approximately 10 minutes. Turn off the heat and leave to simmer for another 10 minutes. Take out the langoustines and place them on their backs, to keep the juices from escaping. Cover them up and place in the fridge to cool. Then split the langoustines and serve with toasted country bread and *aïoli*.

TUNA PASTE

THOIONNADE

Sadly, fishing for tuna has more or less ceased along the coast of the French Mediterranean. Luckily for us, this classic dish is also delicious when using tinned tuna – as long as you remember to use good quality olive oil.

250 g tuna in oil
3 cloves of garlic
50 g capers
50 ml olive oil
A few black olives

Crush the garlic cloves and remove the stones from the olives. Pound the ingredients in a mortar or blend to a paste in a blender. The paste should be relatively solid. Serve on toast, with tomatoes or hard-boiled eggs.

GRILLED SARDINES

SARDINES GRILLÉES

Most people think of sardines as a cheap but tasty ingredient bought in tins, and indeed they are, if served on toasted country bread and drizzled with lemon juice. However, freshly caught sardines are a world away from the tinned variety, and much more delicious. For the best result, make sure you buy them as fresh as possible from the harbour markets along the Mediterranean. Sardines do not require much preparation; the Provençal don't even remove the innards, preferring to cook and eat them whole.

Grilled sardines are very delicate when brushed with olive oil and lemon juice prior to a couple of minutes each side on a charcoal grill, but, as shown in this recipe, you can also fry them.

200 g wheat flour
1 twig of thyme
500 g sardines
Salt and freshly ground pepper
Lemon juice
Olive oil

Coat the sardines in flour and thyme and fry them in a pan with olive oil for a couple of minutes on both sides. The fish themselves are quite oily so be careful not to use too much oil. Do not fry them for too long either, as they will quickly lose their lovely taste and become quite dry. Drizzle some lemon juice on top and serve directly from the pan. Enjoy with a glass of rosé wine.

MONKFISH WITH GARLIC

BAUDROIE À L'AIL

1½ kg monkfish
6–8 shallots
4 cloves of garlic
1 twig of thyme
200 ml white wine
Salt and freshly ground pepper
6 tbsp olive oil

Peel the shallots and slice them before gently frying them in olive oil – they must not turn brown.

Pierce the monkfish with halved garlic cloves – as if it were a leg of lamb. Place in an ovenproof dish and cover the entire fish in the sautéed shallots.

Add thyme and white wine and bake in the oven for 25–30 minutes at 180°C or until the meat effortlessly flakes off the bone. Be sure to keep an eye on the fish, as you want it to be succulent and not the least bit dry.

KING PRAWNS WITH WINE AND GARLIC

GAMBAS AU VIN ET À L'AIL

The king prawns of the Mediterranean are caught in deep waters and kept on ice from the moment they are caught. When fresh, they're a greyish-brown but after boiling they turn a gorgeous red colour, rather like lobsters. They're impressive creatures that can be as long as 20 cm and are far superior in taste to the cultivated version from Southeast Asia, which unfortunately are much easier to get hold of.

4 large freshly caught king prawns
200 ml rosé wine
3 shallots
2 cloves of garlic
Parsley
1 twig of thyme
Salt and freshly ground pepper
Olive oil

Chop the shallots, garlic and parsley finely. Fry the prawns in a deep pan with olive oil until beautifully red. Add the shallots and thyme and leave to simmer for a moment. Then add the wine, garlic, and parsley and leave to simmer under a lid for approximately 20 minutes. Try not to reduce the sauce completely. Serve with fresh country bread.

SCALLOPS AU GRATIN

COQUILLES SAINT JACQUES À LA PROVENÇALE

4 large scallops
  (with coral if possible)
1 clove of garlic
2 tbsp lemon juice
1 tbsp parsley
4 tbsp olive oil
100 g bread crumbs
Salt and freshly ground pepper

Place the scallops in their shells or in a small ovenproof dish.

Mix the oil, lemon, crushed garlic, salt and pepper and cover the scallops, thus ensuring that they do not dry out while cooking.

Sprinkle a few breadcrumbs and some olive oil on top before placing the shells in the oven at 225°C for approximately 10–15 minutes or until nicely golden. Sprinkle finely chopped parsley on top and serve immediately.

SALT COD PURÉE

BRANDADE DE MORUE

1.2 kg salt cod
200 ml whole milk
200 ml olive oil
3 cloves of garlic
Juice of 1 lemon
A pinch of grated nutmeg
½ bunch of parsley
2 tbsp whipping cream
 (can be left out)
Salt and white pepper

Court bouillon
2 litres of cold water
Peppercorns
1 celery stalk
1 carrot
1 onion
Twigs of thyme and parsley

Steep the cod in water for 24 hours (changing the water several times). Then boil in the *court bouillon*, which you make in a pot with water, peppercorns, celery, carrot, onion and a little thyme and parsley. Boil for approximately 8 minutes once the bouillon reaches boiling point.

Leave the cod to drip dry. Remove what skin and bones may be left before flaking the fish. Heat the milk and oil in two different saucepans. Add the cod to a bowl with 2 tbsp olive oil and the crushed garlic cloves. Stir with a wooden spoon while you add the milk and olive oil. Continue stirring until the cod becomes a soft, white, solid pulp.

Season with whipped cream, nutmeg and white pepper. Add a little lemon juice if the cod purée is too bland.

Sprinkle with chopped parsley and serve at once, accompanied by boiled potatoes, bread croutons or whole wheat bread.

Potatoes with Brandade

POMMES DE TERRE À LA BRANDADE

6 baking potatoes
3 tbsp olive oil

Make the brandade as shown on page 188.

Scrub the potatoes thoroughly and bake in the oven for approximately 1½ hours, depending on size. Then halve the potatoes lengthwise and carefully scoop out the pulp, without ruining the skins. Mash the pulp and mix with the warm brandade. Add it all to an icing bag and squeeze back into the potato skins (you can also use a spoon).

Drizzle olive oil on top of the potatoes and bake in the oven at 200°C for approximately 15 minutes or until they are nicely golden. Serve directly from the oven with some fresh bread and a green salad.

Red Peppers with Brandade

POIVRONS ROUGES À LA BRANDADE

6 red peppers
Olive oil

Make the brandade as shown on page 188.

Cut off the tops of the peppers and remove ribs and pips. Smear them with olive oil and bake in the oven at 200°C for 8–10 minutes. Then fill with the warm brandade, drizzle a little olive oil on top and bake for another 10–12 minutes, until the top is nicely golden. Remember to leave the top of the peppers in the dish. Place at an angle when serving.

Salt Cod with Garlic Mayonnaise

LE GRAND AÏOLI

Le grand aïoli is a traditional dish, which is always served on festive occasions. It is practically obligatory on Good Friday and Christmas Eve (December 24th).

1 kg salt cod	*Court bouillon*
4 hard-boiled eggs	2 litres of cold water
4 small violet artichokes	Peppercorns
1 lemon	1 celery stalk
1 fennel root	1 carrot
½ bunch of new carrots	1 onion
8 turnips	Twigs of thyme and parsley
½ cauliflower	
100 g green beans	

Steep the cod in water for 24 hours (changing the water several times).

Rinse and clean all vegetables before boiling them in lightly salted water. They must not boil for too long, as you want them to remain crunchy. Boil the artichokes separately, with lemon juice in the water, or they will discolour.

Boil the steeped cod in *court bouillon*, which you make in a saucepan with water, peppercorns, celery, carrot, onion and a little thyme and parsley. Boil for approximately 8 minutes once the bouillon reaches boiling point.

Serve the cod while steaming hot on a dish with all the vegetables and a bowl of *aïoli* (please refer back to page 30).

FISH SOUP

SOUPE DE POISSON

*This soup will be at its best when made with Mediterranean fish,
but you can also use small, white fish such as greater weaver, mullet
and gurnard.*

100 ml olive oil

1 kg fish, without innards,
  skin or scales

4 ripe, skinned tomatoes
  (can also be tinned)

5–6 small crabs
  (can be left out)

2 leeks

2 onions

2 cloves of garlic

1 fennel stalk

A little dried orange zest
  (can be left out)

1 twig of thyme

1 bay leaf

1 pinch of saffron

Salt and freshly ground pepper

200 g Gruyère

Garlic croutons

Add the oil to a large saucepan and sauté the leeks, onions and garlic.
Add 2 litres of water to the pan. Then add the fish, crabs, skinned
tomatoes and herbs. Boil over a high heat for 15 minutes.

Purée the soup in a food processor, a little at a time. Add saffron
and bring the soup to a boil again. Season with salt and pepper.

Serve the soup steaming hot with little garlic croutons, grated
cheese and *rouille* (please refer to page 197).

GARLIC SAUCE WITH SAFFRON

ROUILLE

Serve rouille *with fish soups. Don't make it too strong though.*

3 cloves of garlic
1 slice of fresh bread
1 small boiled potato
200 ml olive oil
3 tbsp fish soup
  (can be left out)

1 egg yolk
½ tsp ground saffron
1 tsp cayenne pepper
1 pinch of coarse salt

Chop the garlic cloves in a food processor. Add the bread and then the potato, mashed. Blend thoroughly. Leave the machine running while you add 1 tbsp olive oil, the egg yolk and 1 tbsp fish soup. Add the remaining olive oil slowly, while the blender is still running, as if you were making mayonnaise.

Dissolve the saffron in a little boiling water. Add the rest of the fish soup to the mixture in the food processor before adding the saffron mixture, cayenne pepper and a decent pinch of salt.

BOUILLABAISSE

BOUILLABAISSE

2½ litres of cold water

100 ml olive oil

1 kg fish, without innards
   or scales

6 ripe and skinned tomatoes
   (can also be tinned)

2 leeks

1 carrot

1 dried fennel stalk or
   1 fresh fennel root

A little orange zest
   (can be left out)

Fresh thyme

2 bay leaves

A little saffron
   (its taste is quite
   penetrating)

2 tbsp tomato purée

50 ml pastis

200 ml white wine

Salt and freshly ground
   pepper

200 g Gruyère

Garlic croutons

You'll achieve the best results here if you use 7–8 different kinds of Mediterranean fish such as scorpion-fish (la rascasse), greater weaver, sea bass, mullet, gurnard, conger eel and John Dory. These can all be ordered at your local fishmonger.

Bouillabaisse *was originally a rather primitive dish, which the fishermen from Marseilles made from the small catch that no-one wanted to buy. It needs a quick parboiling (bouillir), then you turn the heat down and leave it to simmer (baissir), which is how the dish got its name. The* bouillabaisse *is often served on two separate plates, one with soup and one with fish. It's very important not to overcook the fish.*

Add oil and garlic to a large saucepan, the garlic must not turn brown. Add leeks, onion, carrot and sauté. Then add tomato purée, pastis and white wine.

Add 2½ litres of cold water and bring to the boil. When boiling, add the fish (whole or in big pieces) and the herbs, except saffron. Skim the soup regularly. Leave to simmer over low heat for approximately 1 hour. Make sure the fish is not overcooked. Take out the pieces of fish and remove any skin and bones. Keep them warm, so they can be served separately or with the soup.

Purée the soup in a blender and strain through a medium sized strainer; it is important that it is not too finely meshed. Season with saffron, salt and pepper. Chop the tomato into nice little squares and add to the steaming hot soup. Serve with grated Gruyère and garlic croutons. This can also be served with rouille (please refer back to page 197).

FISH STEW WITH GARLIC SAUCE

BOURRIDE

Bourride *is the lesser-known cousin of* bouillabaisse, *and is equally delicious.*

4 fillets of firm, white
   fish of 150–200 g
   (monkfish, turbot,
   halibut, sea bass
   or mullet)
½ carrot
½ courgette
¼ leek
3 cloves of garlic
1 bay leaf

1 twig of thyme
2 short fennel stalks
1 litre of fish stock
100 ml dry white wine
15 small, firm potatoes
1 portion *aïoli* (please refer
   back to page 30)
1 tbsp olive oil
2 egg yolks
Garlic croutons

Slice the carrot, courgette and leek very finely. Chop the garlic cloves finely. Heat some olive oil in a saucepan over a medium heat and sauté the vegetables. Place the fish fillets on top of the vegetables and the herbs on top of the fish. Cover with fish stock and white wine. Sprinkle a little salt on top. Leave to poach for approximately 15 minutes over a very low heat.

Meanwhile, boil the potatoes, peel them and keep them warm. Put the fish fillets on a heated dish and keep warm. Strain the soup into another pot and reduce by half. Add approximately ⅔ of the *aïoli* into a bowl and mix in one egg yolk and 2 tbsp soup. Mix thoroughly and then add the second egg yolk and a little more soup. Add this mixture to the remaining soup and heat carefully. Do not bring to a boil. Place the fish on soup plates, pour in soup and serve with the remaining *aïoli*, garlic croutons and potatoes on the side.

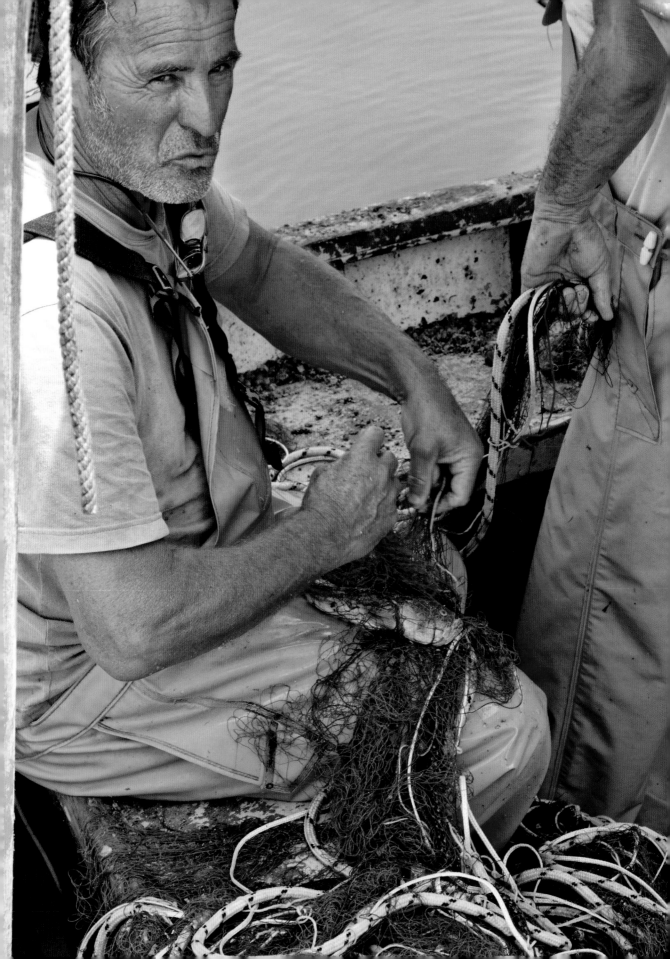

PROVENÇAL SQUID

ENCORNETS À LA PROVENÇALE

1 kg squid
1 onion
3 tbsp olive oil
350 g skinned tomatoes
300 ml dry white wine
2 cloves of garlic
Potherbs with thyme,
  bay leaf and 1 fennel stalk
Salt and freshly ground
  pepper

For this dish, use tubular squid called encornets *or* calamars *in French. Ask your fishmonger to clean them, which involves removing the beak and taking out the cartilage.*

Cut the squid into slices approximately 3 cm wide. Chop the onions, garlic and tomatoes finely.

Heat the oil in a thick-bottomed saucepan and sauté the onions until soft but not brown. Turn the heat up and add the squid. Stir until the juice from the squid evaporates. Add the white wine and bring to a boil. Then add the tomatoes, garlic and potherbs. Bring to a boil once again and season with salt and pepper. Place a lid half way across the pot and leave to simmer for approximately 45 minutes. If there is too much liquid, take out the squid and reduce over a high heat. Then put the squid back in the pot and serve at once with rice (from Camargue, if you have it) on the side.

FRIED CALAMARI

CALAMARS

For this dish, use tubular squid called encornets *or calamars in French. Ask your fishmonger to clean them, which involves removing the beak and taking out the cartilage. You can also deep-fry them; however, if you follow this recipe, you will use much less oil.*

8–10 squid

200 g wheat flour

Some breadcrumbs
  or broken wheat

Olive oil

Lemon

Salt and freshly ground pepper

Aïoli (please refer to page 30)

Cut the squid into slices approximately 1 cm wide. Add the bread-crumbs or broken wheat to the flour and roll the squid in the flour mixture. Fry in a cast iron saucepan or in a heavy frying pan. Fry for a couple of minutes on both sides until beautifully golden. If the squid seems a little tough, give it a bit longer. Serve directly from the pan with lemon and *aïoli* on the side.

OCTOPUS SALAD

SALADE DE POULPE

In spite of its alarming looks, the large eight-armed octopus is a very popular ingredient in all Mediterranean countries. It can weigh up to several kilos and its arms can be as long as one metre. If prepared properly, the meat is very tender and extremely delicious. The Greeks bash the beast energetically against the rocks before throwing it on a charcoal grill. However, it is equally effective if you freeze the octopus for a couple of days before boiling it. The cooking time is naturally dependent on the size of the animal, but half a kilo's worth of octopus should be cooked in 40 minutes. The easiest way to be sure your octopus is tender is to cut it with a knife.

1 octopus of around 1 kg
200 ml olive oil
3 tbsp lemon juice
1 clove of garlic
Salt and freshly ground pepper
1 tbsp parsley

Pickle
Thyme
Salt and freshly ground pepper
Bay leaves

Boil the octopus in the pickle until tender. Then remove the octopus and leave to cool. Cut it into slices approximately 3 cm wide though slice the arms into slightly bigger chunks – it looks good. Add the octopus to a bowl with oil, lemon juice, finely chopped garlic and parsley as well as salt and pepper. Leave to set for a while in the fridge and serve with toasted country bread.

OCTOPUS IN A RED WINE SAUCE

POULPE AU VIN ROUGE

An octopus weighing 1 kg

4 onions

2 cloves of garlic

500 ml red wine

2 tbsp flour

4 tbsp olive oil

Salt and freshly ground pepper

Freeze the octopus for a couple of days before cooking, to tenderise it. Then boil the thawed octopus for approximately 1½ hours or until it is completely tender. Cool and cut into slices of approximately 3 cm width.

Chop the onions finely. Braise the octopus in olive oil. Remove the octopus and sauté the onions until golden. Add the flour and mix before adding the wine and crushed garlic. Put the octopus back in the saucepan and leave to simmer for 40 minutes. Make sure the sauce is not too thin. Season with salt and pepper and serve with rice or pasta.

STUFFED CALAMARI

CALAMARS FARCIS

1 kg squid	100 g chopped breadcrumbs
3 cloves of garlic	1 tbsp flour
5 tbsp olive oil	150 ml dry white wine
3 skinned tomatoes	1 bay leaf
2 tbsp parsley	1 tbsp dry breadcrumbs
2 onions	2 tbsp boiling water
3 egg yolks	Salt and freshly ground pepper

Clean and rinse the squid. Chop the tentacles and set aside.

Add 1 tbsp olive oil to a saucepan and sauté one of the chopped onions over a low heat. Add the bay leaf, 1 chopped garlic clove and 1 tbsp flour. Mix thoroughly and add the wine and 2 tbsp boiling water. Season with salt and pepper and bring the sauce to the boil. Leave to simmer for 15 minutes.

Fry the other chopped onion for 3 minutes in olive oil until soft but not brown. Add the chopped squid tentacles and chopped tomatoes. Season with salt and pepper and leave to simmer while stirring until the tomatoes have reduced. Take the saucepan off the heat before adding the fresh breadcrumbs, 2 chopped garlic cloves and parsley. Mix the stuffing thoroughly and add a little boiled water if necessary. Then add the 3 egg yolks. Stuff the squid-tubes, close them and place in a greased ovenproof dish. Pour the sauce over the squid and sprinkle dry breadcrumbs and some olive oil on top before baking in the oven for approximately 50 minutes at 190°C.

MUSSELS WITH PASTIS

MOULES AU PASTIS

2½ kg mussels

3 tbsp olive oil

2 leeks

3 cloves of garlic

3 carrots

600 ml dry white wine

100 ml pastis

½ bunch of parsley

1 bay leaf

Salt and freshly ground pepper

Scrub and rinse the mussels. Those that are cracked or do not close while scrubbing should be discarded.

Add the olive oil and finely chopped leeks to a saucepan and sauté until soft but not brown. Add crushed garlic, finely chopped carrots, salt and pepper. Then add the wine, pastis and bay leaf and leave to simmer without a lid until the liquid is reduced by about half.

Add the parsley and mussels. Put a lid on the pot and shake to ensure that all the mussels make contact with the liquid. The dish is ready when the mussels open, which should take 5–8 minutes. Throw away mussels that have not opened.

Serve the mussels and soup together in small bowls with fresh bread on the side.

MUSSELS IN WHITE WINE

MOULES MARINIÈRES

2½ kg mussels

3 tbsp olive oil

4 shallots

3 cloves of garlic

3 carrots

600 ml dry white wine

½ bunch of parsley

1 bay leaf

Salt and freshly ground pepper

Scrub and rinse the mussels. Those that are cracked or do not close while scrubbing should be discarded.

Add the finely chopped onions to a saucepan with olive oil and sauté until soft but not brown.

Add the crushed garlic, finely chopped carrots, salt and pepper. Then add the wine and bay leaf and leave to simmer without a lid until the liquid is reduced by about half.

Add the parsley and mussels. Put the lid on the saucepan and shake to ensure that all the mussels make contact with the soup. The dish is ready when the mussels open, which should take 5–8 minutes. Throw away mussels that have not opened.

Serve the mussels and soup together in small bowls with fresh bread on the side.

MUSSELS AU GRATIN

MOULES GRATINÉES

2 kg mussels	*Gratin*
2 tbsp butter	2 tbsp butter
2 shallots	3 tbsp flour
1 carrot	2 shallots
1 tsp parsley	2 slices of dry bread
1 bay leaf	3 tbsp milk
200 ml dry white wine	200 ml reduced mussel stock
	300 g spinach
	Salt and freshly ground pepper
	3 tbsp grated Swiss cheese

Scrub and rinse the mussels. Those that are cracked or do not close while scrubbing should be discarded. Add some butter, finely chopped shallots, bay leaf, chopped parsley and wine to a large saucepan and bring to the boil before adding the mussels and leave to simmer over high heat for 5–8 minutes, until the mussels have opened. Shake well while cooking. Throw away mussels that have not opened.

Rinse the spinach and remove the coarsest stalks. Then chop and blanch the spinach in a little water. Drain the water. Soak the bread in milk. Melt some butter in another saucepan and sauté the shallots for a few minutes until soft but not brown. Add flour and the hot mussel soup. Stir thoroughly until the sauce is hot. Squeeze the milk from the bread before adding to the sauce with the chopped and blanched spinach. Season with salt and pepper.

Place the mussels in their shells and fill up with the spinach mixture. Sprinkle with some Swiss cheese. Bake in oven at 250°C until golden.

MUSSELS WITH CAMARGUE RICE

RIZ DE CAMARGUE AUX MOULES

A great deal of the rice used in France comes from Camargue at the Rhône Estuary. The rice is cultivated on huge, flat, and at times swampy, plains, where it is practically impossible to grow anything else. The local production of rice increased greatly when France had to give up its territories in Indochina in the 1950s.

125 g Camargue rice	A pinch of saffron
1 kg mussels	200 ml dry white wine
2 tbsp olive oil	1 tbsp flour
1 onion	25 g butter
2 cloves of garlic	100–200 ml stock
1 tomato	Salt and freshly ground pepper
1 shallot	

Boil the Camargue rice according to the instructions on the packet.

Scrub the mussels and rinse in lots of cold water. Discard the mussels that do not close. Steam the mussels in white wine until they open. Throw away those that do not open. Save the stock from the mussels and add the rice, before boiling for approximately 10 minutes over low heat, making sure the rice doesn't dry out.

Add the olive oil to a pot along with the butter, finely chopped onion, shallot, tomato and garlic. Leave to simmer for a short while before adding the flour. Stir thoroughly. When it is all golden, add the stock. Leave to simmer and add the rice. Season with salt, pepper and saffron. Pour the mussels over the rice and serve.

Soft Clams

TELLINES

Where the sandy beaches of Camargue meet the Mediterranean, you'll find little tellines, *soft clams. When steamed in white wine they're considered one of the great Provençal delicacies. The clams are buried in the sand and can be fished all year around, but summertime is high season. The fishermen –* les tellinaires *– catch them in the mornings, waist-deep in water, using a special tool to rake the sandy bottom. If there is no wind, this is easy, but after a storm, the clams are sometimes buried as far as 20 cm down and that makes them difficult to catch.*

For the best results, rinse the clams in plenty of cold, salty water, to eliminate any traces of sand. But if you don't feel like cooking this dish yourself, you can always venture out to Saintes-Maries-de-la-Mer, a fishing village in Camargue, where the restaurants specialise in serving freshly caught soft clams.

1 kg soft clams
2 shallots
3 cloves of garlic
5 tbsp olive oil
1 bunch of parsley
Salt and freshly ground pepper
100 ml white wine

Clean the clams thoroughly in several lots of cold, salty water and leave them long enough to open. It can take hours to get rid of all the sand. However, like mussels, the clams must close when stirred vigorously. Discard clams that do not close.

Chop the shallots and garlic finely. Heat the oil and sauté the shallots until golden. Add the garlic, chopped parsley, salt, pepper and white wine. Then add the clams and leave to simmer under a lid until they open – this should take approximately 5 minutes. Throw away the soft clams that do not open. Serve as a starter with fresh bread on the side.

Fried Red Mullet

ROUGET DE ROCHE

A tiny red mullet doesn't look as if it could deliver much, but it is highly prized by the fishermen along the rocky coastline. It's not only delicious, but easy to prepare; all you have to do is scrape off the scales and cook it for a few minutes in a frying pan or on the grill.

4 whole red mullet
5 tbsp olive oil
Juice of ½ a lemon
Salt and freshly ground pepper

Remove the scales and smear the red mullet with olive oil. Drizzle with lemon and season with salt and pepper. Fry for a few minutes on both sides and serve with a fresh salad.

Boucherie

Christian
SEIGNOUR

MEAT, VENISON AND POULTRY

Traditionally, meat has never been terribly important in Provençal cuisine. This is quite obvious when you go around the different markets, where you only come across a few recipes containing meat. There are areas though where the inhabitants have had fairly easy access to beef. The Carmargue in western Provence is one of them, and here they use the half-wild black bulls in a dish called *Gardianne de taureau*, named after the tough cowboys who ride the small, white Camargue horses while minding the cattle. It simmers over a low heat for hours and can be compared to the delicious *daubes* (pot roasts) that are familiar throughout Provence. Outside the Camargue, mature beef is often replaced with regular beef, lamb, pork or rabbit – and some even use octopus. Daubes are a wonderful way of preparing meat, which can otherwise be tough and hard. Every family has its own version but the overriding principle is that the meat must stew over low heat for a very long time.

Arles and several of the little hinterland villages are well known for their delicate air-dried sausages which can be made from just about anything, including donkeys, sheep, goats, horses, pigs and bulls.

Many farms breed rabbits and poultry, which they bring to the markets while still alive, leaving the customers in no doubt about the quality of produce. You can simply order a chicken or rabbit to be delivered ready for the pot on the following market day.

However, lamb is the reigning speciality. The sheep feed on wild herbs in the mountains, which gives the meat its unique taste. The desolate areas around Sisteron in Haute-Provence produce the most sought after lamb, but lamb from les Alpilles and Lubéron is also highly valued. Lamb dishes don't require much preparation, involving only a little thyme, rosemary and lots of garlic.

In the old days, huge herds of sheep were shepherded up to the lush pastures on the mountainsides in spring and not brought back down again until the autumn. To a certain extent, this still happens, although many a sheep will have to settle for experiencing at least part of this *transhumance* from the back of a lorry.

VOLAILLES

GIBIERS

BEEF STEW FROM CAMARGUE

BŒUF À LA GARDIANNE

This is how you would prepare such gorgeous meat. You can easily make the dish a day in advance; leaving the flavours to marinate for a day only improves it.

1.2 kg beef, chuck rib or shoulder	Peel of 1 orange in strips
1½ kg potatoes	1 bottle of red wine
150 g smoked bacon	150 g black olives
4–5 onions	1 twig of basil
5 cloves of garlic	3 tbsp olive oil
1 bunch of potherbs with thyme, rosemary and a bay leaf	Salt and freshly ground pepper
	Dough from 6 tbsp flour and water to keep the lid firmly closed

Chop the meat into cubes of 4 x 4 cm. Heat the oil in an ovenproof casserole, add the meat and braise on all sides. Take the meat out again and leave to one side. Peel the potatoes and slice thickly. Dice the bacon and slice the onions.

Add the bacon and onions to the casserole and brown for 5 minutes. Add the meat and its juices along with crushed garlic, potherbs and orange peel. Sprinkle with salt and pepper. Cover in wine and bring to a boil. Then add the potatoes and mix thoroughly.

Make a soft dough from the flour and water and roll it into a sausage the length of the rim of the casserole. Press it down along the rim of the pot and squeeze the lid down on top. This will make sure the lid is completely airtight.

Place the pot in the oven, heated to 180°C, and leave for at least 4 hours. Then remove the lid and add the whole olives without stones shortly before serving. Give the stew a good stir and season with salt and pepper. Garnish with basil and orange peel. Serve in the casserole.

What sets this dish apart from similar dishes in any other region of France is the use of olives. In order for them not to lose their fruity taste, it is important that they are not boiled for more than a few minutes.

CHEVREUIL
100g - 1F50

COIN DE
JAMBON
1KG / 15€

BEEF STEW

BŒUF EN DAUBE

1½ kg beef, chuck rib
  or shoulder
2 onions
1 carrot
1 bunch of potherbs
  with thyme, parsley
  and a bay leaf
1 piece of dried orange peel
Whole peppercorns
1 tbsp wine vinegar
1 litre of red wine
100 ml cognac
250 g lean smoked bacon
1 tsp tomato purée
6 cloves of garlic
250 g small onions
Wheat flour
Sugar
Butter
8 tbsp olive oil
Salt and freshly ground
  pepper
1 tsp chopped Parsley

Cut the meat into cubes of 4 x 4 cm. Chop the onions and dice the carrot. Marinate the meat, carrot, onion, potherbs, orange peel and peppercorns in wine mixed with vinegar and cognac for at least 5 hours in a bowl with an absolutely airtight lid – leaving it overnight will only improve it.

Drain the marinade and keep it separately. Heat 6 tbsp olive oil in a huge pan and brown the meat. Remove the rind from the bacon and dice finely before browning in a separate pan.

Place the bacon rind in the bottom of a large oven-proof pot. Then add the rest of the bacon and the browned meat along with the onions, potherbs, orange peel and crushed garlic. Pour in the marinade and tomato purée. The meat should be completely covered. Sprinkle salt and pepper on top. Stir thoroughly and bring to a boil. Skim the sauce and turn the heat down. Leave to simmer over low heat for at least 6 hours. Alternatively, you could leave it in the oven at 150°C.

After 4–5 hours, skim off any fat and mix in with flour – this is called a *roux*. Drain all the sauce from the dish and cook the sauce for at bit longer in a separate pot. Skim any remaining fat off and use the *roux* as thickening by whisking it into the sauce, then leave to boil for 5–8 minutes. Season with salt and pepper and pour the sauce over the meat before heating again.

Peel the small onions. Add to a pot with a little butter and sugar. Pour in 100 ml of water and leave to simmer over a low heat until soft and slightly caramelised.

Add the caramelised onions to the stew 15 minutes before serving. Serve with freshly chopped parsley and gnocchi or pasta.

BLANQUETTE OF LAMB

BLANQUETTE D'AGNEAU

1 kg breast of lamb	300 ml vegetable stock
or shoulder off the bone	300 ml white wine
3 tbsp olive oil	Salt and freshly ground pepper
3 onions	2 tbsp flour
1 twig of thyme	1 egg yolk
3 cloves of garlic	Parsley

Cut the meat into pieces of 3–5 cm. Add to a saucepan with the olive oil and brown lightly.

Add the finely chopped onion and thyme. Sprinkle with salt and pepper. When the onions are soft, add the crushed garlic, vegetable stock and white wine and make sure the meat is completely covered. Cover the saucepan with a lid and leave to simmer over a low heat for 2½–3 hours.

When the meat is tender, use the flour to thicken the sauce a little and then pour the mixture back into the pan while stirring thoroughly. Take the pan off the heat and use the egg yolk to thicken the dish further. Garnish with parsley and serve with freshly boiled peas and rice from the Camargue.

ROAST SHOULDER OF LAMB WITH GARLIC AND THYME

ÉPAULE D'AGNEAU À L'AIL ET AU THYM

1 shoulder of lamb on the bone

4 cloves of garlic

3 twigs of thyme

1 tbsp lemon juice

4 tbsp olive oil

200 ml white wine

100 ml water

Salt and freshly ground pepper

Rub the shoulder of lamb with salt and pepper. Mix the crushed garlic with thyme, lemon juice and olive oil. Smear the shoulder of lamb with this mixture and place in an ovenproof dish. Drizzle a little more olive oil over the meat and add the wine and water to the dish before baking in the oven for approximately 3 hours at 160°C. Pour the fat drippings over the lamb to keep it moist whilst cooking. Leave to settle for 15 minutes before carving.

LAMB CHOPS WITH GARLIC AND THYME

CÔTELETTES D'AGNEAU À L'AIL

16 lamb chops on the bone
1 bulb of garlic
¼ bunch of thyme
2 tbsp balsamic vinegar
Salt and freshly ground pepper

Trim any superfluous fat off the lamb chops, and scrape the sinews and fat off the bone. Halve the garlic bulb and rub the chops thoroughly before sprinkling salt and pepper on top.

Then fry the chops in heated olive oil for approximately 3 minutes on both sides. While frying sprinkle thyme on the pan, flavouring both oil and meat.

Finally, drizzle balsamic vinegar on top of the meat and the chops are ready to be served. Ratatouille makes for an excellent side dish (please refer back to page 120).

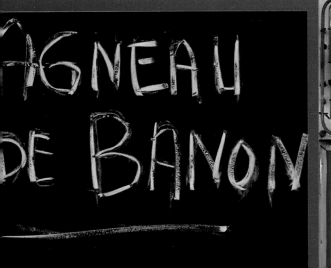

Roast Leg of Lamb with Herbs

GIGOT RÔTI AUX HERBES

A leg of lamb weighing 1½ kg
3–4 tbsp olive oil
4 cloves of garlic
2 fresh sage leaves
2 twigs of fresh rosemary or 1 tsp dried rosemary
2 bay leaves
2 twigs of fresh thyme or 1 tsp dried thyme
Salt and freshly ground pepper
150 ml dry white wine

Peel and halve the garlic cloves. Smear the leg of lamb with olive oil. Make little incisions in the lamb with a sharp knife and fill with garlic and fresh herbs. If you use dried herbs then sprinkle them on top of the lamb. Spread the remaining fresh herbs on top of the lamb and set aside somewhere cool for 2 hours.

Place the leg of lamb in an ovenproof dish and pour a little olive oil over the meat. Sprinkle salt and pepper on top before placing in the oven at 220°C. Turn the heat down to 175°C when the meat is nicely brown (after approximately 15 minutes). Pour in the wine and leave to cook.

The leg of lamb should be cooked for approximately 1 hour (about 20 minutes per ½ kg). Pour the fat drippings over the leg of lamb to keep it moist whilst cooking.

Leave the lamb to settle for 15 minutes before carving. Serve with oven-baked potatoes and tomato salad.

244

WILD BOAR STEW

DAUBE DE SANGLIER

The wild boar season lasts from September until January. It can be strangely difficult to get hold of the meat when in Provence, and you have to know a good butcher or have friends among the local boar hunters to get your hands on this delicacy. Luckily there are many wild boar suppliers throughout the rest of Europe, particularly online.

1.2 kg wild boar	600 ml white wine
150 g smoked bacon	1 bunch of potherbs with
3 onions	thyme, a clove and a bay leaf
3 shallots	Peel from 1 organic orange
5 cloves of garlic	Salt and freshly ground pepper
2 tbsp olive oil	

Cut the meat into cubes of approximately 3 x 3 cm. Dice the bacon finely. Quarter the onions and slice the shallots.

Mix the meat, bacon, onions and crushed garlic with the wine and leave to marinate for 3–4 hours in a bowl. Drain the marinade and save for later.

Heat the oil in a thick-bottomed casserole and brown the meat. Then add the potherbs and orange peel. Stir well and braise for a couple of minutes. Then add the marinade and sprinkle with salt and pepper. Stir thoroughly. Turn the heat down and leave to simmer for 4–6 hours. You can add more wine if the sauce is too thick.

The meat should be so tender you can cut it with a fork. Serve with rice or pasta. Many a Provençal will use red wine instead of white wine in this dish.

CHICKEN WITH 40 CLOVES OF GARLIC

POULET AUX 40 GOUSSES D'AIL

1 chicken weighing at least 1½ kg
40 cloves of garlic
3 twigs of thyme
3 stalks of basil
3 stalks of tarragon
100 ml olive oil
Salt and freshly ground pepper
Dough made from 6 tbsp flour and water
  to keep the lid airtight

Peel the garlic cloves. Rub the insides of the chicken with salt and pepper., then stuff with 15 garlic gloves and half the herbs.

Grease an ovenproof casserole with 50 ml of olive oil and spread the rest of the garlic cloves over the bottom. Place the chicken on top. Put the remaining herbs on top as well as the remaining olive oil.

Make some dough with flour and water and place along the rim of the pot. Press the lid tightly down on the pot to make sure it is completely airtight. Roast in the oven for 1½ hours at 225°C.

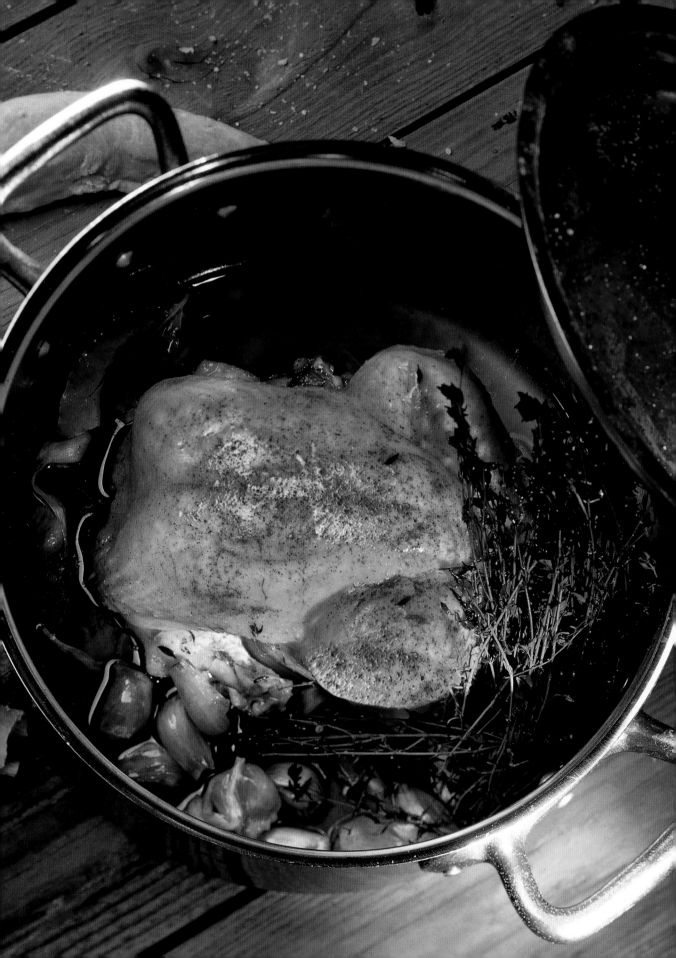

CHICKEN STEW WITH BASIL AND TOMATOES

COCOTTE DE POULET AU BASILIC ET AUX TOMATES

1 fresh country chicken weighing at least 1.7 kg	2 cloves of garlic
3 tbsp olive oil	100 ml dry white wine
4 large skinned tomatoes	1 bay leaf
2 onions	1 bunch of basil
1 tsp *herbes de Provence*	Salt and freshly ground pepper

Slice the onions and garlic and chop the tomatoes. Cut the chicken into 8 pieces and brown in a pot along with the onions. Add the chopped tomatoes, garlic, bay leaf, finely chopped basil and white wine. Sprinkle with *herbes de Provence*, salt and pepper. Turn the heat down, place a lid on top and leave to simmer for approximately 40 minutes, until the chicken is well done and the meat juice is clear. Garnish with fresh basil leaves and serve with rice.

CHICKEN WITH THYME

POULET AU THYM

1 fresh country chicken weighing at least 1.7 kg	1 onion
1 bunch of fresh thyme	100 ml olive oil
2 cloves of garlic	Salt and freshly ground pepper

Place the halved garlic cloves in the chicken's stomach along with chopped onion and 2–3 twigs of thyme. Mix the remaining thyme with olive oil and smear the chicken with this mixture. Sprinkle salt and pepper on top. Place the chicken in an ovenproof dish with ½ cm of water in the bottom. Roast in the oven at 200°C for approximately 1 hour or until the meat juice runs clear when a roasting fork is stuck into the chicken.

Coq au Vin

COQ AU VIN

1 large cockerel weighing
   1½–2 kg
20 small shallots
30 mushrooms
6 cloves of garlic
2 carrots
1 aubergine
200 g lean air-dried ham
100 g lean bacon
Olive oil
Salt and freshly ground
   pepper
40–50 ml cognac
2 twigs of thyme
1 twig of rosemary
1½ bottles of heavy
   Provençal red wine
2–4 tbsp wheat flour
Parsley

Cut the legs and wings off the chicken. Separate the legs into drumsticks and thighs. Cut off the breasts and quarter. Sprinkle a little salt on top of the chicken pieces and set aside for about 1 hour.

Place the onions in cold water to soften the skin. Peel the onions and slice the mushrooms. Peel the garlic cloves and chop 1 clove finely. Dice the carrot and aubergine quite coarsely. Cut the ham and bacon into smaller cubes and fry gently in olive oil in a big roasting pot. Then take the meat out and sauté the onions and mushrooms in the leftover fat along with the chopped garlic clove. Add salt and pepper. Take out the onions, mushrooms and garlic, then put to one side along with the ham and bacon.

Brown the chicken pieces in a little bit of olive oil. Add the cognac and light a match to flambé. Add thyme and rosemary to the pot along with the carrots, auber-gine, the remaining garlic cloves and the mushrooms. Add wine until all is covered and leave to simmer under a lid for approximately 30 minutes before placing eve-rything in a dish. Give the chicken thighs and wings about 20 minutes more than the breasts before taking them out. Leave the rest of the bird in the pot to simmer for another 30–40 minutes without the lid. Then throw away the bones and herbs before straining the red wine gravy into a bowl. Skim the fat from the gravy but save a little. Add a couple of spoonfuls of fat and 1 tbsp of butter to the pot and then add flour. Use the gravy to dilute. Then add the bacon, onions and mushrooms to the pot and reduce the sauce. It is important that the sauce is not too thin. Leave to simmer for 15–20 minutes over a low heat. Add the chicken pieces to the pot and leave to simmer for another 5–6 minutes. Garnish with finely chopped parsley.

Producteur
d'œufs et de volailles
élevées aux céréales
et en plein air
VIDAUBAN

PINTADE
8.8€ei le kg

SKEWERS OF PORK WITH FRESH SAGE

BROCHETTES DE PORC À LA SAUGE FRAÎCHE

600 g pork tenderloin
2 tbsp fresh sage
2 tbsp olive oil
24 cherry tomatoes
24 medium sized mushrooms
Salt and freshly ground pepper

Cut the meat into cubes and add to a bowl with olive oil, sage, salt and pepper and leave to marinate for 30 minutes. Use 12 skewers and alternate the meat cubes with tomatoes and mushrooms. Place the skewers under the grill in the oven for 10–12 minutes. You can also use an outdoor charcoal grill.

Turn the skewers over regularly and add marinade as needed. Place the finished skewers on a dish and garnish with freshly chopped sage.

CHEESE

There are numerous goat's cheeses sold directly from farms themselves or a short distance away in the local markets. While the goat used to be the poor man's cow – a Provençal peasant could rarely afford a real cow – both sheep and goats actually manage much better in the *garrigue*, where herbs provide a sparse but highly aromatic feed. It is, however, those very herbs that give the goats milk its characteristic and strong taste. Young cheeses can be quite mild though, and are highly suitable for cooking.

Brousse is a round, unsalted cheese, rather similar to ricotta. It used to be made from goat's milk, but these days, you'll be more likely to come across *Brousse* made from sheep's milk. This cheese can be served with a sprinkling of sugar and a dash of orange blossom water or with oil, vinegar, garlic, herbs and onions.

Picodon is a small, round cheese made from goat's milk, roughly 8–9 cm in diameter and primarily produced in the Drôme Provençale and in Valréas in Vaucluse. The *Picodon* was awarded an *Appellation Contrôlée* in the early 1980s. The young *Picodon* is much like an ordinary goat's cheese, while the mature *Picadons*, rinsed in white wine, are noticeably stronger in taste.

Banon is a small, quiet village in Haute-Provence. On the small, desolate farms, scattered across the surrounding countryside, they produce the famous *Banon* cheeses: small, round goat's cheeses that mature for a few weeks prior to being wrapped in chestnut leaves soaked in marc. Some of the cheeses are only garnished with a twig of summer savory, which then adds a little of its characteristic peppery taste to the cheese.

The *Banon* cheeses are extremely delicate, even when young. As they mature, they become quite piquant and almost fluid. Finding a genuine *Banon* can be a little tricky though, as there are so many copies around.

In Camargue, you will find one of the few Provençal cheeses made from cow's milk, the *Tomme de Camargue*. It is a delectable, small, oblong or round cheese, usually covered in thyme.

SALAD WITH WARM GOAT'S CHEESE

SALADE AUX FROMAGES DE CHÈVRE CHAUDS

The best results occur if the goat's cheese is neither too young nor too mature. If it is too young, the taste will be too bland, and if too mature, it will be gritty and hard.

4 youngish goat's cheeses
Rocket or lettuce
Baguette or country bread

Dressing
1 part white wine vinegar
5 parts olive oil
Salt

Grill 8 little pieces of baguette in the oven until light brown. Then smear with olive oil and place half a small goat's cheese on each piece. Place in the oven under the grill, but only for a short while as it is important that the cheese is not overcooked or it will turn gritty. Spread the cheese croutons over the lettuce and drizzle the dressing on top.

SMALL GOAT'S CHEESES IN OLIVE OIL

BOCAL DE FROMAGES DE CHÈVRE À L'HUILE

Summer savory is small herb with narrow, pointy dark-green leaves, reddish stalks and tiny pink flowers. It originates in southeast Europe and it was most likely brought to France by the Romans and the monks, who used it in food as well as medicine. It thrives on the rather barren plains in the mountains and it is the herb most frequently used with Provençal goat's cheeses because it gives the cheese a characteristic and delicately peppery taste. Locally, they call summer savory, poivre d'ane *(donkey pepper). If you are unable to get your hands on some summer savory, you can use thyme and rosemary instead.*

500 ml of olive oil
25 small, slightly mature goat's cheeses (*demi-sec*)
5 tbsp dried summer savory

Put a layer of summer savory in the bottom of a large pickle jar and add a layer of goat's cheeses. Repeat this layering until there are no cheeses left. Pour the olive oil into the jar and leave to marinate for a few weeks before using. Serve with a fresh salad and white wine.

QUICHE WITH FRESH GOAT'S CHEESE

QUICHE AU CHÈVRE FRAIS

Pastry
200 g plain flour
50 ml olive oil
Possibly a little water
Salt

Filling
3 small onions
3 slices of air-dried ham
4 eggs
100 g fresh, soft goat's cheese
150 ml milk
Salt and freshly ground pepper

Heat the oven to 180°C and mix the pastry in a food processor until smooth, then spread it over the bottom and along the sides of a greased tart mould. Prick the pastry with a fork and leave to cool in the fridge for 15 minutes. Pre-bake the pastry for 10–15 minutes.

Chop the onions and fry in olive oil in a hot pan until golden. Turn the heat off, chop the ham and mix in with onions. Spread the filling over the bottom of the tart. Mix the eggs, milk, goat's cheese, salt and pepper and pour over the filling. Bake at the bottom of the oven for approximately 30 minutes, until nicely golden.

Toast with Goat's Cheese

PAIN DE CAMPAGNE GRILLÉ AU
FROMAGE DE CHÈVRE

8 half slices of country bread
8 goat's cheeses of approximately ½ cm

Grill the bread in the oven until just golden. Add the goat's cheese and grill until the cheese turns golden.

You can easily vary this dish by adding a teaspoonful of honey on top of each cheese before you grill it for the second time, or by adding some thyme. Whichever way you chose to prepare this dish, always serve with a glass of chilled rosé wine.

Scrambled Eggs with Fresh Goat's Cheese

BROUILLADE AU CHÈVRE FRAIS

8 eggs
50 g mild and soft goat's cheese
Salt and freshly ground pepper
Olive oil

Whisk the eggs and goat's cheese together. Add the egg mixture to a hot frying pan and stir frequently. Serve with fresh bread.

GOAT'S CHEESE WITH PEAR AND ACACIA HONEY

*FROMAGE DE CHÈVRE AVEC POIRE
ET MIEL D'ACACIA*

*If the goat's cheese is not too mature, this is a great way to create
a not only beautiful but also very delicate cheese plate to complete
a meal.*

4 goat's cheeses
4 small pears
4 large tbsp acacia honey

Peel the pears and place a pear and a cheese on each plate. Pour the
honey on top.

TOMATOES STUFFED WITH FRESH GOAT'S CHEESE

TOMATES FARCIES AU CHÈVRE

4 small, ripe and sweet tomatoes	100 g fresh goat's cheese
2 tbsp olive oil	Salt and freshly ground pepper

Hollow out the tomatoes, then dip in olive oil, sprinkle salt and pepper
on top and stuff with fresh goat's cheese. Serve cold as a starter.

It is also worth trying this variation of the dish: Add a little oil
to the hollow tomatoes and bake in the oven at 200°C until soft –
should take approximately 30 minutes. Then stuff them with fresh
goat's cheese and sprinkle a little thyme on top before cooking them
au gratin in the oven until the cheese is golden. Serve while hot.

Fromages de chèvre · à 30

Banon à l'ancienne

DESSERTS

A meal in Provence will often finish with some fresh fruit and nothing else. This is perfectly acceptable because the selection of sweet and delicious fruit in this region is abundant and the markets are bursting with locally grown produce almost all year around. Different fruits can also be used in tarts which are very easy to make. Or the locals will make crystallised fruits, using cherries, melons and apricots, as they do in Apt, or mandarins, as they do at *Confiserie Florian des Gorges du Loup* behind Grasse.

There are numerous almond trees around Aix and Salon-de-Provence – the first of them arrived from Asia as far back as 1548 – and in spring they cover the area in a sea of pink flowers. The almonds from Aix are used in the famous almond cakes, *les Calissons d'Aix*, so legendarily mouthwatering that they have been awarded their very own *Appellation Contrôlée*. Almonds are also put to excellent use in Sault by Mon Ventoux, where André Boyer makes the most exquisite white and dark nougat with almonds and honey. The dark nougat is particularly delicious. The Boyer's have had their shop in Sault for more than a century and they strictly adhere to the finest of Provençal traditions. Please do not mistake the nougat made here for the better known but also far more bland and mass-produced white nougat from Montélimar.

Honey is a very important speciality, and you find different varieties all the way from the coast and the chestnut forests around les Maures to the lavender fields way up in the hinterland. The beehives are moved around to different flowery fields depending on the season and on which kind of honey the beekeepers want to produce. The beekeeper will often pay the farmer in honey for the use of his fields. The bees are flower-consistent, which means that once they realise that they are on to a good source they keep going back to the same sort of flower until there is nothing left. Thus the beekeepers can name their honey after specific flowers, which is also absolutely as it should be, because each flower has a distinct scent that produces a distinctly flavoured honey.

CHARD PIE

TOURTE DE BLETTES

Short crust pastry
250 g plain flour
120 g butter
100 g sugar
A pinch of salt
1 whole egg
1–2 tbsp water

Filling
1 kg chard (can be
  replaced by spinach)
50 g grated Parmesan
150 g light muscovado
  sugar
100 g raisins (soaked
  in marc)
1 tbsp olive oil
100 g pine nuts
2 eggs
1½ kg apples
4 tbsp icing sugar

Mix the flour, butter, sugar and salt in a food processor. Use egg and water to bind the pastry and place somewhere cool for half an hour. Halve the pastry and use one part to cover a tart mould. Use a fork to prick holes in the bottom and leave somewhere cool for another hour, before baking it.

Rinse the chard thoroughly using several lots of cold water and blanch for a moment in boiling water. Then dip in cold water and squeeze out all water, so they end up completely dry. Cut into strips. Whisk the eggs, muscovado sugar, oil and grated Parmesan thoroughly before adding the chard, raisins and pine nuts.

Peel and slice the apples. Spread the filling over the pastry and add a layer of apples. Roll out the other half of pastry and place on top. Press the pastry firmly down along the edges, piercing in a few places to allow steam to escape.

Bake the pie in the oven for approximately 40 minutes at 180°C until it is nicely golden. Take it out and sprinkle with plenty of icing sugar. Serve while hot.

ALMOND AND HONEY PIE

TARTE AUX AMANDES ET AU MIEL

Short crust pastry
250 g plain flour
125 g soft butter
100 g sugar
A pinch of salt
1 whole egg
1–2 tbsp water

Filling
150 g almonds
100 g honey
3 eggs

Mix the flour, butter, sugar and salt in a food processor. Use egg and water to bind the pastry and place somewhere cool for half an hour. Halve the pastry and use one part to cover a tart mould. Use a fork to prick holes in the bottom and leave somewhere cool for another hour, before baking it.

Mix the honey and coarsely chopped almonds together. If the honey is too solid, you can soften it over a hot bain-marie. Separate the eggs and add 2 yolks to the honey mixture. Whisk the 3 egg whites until stiff and carefully mix in with the honey mixture. Pour this mixture into the tart mould. Roll out the other half of the pastry and place over the filling. Make little cuts in the pastry-lid and use the last egg yolk to glaze.

Bake in the oven for approximately 35 minutes at 180°C until nicely golden.

You can also use pine nuts instead of almonds and sugar instead of honey. You can even add a small cup of sour cream to the filling.

APPLE TART

TARTE AUX POMMES

Short crust pastry
250 g plain flour
125 g soft butter
100 g sugar
A pinch of salt
1 whole egg
1–2 tbsp water

Filling
1 kg apples
125 g sugar
3 tbsp apricot marmalade

Mix the flour, butter, sugar and salt in a food processor. Use egg and water to bind the pastry and place somewhere cool for half an hour. Halve the pastry and use one part to cover a tart mould. Use a fork to prick holes in the bottom and leave somewhere cool for another hour, before baking it.

Peel and slice the apples and place neatly on the pastry in the mould, each overlapping the next. Sprinkle with the sugar. Bake in the oven for approximately 35 minutes at 180°C until both apples and pastry are nicely golden. Take the tart out of the oven and brush the apples with apricot marmalade so they become nice and shiny. Serve while warm.

Apricot Tart

TARTE AUX ABRICOTS

Short crust pastry
250 g plain flour
125 g soft butter
100 g sugar
A pinch of salt
1 whole egg
1–2 tbsp water

Filling
1 kg apricots
　(can be tinned)
2 tbsp sugar
3 tbsp apricot marmalade

Mix the flour, butter, sugar and salt in a food processor. Use egg and water to bind the pastry and place somewhere cool for half an hour. Roll out the pastry and cover a greased tart mould. Use a fork to prick holes in the bottom and leave somewhere cool for another hour, before baking it.

Halve or quarter the apricots and take the stones out. Place the apricots closely together on the pastry in the tart mould and sprinkle sugar on top. Bake in oven for approximately 35 minutes at 180°C. Take the tart out of the oven and brush with apricot marmalade.

FIG TART

TARTE AUX FIGUES

Short crust pastry
250 g plain flour
125 g soft butter
100 g sugar
A pinch of salt
1 whole egg
1–2 tbsp water

Filling
75 g sugar
16 fresh figs

Mix the flour, butter, sugar and salt in a food processor. Use egg and water to bind the pastry and place somewhere cool for half an hour. Roll out the pastry and cover a greased tart mould. Use a fork to prick holes in the bottom and leave somewhere cool for another hour, before baking it.

Rinse the figs and dry off. Sprinkle some sugar over the pastry in the tart mould. Cut each fig at the top and place close together in the mould, bottoms down. Sprinkle a little sugar on top and bake in the oven for approximately 30 minutes at 180°C. Serve while warm.

LEMON TART FROM MENTON

TARTE AU CITRON DE MENTON

Short crust pastry	Filling	Meringue
250 g plain flour	4 egg yolks	4 egg whites
125 g soft butter	200 g sugar	2 tbsp sugar
100 g sugar	2 tbsp flour	
A pinch of salt	3 dl milk	
1 whole egg	3 organic lemons	
1–2 tbsp water		

Mix the flour, butter, sugar and salt in a food processor. Use egg and water to bind the pastry and place somewhere cool for half an hour. Roll out the pastry and cover a greased tart mould. Use a fork to prick holes in the bottom and leave somewhere cool for another hour, before pre-baking it for 20 minutes at 175°C.

For the filling, whisk the egg yolks with the sugar. Add the flour. Heat the milk until boiling and pour it into the egg mixture little by little. Add juice and zest from the 3 lemons. Pour the mixture back into the pan and heat slowly, until the mixture thickens. Leave to cool while stirring frequently.

For the meringue, whisk the egg whites until stiff and add a little sugar to make the meringue shiny. Spread the lemon mixture over the tart mould and cover with meringue. Bake in the oven for 10 minutes at 175°C until the meringue is lightly golden.

282

CHRISTMAS LOAF

POMPE À L'HUILE

This bread and the dark nougat are the most important of the 'thirteen desserts'. (See following page for more on this)

25 g yeast
200 ml tepid water
500 g strong flour
150 g sugar
A pinch of salt
125 ml olive oil
Zest from 1 organic orange
2 tbsp orange blossom water (which
   you can buy from select shops)

Dissolve the yeast in tepid water. Add the flour, sugar, salt, oil, orange zest and orange blossom water. Knead thoroughly and make into a ball. Cover with a tea towel and leave to prove for 3 hours.

Knead thoroughly again and form into a round loaf. Place on a greased baking sheet. Make a few deep cuts in the bread and bake in the oven for approximately 30 minutes at 200°C.

THE THIRTEEN DESSERTS

LES TREIZE DESSERTS DE NOËL

On Christmas Eve, tradition dictates that you serve Le Gros Souper *before midnight mass. It is a modest meal, but still quite filling because it consists of many different dishes.*

In Provence, it is considered the most important meal of the year, when the whole family gets together and leaves all private bickering aside for a while. The dessert must consist of thirteen different offerings, symbolising Jesus and the twelve disciples.

You can expect to be served raisins, dried figs, walnuts, almonds, dried apricots, dates, grapes, mandarins, oranges, apples, pears, white and dark nougat, crystallised fruits, quince, melon, *fougasse* or the Christmas loaf *pompe á l'huile*. The selection is hugely varied. Raisins and nuts are called *les mendiants*, the beggars, because their colour resembles that of the habits of the mendicant friars – the Capuchins, the Dominicans and the Franciscans.

DARK NOUGAT

NOUGAT NOIR

Dark nougat is considered the real thing in Provence. It's crunchy and not as tough as the white nougat. Lavender honey is most often used when making nougat. The honey is a much valued side benefit of growing lavender and each spring nearly 40,000 beehives are positioned close to the lavender fields for this very reason.

1 kg honey
1 kg almonds in their skins
Mild olive oil

Grease a baking sheet with oil. It is important to do this in advance.

Pour the honey into a heavy-bottomed saucepan and heat while stirring constantly. Once the honey reaches boiling point it changes colour and becomes darker. Then add the almonds. Keep stirring all the time. Take the pan off the heat as soon as the almonds start making little snapping noises and the honey is a nice, deep brown colour.

Pour the nougat onto the greased baking sheet. Be careful – the nougat is very hot. This is the tricky bit: if the mixture is undercooked it will stick, if overcooked it will become hard.

ALMOND BISCUITS

CROQUANTS

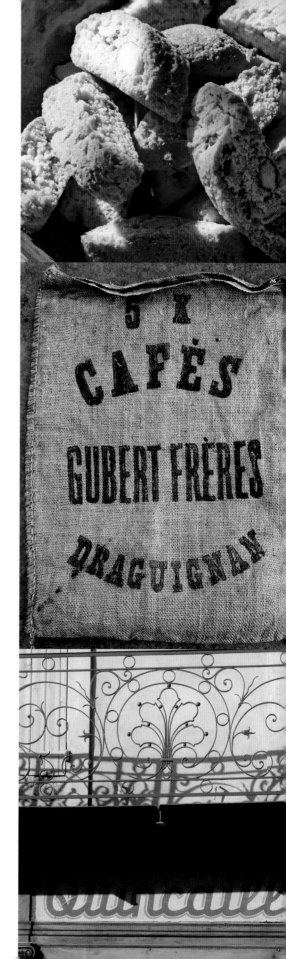

These almond biscuits are inspired by Italian biscotti, but you can buy them at practically every baker's shop in Provence. The amount of sugar used can vary a great deal.

250 g plain flour
100 g sugar
½ tsp baking soda
A pinch of salt
2 large, whole eggs
150 g almonds in their skins
1 egg for glazing

Mix all the ingredients, putting the almonds in last. Divide the dough into four portions, roll them into long sausages and place them on a baking sheet. Brush the rolls with egg to make them beautifully golden. Bake in the oven for 15–20 minutes at 180°C. Take out and slice at an angle into biscuits of 2–3 cm. Then bake for another 5 minutes or until sufficiently crunchy.

ORANGE MARMALADE

CONFITURE D'ORANGE

1 kg organic, thin-skinned oranges
1 kg sugar
Preservative (optional)

Rinse the oranges well and quarter them. Add to a saucepan and add enough water to cover them. Boil the oranges for approximately 1 hour over low heat. Pour the oranges into a colander held over another pan. Add sugar to the fluid and boil until reduced by approximately 1/3. In the meantime, slice the oranges finely. When the fluid has reduced, add the oranges and leave to boil for approximately another half an hour or until the marmalade has the right texture. Finally, skim the marmalade and pour into clean jars. You can also choose to rinse out the jars with preservative before pouring marmalade into them.

APRICOT JAM

CONFITURE D'ABRICOTS

The apricot season starts at the end of June. It's a wonderful time of year, and the fresh fruits themselves possess a light and delicate flavour. This recipe is a good way to preserve whatever apricots you have left over, and prolongs the season, even if in a jar.

1 kg very ripe apricots
1 kg sugar
Juice of 1 lemon
Preservative (optional)

Halve the apricots and take out the stones. Pour the sugar and lemon juice over the apricots and leave until the following day. Boil the apricots over low heat for 10 minutes. Remove the fruit and put into clean jars. You can also rinse the jars out with preservative prior to filling them. Reduce the syrup a little and pour over the fruit. Seal the jars at once.

HONEY CAKE WITH HAZELNUTS

GÂTEAU DE MIEL AUX NOISETTES

6 eggs

300 g liquid honey

100 g self raising flour

100 g hazelnuts

1 tbsp butter

Roast the nuts in a dry pan and get rid of as much of the brown skin as possible by rubbing them in a clean tea towel. Then chop the nuts finely.

Separate the eggs and mix the yolks with the honey. If the honey is a little stiff you can soften it over a hot bain-marie. Add flour little by little while stirring and then add the chopped nuts. Whisk the egg whites until stiff and carefully mix in with the rest. Pour the mixture into a greased cake tin and bake for approximately 35 minutes at 180°C. You may have to cover the cake with a piece of baking paper after the first 20 minutes.

HONEY LOAF

PAIN D'ÉPICES

350 g honey

300 ml boiling water

1 tsp ground cinnamon

1 tsp lemon zest

1 tsp orange zest

A pinch of salt

2½ tsp baking soda

4 eggs

200 g rye flour

200 g wheat flour

1 tbsp butter

Mix the honey, water and spices and leave this mixture to cool down. Then add the eggs, one at a time, and then flour and baking soda. Pour the relatively runny mixture into a greased baking tin and bake for approximately 1¼ hours at 170°C.

SMALL LOAVES OF FOUGASSE

FOUGASSETTES

500 g plain flour
25 g yeast
2 eggs
1 tbsp orange blossom water
(can be left out)
150 g sugar
200 ml tepid water
50 ml olive oil
A pinch of salt

Dissolve the yeast in 100 ml of tepid water, sift in 250 g flour and mix. Leave the dough to prove somewhere warm for 2–3 hours.

Sieve the remaining flour into another bowl along with the salt, eggs, orange blossom water, sugar, 100 ml of water and olive oil. Knead thoroughly and then add to the already proved dough and knead until smooth and shiny. Leave the dough to prove for another 3 hours.

Knead the dough and divide into 3 parts, then shape into round balls, which you then use a rolling pin to roll into oval shapes that are approximately 2–3 cm thick. Make several deep cuts in the loaves and bake in the oven for approximately 15 minutes at 200°C.

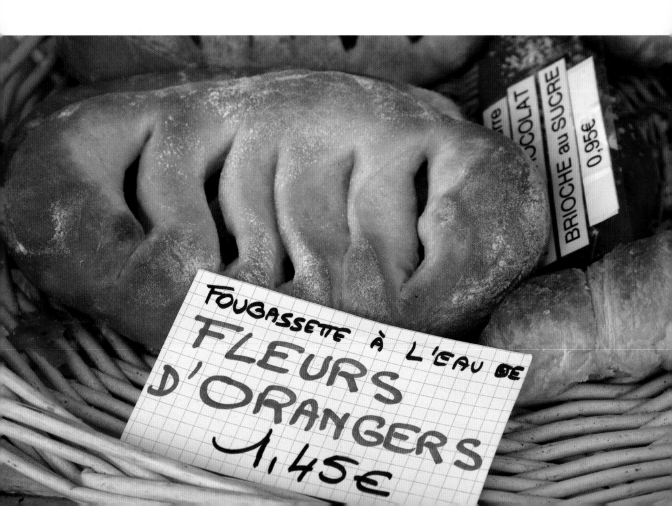

RASPBERRY COULIS

COULIS DE FRAMBOISE

200 g raspberries
100 g sugar
Grains from ½ a vanilla pod
100 ml water

Bring the berries, sugar, water and vanilla to a boil and leave to simmer for approximately 5 minutes. Blend the coulis and then squeeze it though a very finely meshed strainer. Add more sugar if needed.

Serve with ice cream or cake – chocolate cake for example.

CHOCOLATE CAKE

GÂTEAU AU CHOCOLAT

100 ml all purpose (plain)
  flour
½ tsp baking powder
75 ml cocoa
3 tsp vanilla sugar
3 eggs
250 ml sugar
200 g fromage frais or
  sour cream
2 tbsp mild olive oil
2 tbsp strong coffee

Heat the oven to 200°C. Mix the flour, baking powder, cocoa and vanilla sugar. Whisk the eggs and sugar until white. Add the fromage frais to this mixture and then add all of this to the flour mixture. Then add olive oil and coffee and mix thoroughly. Pour the mixture into a greased tart mould and bake at the bottom of the oven for 25 minutes. Serve with a coulis made from fresh berries.

Pears in Red Wine

POIRES AU VIN ROUGE

8 small, firm pears
800 ml red wine
1 tsp lemon zest
1 tsp orange zest
6 tbsp orange juice
225 g sugar
2 whole cloves
1 vanilla pod
1 cinnamon stick
100 ml port (can be left out)

Peel the pears and remove the flower but leave the stalk. Halve the vanilla pod and scrape out the grains.

Bring all the other ingredients, except for the port, to a boil. Turn the heat down before adding the pears, then leave to simmer over very low heat for approximately 20 minutes.

Take out the pears and place in a dish. Reduce sauce by half and strain over the pears. Add port and place somewhere cool until ready to serve.

PRIX▶

Produit

Variété

Origine FR...

Calibre

Catégorie II

1Kg

€

TERRE DE POMMES®

CHERRY CAKE

CLAFOUTIS

Clafoutis *is a classic, and is often made with sweet cherries from the Lubéron. However, you can also get perfectly agreeable results by using other fruits, such as apples, apricots or ripe plums.*

500 g very ripe cherries
1 tbsp butter
300 ml milk
100 g wheat flour
4 eggs
50 g sugar
Grains from 1 vanilla pod
2 tbsp icing sugar

Halve the cherries and take out the stones. Grease a tart mould and heat the oven to 180°C. Add the milk, flour, eggs, sugar and vanilla grains to a bowl and whisk until frothy. Pour a little of the mixture into the mould, leaving a thin layer of approximately ½ cm. Bake in the oven for approximately 10 minutes or until it sets.

Place the cherries on top and pour the remaining mixture over the cherries. Bake in the oven for approximately 30 minutes until beautifully light brown.

Sprinkle with icing sugar. Serve while hot and possibly with vanilla ice cream.

MOUNTAIN VILLAGES

Most Provençal villages were founded in the Middle Ages, a lawless era when bandits roamed the hills and the local inhabitants had to guard against every form of attack. The importance attributed to this external threat is substantiated by the strength of the villages' fortifications and the fact that most are positioned on inaccessible mountaintops. It is awe-inspiring to contemplate the effort that has been put into building houses on these incredibly steep slopes. Construction work in such difficult conditions must have been extremely hard. The Provençal talk of *les villages perchés* – villages perched high up on mountaintops – or *nids d'aigles* (eagles' nests) when referring to villages in extreme locations such as Goudon and Èze in the Alpes-Maritimes.

While there was no doubt that their northern neighbours were hostile, the greatest threat came from the Saracens in North Africa, who had gained a foothold in Spain, and from there they attacked and conquered large parts of Provence. The first wave of attacks began around the year 800, and as the Saracens would also attack from the sea, it meant that life in the villages along the coast was not safe either. Around the year 1000 the Saracens were eventually pacified, only this meant lasting peace. Provence has always been a battleground, and if the Provençal were not attacked from the outside, they could easily find something to fight about amongst themselves. And it is this highly dramatic period that one is constantly reminded of when visiting the little Provençal villages with well-preserved fortifications, although over the years, the large fortresses and castles have also had to provide building material for additional housing in the villages.

Most of the building materials, primarily stone, would have been locally produced, which is why the villages blend in with their sur-roundings in such a harmonious way. Sometimes it can be very hard to distinguish the villages from the mountainsides on which they sit, which Les Baux in Bouches-du-Rhône exemplifies beautifully.

In the past, there would not have been many buildings located outside the safety of these compact villages. Farmers would ensure

that their houses were built within the town walls, while their farmland would be scattered around the villages, often comprised of many small plots. They would grow vegetables, grain, olives and wine on terraces supported by stone walls, the so-called *restanques* that prevent erosion during the rare, but heavy rainfall of the region.

The village streets are narrow and there are a number of arcades supporting the buildings. The village houses are rather tall; they would generally consist of 3–4 floors as well as a basement, where oil and wine were kept. The ground floor would house a pig or a mule, while the family would occupy the next couple of floors, leaving the loft for storing hay.

The houses have thick walls, which help keep the temperature cool inside during the hot season, but make it really difficult to heat in winter. In fact, there is very little to indicate that much thought has been given to the concept of heat in winter on any level; none of the doors and windows ever shuts properly.

The house facades are usually made of stone or earth-coloured plaster, most are different shades of ochre. There are, however, quite substantial regional differences in terms of colour schemes. The most colourful houses can be found along the coastline, and with the continuous renovation of village houses further inland, brighter colours are gaining a foothold there. Door and window frames will most often be white though. Not only does it look beautiful, but also originally, as insects don't like to cross white surfaces, white frames proved an efficient way of keeping them out of the house.

At the centre of every town, there is a square, where you also find the speckled plane trees, greatly relished for providing cool shade in summer while letting the sun through in winter. This is also where you will find the village church, fountain and the cafés. And of course, it is also where markets and various festivities are held. In other words, the square is the heart of the village.

The villages and towns of Provence have maintained much of their original charm – in some ways, they are almost like living museums. They have been in no rush to throw out any of their antiques, and they are highly aesthetically aware when it comes to choosing colours for shutters as well as buildings.

Over all, we must conclude that the authorities have been very successful in introducing legislation to preserve the classic Provençal look. Newcomers must not expect to be allowed to change much.

PÉTANQUE

There is hardly a town or village in Provence that does not have a dusty, gravel pitch, where the inhabitants play *pétanque*. The crash of colliding balls and lively debates amongst the players is part of the classic Provençal soundscape – on a par with the persistent chirping of the cicadas.

In the old days, they played *boules à la longue* on a pitch that could be up to 20 meters long, and then you had to run-up before throwing the ball. However, that all changed in 1907 when an old player from the seaside town La Ciotat became so riddled with arthritis that he could no longer participate, and so his friends decided to change the rules. They shortened the pitch and decided that the ball should be thrown from a standing position with legs together, which in Provençal is *pieds tanqués*. It is this game that we today know as *pétanque*.

You either play in teams or each man for himself. It's a very simple game, where you start by throwing the little ball, the *cochonnet* (piglet), 6–10 meters out on the pitch and then you try to place your own balls as close to the *cochonnet* as possible. The only additional equipment you need is a cloth to dry off the dusty balls and a tape measure to settle disputes about who is closest to the *cochonnet*. Perhaps that is also why *pétanque* has been so successful worldwide – it's no longer a game only played by pastis-drinking males, although this group still constitutes the majority of active players.

Originally, the game would be played with balls made from hard wood such as boxwood, but over time it was decided to cover the balls in nails to make them last longer. This was a craft carried out by women – *les ferreuses*. They would mount the player's initials in brass nails on balls of particularly high quality. However, this practice ended when a technique was invented to cast balls in one piece in the 1920s.

CERCLE de la FRATERNITÉ

THE ARTISTS' PROVENCE

An impressive number of some of the greatest artists from the 19th and 20th centuries have come to Provence for inspiration.

Paul Cézanne was a native Provençal from Aix. He was deeply fascinated by the countryside surrounding this beautiful university town. His favourite motif was Montagne Sainte-Victoire, of which he painted more than 60 pictures.

Most other artists were visitors, and just like tourists today, the light, the sun and the azure-blue Mediterranean drew them here.

There is hardly anywhere else in the world with such a concentration of museums and artists' residences – and here are some of the most important ones:

Aix-en-Provence

Musée Granet
Place Saint Jean de Malte,
13100 Aix-en-Provence.
Closed on Mondays.
www.museegranet-aixenprovence.fr
Works by Cézanne, Ingres,
Rubens and Rembrandt.

Atelier Cézanne
9, Avenue Paul Cézanne,
13090 Aix-en-Provence.
www.atelier-cezanne.com
Cézanne's studio is exactly as it
was as if he's just popped out.

Antibes

Musée Picasso
Place Mariéjol, 06600 Antibes.
Closed on Mondays.
50 works by Picasso, including
drawings, paintings and ceramics.

Arles

Musée Réattu
10, Rue du Grand Prieuré,
13200 Arles.
www. Museereattu.arles.fr
The museum is primarily
known for its 57 drawings
donated by Picasso.

BIOT

Musée National Fernand Léger
255, Chemin du Val de Pome,
06410 Biot.
www.musees-nationaux-alpesmaritimes.
fr/fleger/
400 works by Fernand Léger,
including ceramics, coloured glass
and paintings.

CAGNES-SUR-MER

Musée Renoir
Chemin des Collettes,
06800 Cagnes-sur-Mer.
Closed on Tuesdays.
The home of Auguste Renoir is
practically as it was when he died.

GRASSE

Musée Fragonard
23, Boulevard Fragonard,
06130 Grasse.
Closed on Tuesdays.
This museum is housed in a beautiful
Villa, in which Fragonard painted
one of his paintings on the staircase.
All the other paintings are copies.

MARSEILLES

Musée Cantini
19, Rue Grignan, 13006 Marseille.
Closed on Mondays.
Works of Picasso, Bacon, Dufy,
Le Corbusier, Léger and Miró.

Musée des Beaux-Arts
Palais Longchamp, 13004 Marseille.
Closed on Mondays.
Works by Puget, Monticelli and Guigou.

MENTON

Musée des Beaux-Arts
Palais Carnolès,
3, Avenue de la Madone,
06506 Menton.
Closed on Tuesdays.
The Princes of Monaco's old
summer residence is now a museum,
housing among other things,
a collection of modern artists
including Dufy and Kisling.

NICE

Musée des Beaux-Arts Jules Cheret
33, Avenue des Baumettes,
06000 Nice.
www.musee-beaux-arts-nice.org
Closed on Mondays.
Works by Fragonard and Dufy.

Musée Matisse
164, Avenue des Arènes de Cimiez,
06000 Nice.
www.musee-matisse-nice.org
Closed on Tuesdays.
Henri Matisse lived in Nice for nearly
40 years and he left a great
number of his paintings to the city. The
museum houses a lovely collection of
drawings, engravings and paintings.

Musée National Marc-Chagall
16, Avenue du Docteur Menard,
06000 Nice.
www.musees-nationaux-alpesmaritimes.
fr/chagall/
The museum houses a large number
Chagall's biblical works.

SAINT-PAUL

Fondation Maeght
623, Chemin des Gardettes,
06570 Saint-Paul-de-Vence.
www.maeght.com/musee
A beautifully positioned museum with
a fantastic collection of works by
Calder, Miró, Zadkine, Braque,
Giacometti and Chagall.

SAINT-REMY

Centre d'art presence van Gogh
Hotel Estrine, 8, Rue Estrine,
13210 Saint-Remy-de-Provence.
Changing exhibitions about van Gogh's
life and work.

SAINT-TROPEZ

Musée de l'Annonciade
Place Grammont,
83990 Saint-Tropez.
Works of Bonnard, Matisse and Signac.

VALLAURIS

Musée National Picasso
Place de la Liberation,
06220 Vallauris.
Apart from ceramics, it also houses
Picasso's War and Peace, carried
out in a Roman chapel.

VENCE

La Chapelle du Rosaire
466, Avenue Henri-Matisse,
06140 Vence.
There is a Mass Saturdays at 10 AM
and it is closed from mid November
until mid December.
Matisse decorated this chapel,
which is considered one of his
masterpieces: he designed
everything in the chapel, including
the altar and the priest's robes.

POTTERY

For centuries, Provence has been renowned for its pottery and ceramics. Even 2,000 years ago, the Romans had workshops around Marseilles and Fréjus, where they produced amphorae for transporting oil, grain and wine. The soil, which is rich in clay, and the easy access to firewood, has, of course, been vital for the development of the craft of pottery; a craft that is still widespread.

You find the most famous potteries in Aubagne, Apt, Cliousclat, Dieulefit, Poët-Laval, Salernes, Biot, Vallauris, Varages and Moustiers. Apart from building materials such as floor and roof tiles, they have specialised in kitchenware, including plates and bowls, as well as various jars, pots and jugs for wine and water.

Over the years, the different regions started specialising. The large pots or jars – *jarres* – that were formerly used to store olive oil and wine were mostly produced in Biot and Aubagne, where they still keep this tradition alive, only now the jars and pots are used as ornaments in gardens and on terraces. Fréjus also used to be famed for its *jarres*, but stopped producing them many years ago.

For the workshops in Salernes, kitchen and bathroom tiles are an important export. The town is especially known for its *tomettes* – the highly characteristic hexagonal tiles made from red clay that adorn the floors in many older Provençal houses. Production can be traced all the way back to the 17th century, but it did not become a regular industry until half way through the 19th century. The emergence of linoleum and other alternative floorings after the Second World War slowed down production considerably. However, these days the *tomettes* are once again in demand by people who want to add a feeling of heritage to their houses.

Ever since the late 17th century, the village Moustiers, close to Gorges-du-Verdon, has been renowned for its exquisite white tin-glazed earthenware – a technique that requires two firings. Most other places tend to focus on traditional rural pottery, and colours vary greatly from workshop to workshop. The palette is quite simple though, and the most common colours are different nuances of green and yellow as well as reddish brown.

In Poët-Laval, Dieulefit and Cliousclat in Drôme Provençal, you will find the workshops that adhere most stringently to the old traditions. At the *Poterie de Cliousclat* in particular, it is as if nothing has changed. They still do everything by hand, and they take great pride in maintaining the old Provençal style. For close to 500 years, the town's potters have produced pots and jars for the olive farmers in Nyons as well as for the producers of *fruits confits* in Apt. The clay in this area has the great advantage that it does not give off taste, which has helped make pots and jars from Cliousclat highly coveted.

In the 19th century, the village Vallauris in the Alpes-Maritimes started producing dishes, bowls and other earthenware for use in the kitchen in large numbers and the goods would then be shipped out of Juan-Les-Pins to North Africa, Italy and Spain.

In the late 1940s, Picasso ventured to Vallauris to try his hand at pottery, and the results of his efforts can be found in the *Musée Municipal de Céramique et d'Art Moderne*, among other places. Picasso was, as always, incredibly productive, and his presence helped establish the village even more firmly on the pottery map. Following in Picasso's footsteps, other artists have also spent time in Vallauris, which has inspired the local producers to experiment more whereas before they focused only on products for everyday use.

Entrée de la Poterie.

FAÏENCERIE

Madeleine
Anduze

RAVEL
RD
AUBAGNE

GLASSBLOWERS

From the 15th century, Provence was home to a successful glassware industry. Many towns were renowned for their glassblowers and numerous place names bear witness to the fact that this was indeed once a widespread craft.

Saint-Paul-en-Forêt in Var is one such village. Apart from producing bottles for wine and oil, this was the village that initiated the production of the hugely popular carboys that could hold as much as 10 litres of wine – the so-called *dames-jeannes*.

Glassblowing is energy-intensive, and the huge Provençal forests made it easy to secure firewood for its insatiable ovens. However, as new sources of energy took over, having easy access to firewood became less important and gradually the craft dwindled away.

Today, it's the glassblowers from *La Verrerie de Biot* who have caught the world's attention. Their characteristically thick, mouth blown glassware is highly valued all over Provence, and their work features in lifestyle magazines everywhere. The glass is unmistakably hand made, which gives each piece a unique, rustic look. The glass-blowers also produce everyday items such as jugs, tumblers, dishes and bowls in many different colours and with visible bubbles, the so-called *verres à bulles*.

Glass production started here in 1956 and the workshop has been very successful over the years. *La Verrerie de Biot* is now a large company with many employees and around 700,000 visitors each year. It is no coincidence that it was the town of Biot that gave the art of glassblowing a new lease of life, as the town's production of other arts and crafts goes back a long time.

SOAPS

Ever since the Middle Ages, Marseilles has been renowned for its soap. It contains only the finest natural ingredients, which makes it particularly soft on your skin. As far back as 1688, a decree was issued that all soap from Marseilles must contain at least 72% vegetable oil. The stamp on the sides must convey information of contents, weight and origin – and if there is no stamp, it's not the real thing. And one must be careful, because unfortunately, soap manufacturers from Marseilles haven't managed to secure an *Appellation Contrôlée*, which is the official guarantee of origin we're so familiar with from olive oil and wine. This is why you come across pirated products that don't come close to the high quality of the genuine *savon de Marseille*.

Some of the best soaps are made from oil extracted from the hot pressing, in other words, oil not used for cooking, and this easy access to huge quantities of olive oil has undoubtedly played a vital part in Marseilles becoming the centre of the soap industry.

Another reason has been the large amounts of salt available from the Camargue, which constitutes the raw material for caustic soda (NaOH), another important ingredient in the production of soap.

From 1823 and onwards, soap producers were also permitted to use coconut, palm and groundnut oil. Colours and scents vary greatly. Soaps made from olive oil, by many considered the best, are quite often of a greenish hue, while soaps made from palm oil are of a much lighter colour.

It takes 14 days to produce soap and, briefly explained, it's produced in enormous containers where oil is mixed with a strong base and periodically heated to 100°C. During this process, the soap is cleaned several times before it is cooled and cut into smaller pieces that are finally stamped on all sides. The soap manufacturers have been up against hard times more than once, not least with the invention of the washing machine and modern detergents. In the early 19th century, there were about 65 soap factories, today only a handful remain, but they can probably look forward to a brighter future, as people are once again taking an interest in natural products that are soft on the skin.

TISSUS **CLAUDINE** VOILAGE

TISSUS CLAUDINE

boutis
+ 2 faces
930 x 250

TEXTILES

It was along the quays of Marseilles harbour that the Dutch and Portuguese ships landed the first consignments of colourful textiles from India in the early 17th century. Never before had such bright and strong colours been seen. The textiles – *les indiennes* – quickly became so popular that the locals initiated their own production of colourful cottons with prints of leaves, flowers, insects and other Provençal motifs. The printed textiles were of such high quality that they were not damaged when washed, which meant that they could be used for a great variety of things. The new material excited even the French Court, despite its having silk in rich supply.

In time though, the privately owned Provençal production of textiles became so successful that it posed a threat to the royal production of silk, wool and flax. In order to curtail this development, the French Minister of Finance, Jean-Baptiste Colbert, banned the production and import of *les indiennes* around 1686. However, the strategy was only partly successful, as the ban increased demand and thus moved manufacture into the hands of merchants who were outside the reach of the authorities.

For example, textile mills were established in Le Comtat Venaissin, an enclave in northern Provence that belonged to the popes of Avignon (it had not yet been annexed by France). The ban was finally lifted in 1759 and this revived the local production. However, as the industrial revolution got under way, many of the smaller mills couldn't keep up as they were still making everything by hand. Today, there are only a few mills left. The most famous manufacturers are *Les Olivades* in Saint-Etienne-du-Grès and *Souleiado* in Tarascon.

The *boutis,* quilts embroidered by hand, are also artefacts particular to Marseilles. The name derives from the needle used to make these quilts and it is a tradition that goes all the way back to the 17th century. The quilts are often used as bedcovers. It is time-consuming work though, which is why they are primarily manufactured in India these days.

LAVENDER

From early June until August, rows and rows of lavender fields come into bloom in the highlands of Provence, far from the coast. They are to be found once you get to 400 m above sea level – where the vineyards stop. The spectacle, the scent and the sound of the humming bees are quite overwhelming.

The colours vary from light-grey to blue to lilac, depending on the time of year and which sort of lavender. Lavender is mainly cultivated for its scented oil, which is distilled locally and then sold on to the perfume industry in Grasse as well as the rest of the world. This oil is also used in soaps and by the pharmaceutical industry because of its disinfectant properties. The flowers are also sold freshly cut or dried in little bags that will scent your washing and linen beautifully.

The use of lavender is hardly a new development; the Romans used it to wash and scent clothes, and lavender actually gets its name from the Roman word for washing, *lavare*. In folk medicine, lavender is respected as a medicinal plant with numerous qualities – it is supposedly very soothing and it has a beneficial effect on cramps.

There are quite a few different sorts of lavender. The most highly esteemed lavender is the *Lavandula angustifolia* (true lavender), which you find growing in the wild all over Provence, particularly between 600 and 1,400 meters above sea level. It can also be cultivated, but it does not yield much oil and is becoming increasingly rare. On the other hand, the producers of true lavender can pride themselves on being allowed to stamp their products with an *Appelletion d'Origine Contrôlée*.

Another sort of lavender is the *Lavandula latifolia*, which has a very potent scent and yields lots of oil, only it is not terribly sought after by the perfumeries. Ever since the 1930s, a hybrid of the latifolia and angustifolia – *le lavandin* – has been cultivated. *Le lavandin* is easy to grow and it yields much more oil than either of its parents. A producer of true lavender must harvest 150 kg of flowers in order to get 1 litre of oil, whereas *le lavandin* will yield 1 litre of oil from only 50 kg of flowers. This hybrid thus becomes a popular choice for

lavender farmers; only the quality of oil is nowhere near the quality of true lavender oil. The entire production of true lavender oil is approximately 50 tonnes while the production of *le lavandin* is approximately 1,200 tonnes.

Lavender is incredibly sturdy; not only will it survive the frost in winter and early spring, it will also survive the scorching sun and dry summer.

In the old days, shepherds would collect the wild lavender and sell it on. The intense cultivation of lavender did not start until the 19th century, and it especially took off in the 1920s, when it gave the mountain farmers a welcome chance to utilise the stony and barren soil that was otherwise difficult to cultivate.

At the beginning, it was mainly itinerant workers from Italy and Spain who did the harvesting. Their work was made difficult by the presence of both bees and vipers, plus it was hard and hot. However, the cost of housing, feeding and paying this human workforce drove the lavender framers towards increased mechanisation, and since the 1960s, the harvest has been completely machine cut.

Unfortunately, the future for lavender farmers is rather bleak. Artificially produced scents as well as competition from farmers and producers in Russia, China, India and Bulgaria cause the French farmers genuine concern.

Most tourists visit the lavender fields in summer; however, they are definitely also worth a visit throughout the rest of the year, and the great lavender fields around the Plateau de Valensole, Gap, Digne, Forcalquier, Sault, Apt, Dieulefit, Nyons and Die are the ones to go and see.

15 AOUT
FETE DE LA LAVANDE

COOPERATIVE
AGRICOLE

La Maison
des Producteurs

SAULT
DE
VAUCLUSE

PASTIS

In the late afternoon, when the heat of the day is at its height, an unearthly calm descends upon the cafés as people sip pastis, that magic, yellow aniseed drink, in what is known as *l'heure du pastis*.

Pastis is a unique symbol of Provence – along with *pétanque* it embodies the essence of the Provençal lifestyle. For many, it's not really about the taste, it's much more about the calm, relaxed and thoughtful ambience that is created as soon as the drink is served. But whatever the reason, pastis does indeed seem to taste different when enjoyed outside Provence.

The first industrially produced pastis hit the markets in 1932, as a substitute for absinthe, which was banned in 1915. For years, the authorities had been reluctant witnesses to the population's profligate consumption of absinthe, which gets its name from wormwood, in Latin *Artemisia absinthium*.

This highly popular drink caused problems because wormwood contains thujone, which is poisonous, and can make people go mad, literally. Whether it was indeed wormwood or the high percentage of alcohol – as high as 70% sometimes – that drove people insane, is impossible to determine. But whatever the reason, the ban on absinthe led to experiments with other aniseed-based drinks during the 1920s, without wormwood and with a much lower percentage of alcohol. The result of these efforts was pastis as we know it today – a mixture of star anise, green anise, fennel, liquorice root and numerous Provençal herbs.

Paul Ricard chose *Le vrai pastis de Marseille* (the genuine pastis from Marseilles) as his slogan and for years he was constantly engaged in fierce competition with his rival Pernod to become the most popular French aperitif – a competition that only came to an end when the two companies merged in 1975.

The proper mixing ratio, incidentally, is 2 parts pastis and 5 parts cold water.

CAFE

BAR DU SOLEIL

PÉRITIF
45
ANISÉ
DEPUIS 1932
PASTIS
de
MARSEILLE
Paul Ricard
45% vol.
CRÉATEUR
FRANCE

BAR

PERNOD
45
Pernod fils

A TOUS LES FRANÇAIS

La France a perdu une bataille!
Mais la France n'a pas perdu la guerre!

Des gouvernants de rencontre ont pu
capituler, cédant à la panique, oubliant
l'honneur, livrant le pays à la servitude.
Cependant, rien n'est perdu!

Rien n'est perdu, parce que cette guerre est
une guerre mondiale. Dans l'univers libre,
des forces immenses n'ont pas encore donné.
Un jour, ces forces écraseront l'ennemi. Il faut
que la France, ce jour-là, soit présente à la
victoire. Alors, elle retrouvera sa liberté et sa
grandeur. Tel est mon but, mon seul but!

Voilà pourquoi je convie tous les Français,
où qu'ils se trouvent, à s'unir à moi dans
l'action, dans le sacrifice et dans l'espérance.

Notre patrie est en péril de mort.
Luttons tous pour la sauver!

VIVE LA FRANCE !

JUIN 1940
LONDRES

C. de Gaulle

GENERAL DE GAULLE

DÉBIT DE BOISSONS

LICENCE

GR

DÉPARTEMENT DU VAR.S.N.S

MARKETS

Visiting the *marché Provençal* is an intoxicating experience. The enormous choice of sun-ripened fruits and vegetables, grilled chickens, goat's cheeses, sausages and freshly baked bread is irresistible.

Most of the goods are locally produced and sold by the farmer or producer directly, creating a very intimate, cheerful and inclusive atmosphere that draws the customer in. The sellers are friendly and more than willing to tell you all about their goods. They take pride in their produce and they know that customers only come back for top quality ingredients. It's here in the market where you suddenly realise why Provençal food is so delicious. The selection of raw produce is magnificent and all of it fresh from the fields.

Apart from food, there are stalls with all sorts of hardware, ceramics, soaps, clothes, music and lots of other useful things. The traders keep up with the times and will gladly sell anything that people want to buy, and it has been this way as far back as anybody can remember. At least the Saturday market in Apt claims that it can be traced as far back as 500 years, back to the days when Good King René ruled out of Aix-en-Provence.

The markets are open until late morning once or twice a week. The traders show up early to get everything ready, but come midday, they start packing everything up again, and they are quick about it too. It is not long before the only signs that there was a market that day are the empty vegetable boxes piled high. So if you want to get something out of going to the markets, you have to get up early – try getting there before 9 AM.

MONDAY

Aix
Bédarrides
Bédoin
Cadenet
Cavaillon
Flayosc
Fontvielle
Forcalquier
Goult
La Valette-du-Var
Les Issambres
Nîmes
Saintes-Maries-de-la-Mer
Saint-Raphaël
Varages

TUESDAY

Aix
Apt
Aubagne
Avignon
Bandol
Banon
Beaumes-de-Venise
Bormes-les-Mimosas
Brue-Auriac
Caromb
Cucuron
Cotignac
Garéoult
Gordes
Fayence

Figanières
Fontaine-de-Vaucluse
Gréoux-les-Bains
Le Tholonet
Le Pradet
Lorgues
Mazaugues
Nice
Saint-Cyr-sur-Mer
Saint-Raphaël
Saint-Tropez
Tarascon
Tourves
Vaison-la-Romaine
Vence

WEDNESDAY

Aix	Nans-les-Pins
Arles	Nice
Aups	Purget-sur-Argens
Avignon	Riez
Besse-sur-Issole	Saint-Maximin
Bormes-les-Mimosas	Saint-Paul-de-Vence
Bras	Saint-Raphaël
Brignoles	Saint-Rémy-de-Provence
Buis-les-Baronnies	Salon-de-Provence
Carcès	Sault
Cassis	Sanary
Cavalaire-sur-Mer	Salernes
Cogolin	Sisteron
Digne	Tourtour
Draguignan	Valréas
La Crau	Vence
La Garde-Freinet	Vidauban
Malaucène	

THURSDAY

Aix	Martigues
Auriol	Mausanne-les-Alpilles
Avignon	Ollioules
Bargemon	Orange
Carquieranne	Pignans
Fayence	Plan-de-la-Tour
Forcalqueiret	Rocbaron
Gonfaron	Pourrières
Grimaud	Ramatuelle
La Cadière d'Azur	Saint-Antonin
Le Lavandou	Saint-Raphaël
Le Muy	Tavernes
Les Arcs	Varages
Les Salles-sur-Verdon	Vence
Méounes	Villecroze
Nice	
Nyons	

FRIDAY

Aix
Avignon
Bonnieux
Châteauneuf-du-Pape
Carnoules
Carpentras
Correns
Cotignac
Cuers
Dieulefit
Entrecasteaux
Flassans-sur-Issole
La Motte

Lourmarin
Le Beausset
Le Luc
Le Pradet
Le Val
Moustiers
Nice
Pontevès
Rians
Roquebrune-sur-Argens
Saint-Raphaël
Vence

SATURDAY

Aix
Apt
Arles
Aups
Avignon
Banon
Brignoles
Brue-Auriac
Callas
Castellane
Coglin
Draguignan
Fayence
Fréjus
Grasse

Hyères
La Roquebrussanne
Manosque
Nice
Ollioules
Oppède-les-Vieux
Pernes-les-Fontaines
Pierrefeu-du-Var
Puget-Ville
Rocbaron
Saint-Raphaël
Saint-Remy-de-Provence
Saint-Tropez
Tourtour
Vence

SUNDAY

Aix
Avignon
Bras
Collobrières
Forcalqueiret
Gardanne
La Londe-les-Maures
L'Isle-sur-la-Sorgue
Jouques
Mormoiron
Nans-les-Pins
Néoules
Nice

Nyons
La Ciotat
La Croix-Valmer
La Garde-Freinet
Le Muy
Régusse
Ramatuelle
Rocbaron
Salernes
Trans
Vence
Vidauban
Vinon-sur-Verdon

FLEA MARKETS

MONDAY

Nice
Nîmes

TUESDAY

Aix-en-Provence, Place Verdun
Avignon
Saint-Raphaël

WEDNESDAY

Vence
Cogolin, Rond Point d'Afrique

THURSDAY

Antibes, Place Nationale
Avignon

SATURDAY

Cannes, Les Allées de la Liberté
Grasse
La Seyne-sur-Mer
Le Cannet-des-Maures
Saint-Remy-de-Provence

SUNDAY

Carpentras
L'Isle-sur-la-Sorgue
Villefranche-sur-Mer
Saint-Remy-de-Provence
Fréjus
Hyères
La Londe-les-Maures
Rocbaron
Six-Fours-les-Plages
Taradeau
Trans
Vidauban

PROVENÇAL WINES
AND VINEYARDS

Provence is known as the home of rosé wine. And it is true that Provence produces endless amounts of dark, dry rosé wines, perfect for quenching your thirst on a hot summer day. However, the best rosé wines are more than that; they are elegant, bright and crisp, on a par with the finest rosé wines in the world. There are also lovely, fresh and young red wines or majestic, soft, rounded ones that keep well. There are fewer white wines, but at their best, they are dry, aromatic and very distinctive. As with both the rosé and red wines, there are plenty of characterful choices, and it's this diversity that ensures each trip to Provence will provide new surprises.

Provence is not renowned for its quality wines, although several districts within the region have been producing excellent wines for some years now, due to increased investment in modern technology and better educated wine growers. And, of course, the climate is perfect for growing wine.

Provence covers the eastern part of the French coastline along the Mediterranean as well as the hinterland, in total 31,400 km². It is one of 22 regions in France and it consists of 6 *départements*: Vaucluse, Bouches-du-Rhône, Var, Hautes-Alpes, Alpes-Maritimes and Alpes-de-Haute-Provence.

Each of the Provençal *départements* encompasses one or more wine districts. Famous and excellent Rhône-wines such as Châteauneuf-du-Pape, Gigondas and a number of the Côte du Rhône Villages wines are from Vaucluse and thus technically from the Provençal region, and even though they are not actually considered Provençal, it gives you an idea of the potential Provence has for producing great wines.

The districts of Côtes du Luberon and Côtes du Ventoux, also in Vaucluse, should be considered transitional areas, as the wines produced here seem to fall somewhere in between a Rhône-wine and a genuinely Provençal wine. The wines traditionally considered Provençal are: Côtes de Provence, Coteaux Varois, Palette, Bandol, Cassis, Bellet, Coteaux de Pierrevert, Coteaux d'Aix-en-Provence and Les Baux-de-Provence.

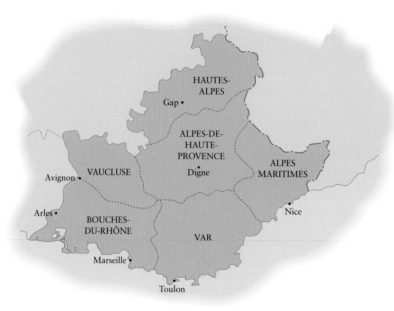

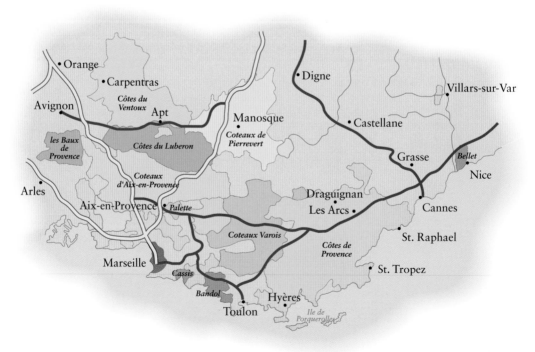

THE STORY OF PROVENÇAL WINE

When, in 600 BC, the Phoenicians and later the Greeks first arrived in Provence, they faced a wild and forested landscape – mainly evergreen pines and oaks – and a population of Celtic-Ligurian origin, who lived within these forests.

Many plants and trees today considered typically Provençal had not yet been introduced to the region. There were no cypresses, planes, agaves, mimosas or palms. However, wild vines grew in the dense woods and it's highly likely that the local population engaged in some sort of wine production even back then. After all, one of the good things about grapes is that it's fairly simple to turn them into wine.

However, the Phoenicians and Greeks preferred their own vines and they started cultivating the cuttings they had brought with them, which belonged to the species *Vitis vinifera*. It's also likely to be the Phoenicians who introduced the olive and fig trees we today consider characteristically Provençal.

Because of the favourable conditions and easy access to the sea, the first major Greek colony settled around Massalia, today known as Marseilles. Later, they established trading posts in Cassis, Bandol, Saint-Tropez, Fréjus, Antibes and Nice, which is why Provence was really the first region in France to start a serious wine industry.

The climate of Provence, with its dry, sunny summers and mild winters, provided the perfect growing conditions for grapes. The Greeks also flourished, and the trade with the Romans ensured that Massalia became an important commercial town, with the river Rhône enabling them to trade further with the Gauls and barbarians in the north. Merchant ships from this era have been located all along the Mediterranean coastline, containing thousands of amphorae for transporting wine. Apart from wine, these amphorae were mainly used for transporting olive oil and grain, and many of them would have been produced in Fréjus.

Unfortunately for the Greek colonists, though, they were better diplomats and merchants than warriors, and Massalia was often

exposed to plundering from local tribes, barbarians from the hinterlands and pirates from the sea. Around 120 BC things were getting out of hand, and so the Greeks asked their close allies, the Romans, for help. They duly arrived and quickly settled in, but instead of just helping the Greeks, the Romans conquered the entire region and named it *Provincia Romana* – the Roman Province – and hence Provence.

The Romans liked the Provençal wine, but they were also competent wine growers in their own right and they both improved and expanded the vineyards. Producing wine, however, was not merely a commercial enterprise; ensuring that there was enough wine for the thirsty Roman legionaries was also important. Furthermore, the Romans introduced new sorts of vines that would later be considered characteristic of the region, such as the *Tibouren* brought in from the banks of the Tiber.

With their usual diligence, the Romans built villages, roads, bridges, viaducts, arenas and villas all over Provence and later also across Gaul. Civilisation was making its mark on France, and in Provence especially there are still numerous well-kept Roman monuments such as the theatre in Orange, the *Tropaeum Alpium* (*Trophée des Alpes*) in La Turbie and the arenas in Arles and Fréjus.

The river Rhône became the Romans' preferred route of transportation through Provence and later also farther north. Wherever they landed, they established towns and vineyards. The Romans could not even contemplate civilisation without wine, and it was actually via Provence that the Romans established practically all the wine districts in Northern Europe.

The Provençal wine was exported to Rome, where it was greatly appreciated. So successful was it that local wine growers proceeded to demand a ban on imported wine to eliminate any competition. So in the year 92 AD, the Roman Emperor issued a decree that banned the establishment of new vineyards in Gaul and also demanded that many of the existing vineyards should be burnt to the ground. Former wine growers were now supposed to grow grain, which was always in short supply.

This might have helped curtail Provençal wine production, but not to any critical extent. After all, it was not only the locals who produced and drank wine, it was also the ex-pat Romans or the pensioned off legionaries, and these Roman pioneers of wine-growing would not have been terribly pleased when told to exchange their vines for grain.

The decree from Rome was in fact a hopeless, purely theoretical decision, because many of the Provençal vineyards were totally unsuitable for growing grain. And so the ban was never really effective and 200 years later Emperor Probus revoked the decree. Ever since then, there has been no doubt whatsoever that wine is indeed the most important crop in Provence.

Following the fall of the Romans in 476 AD, Provence suffered a number troubled years. The barbarians, Huns and Visigoths terrorised, plundered and generally unsettled the region. In the 8th century, Provence became part of the wine-loving King Charles the Great's empire, however, it was a brief respite. Throughout most of the 8th and 9th centuries, the Saracens gained a foothold in Spain from where they successfully conquered Marseilles and Aix and attacked Provence.

In terms of wine, the medieval era was a dark age for most of the South of France, however, due to the Church's increasingly powerful position in society, wine was given a second chance. During the Middle Ages, the Church was instrumental in the development of new and improved vine-growing techniques. They needed supplies for altar wine, but it's also safe to assume this crop, above all others, delivered the greatest profits.

In Provence, churches, monasteries and abbeys sprang up all over the place, and along with them, vineyards. Several of the monasteries were better known for their wine than their religious practices. The vineyards belonging to Domanie de l'Abbaye in Le Thoronet, Commanderie de Peyrassol in Flassans, Château de Saint-Martin in Taradeau, Castel Roubine in Lorgues and Château Sainte-Roseline in Les Arcs-sur-Argens all date back to this era.

It was also about this time that the crusades began, and among other places, they set sail from Marseilles, which meant that the entire region flourished through an increase in trade and export of wine. On their way back from the Holy Land, the crusaders also came across new sorts of vines that they brought back with them.

When Eleanor of Provence married King Henry III, she took advantage of her new position and soon the English Court was enjoying Provençal wine. It was also in the medieval era that the Papacy moved from Rome to Avignon. The popes were very fond of wine and the famous Châteauneuf-du-Pape vineyards date back to this time.

From the 13th to the 15th century, the Counts of Anjou ruled

Provence. They were not particularly interested in wine, being preoccupied with fighting in Italy instead. The only exception was Good King René, who in the 15th century owned a vineyard close to Aix, in what is today known as Palette.

King René was a poet and a passionate wine grower, but not terribly interested in waging wars. Having lost Naples in 1442, he was returning from Italy when he came across a new sort of Muscat grape, which he brought back to Provence. A few years later, this grape made Cassis famous. The Good King himself experimented with the production of new wines and among other things he developed *vin cuit* (where you concentrate the must by boiling it) based on his Italian Muscat grape. However, his greatest achievement is without doubt the introduction of rosé wine. It was René's nephew who bequeathed Provence to the French Crown and since 1481 Provence has been under French reign.

The 16th and 17th centuries witnessed the religious wars between the Catholics and the Protestant Huguenots. This put a stop to the burgeoning development of wine production in Provence, because both the church and the nobility – the two institutions that cultivated vines – were too busy fighting. Among other atrocities, the fighting resulted in the destruction of Châteauneuf in Avignon. Furthermore, Cardinal Richelieu tore the fort in Les Baux to the ground as the nobility in Paris considered the Counts of Les Baux a little too frivolous and wilful.

By the end of the 17th century, the famous correspondent Madame de Sévigné from Entrecasteaux in Var wrote to her aristocratic friends about the brilliance of Provençal wines. But although the wines had excellent reputations, there were also plenty of obstacles. From the 16th to the 19th century, the export of Provençal wine to the north was impeded by the regions of Bordeaux and Burgundy's fear that competition would add additional taxes to the price of imported wines. However, practically all the French vineyards were affected by severe frost in 1709, 1725, 1737 and 1740. Only the Provençal vines were unaffected, and as the rest of France was short of wine, the customs barriers were soon lowered. In Provence, they expanded the vineyards and made a fortune supplying the rest of war-torn France with wine. At the same time export by sea was also flourishing and Provence shipped wine to places as far away as North America and Brazil.

The desire to cultivate new and better vines turned many wine growers' attention to the other side of the Atlantic and they experimented with grafting American and European vines. This would turn out to be fatal.

In the mid-1840s, French vineyards were attacked by a powdery fungus, grape mildew (*Oidium tuckeri*), the first time the disease had entered the region. It was mainly the green part of the vines and their flowers that were infected, but the grapes did not escape unscathed. Although the vines did not necessarily die, they were weakened to such a degree that the total French wine production fell from 45 million hectolitres (hl) in 1850 to 10 million hl in 1854.

The damp regions of France were most severely contaminated, but the Provençal spring can be quite wet and so vineyards there were also quite badly hit. Wine growers were ruined and many Provençal citizens migrated to France's newest colony, Algeria. Others went to America, hoping that conditions there would be better. Those migrating across the Atlantic to avoid the grape mildew went in the wrong direction though, because the fungus originated in America. However, the effect on the American vines was not nearly as harsh as on the European plants. In America, the vines had been exposed to grape mildew for thousands of years and so researchers had developed an antidote to the fungus. A cure for the infection was quickly discovered: a solution of sulphur that is still used on a regular basis today.

However, the wine growers hardly had time to get over the mildew attack before disaster struck again. The vine pest (*Phylloxera vastatrix*) invaded France, in much the same way as the Romans, along the Rhône.

The first infestation was noted around Arles in Provence in early 1863. The vine-leaves turned a strange colour and the new sprouts were lacking vigour. The grapes would not ripen and the plants gradually died. When they pulled the dead vine from the soil, it had hardly any roots. Nobody could come up with an immediate explanation because the lice did not stay with the dead vine; they happily continued their destruction on new and fresh roots. By 1866 the infestation had spread to the entire Midi-area and all over Provence.

The phylloxera infestation meant further loss for wine growers. The rural population starved to death and nobody knew what to do. The situation was desperate and huge rewards were offered to whomever could solve the problem. France's entire wine production was at stake. They tried all sorts of sorcery and witchcraft but, apart from flooding

the wine fields and gassing the vines with sulphur, nothing seemed to have any effect.

In dry Provence, flooding the wine fields is far from easy. There is hardly ever enough water. Furthermore, the best vineyards are situated on slopes or terraces. The explosive sulphur gas not only killed the lice, it also affected the farmers, and on top of that, the poisonous gas would have to be infused into the soil around each individual vine – a dangerous and enormous task to undertake.

It was not until staff at the University of Montpellier started approaching the problem systematically that a solution was found. The wine louse was identified and its cycle described by professor J.E. Planchon. It has a highly complex life cycle with up to twelve different phases, each with its own particular manifestation. The louse itself is tiny, though visible to the naked eye. Furthermore, it is extremely reproductive, which makes it a great coloniser. Theoretically, through parthenogenesis, a single female louse can mother 48,000,000,000 (48 billion) individuals per year – which is no small family.

The wine louse was not of French origin but is thought to have been brought over from North America. Why it infected Provence at that particular time remains an unsolved mystery. One hypothesis is that it happened when the shipping trade was upgraded substantially by the introduction of fast steamships. A trip across the Atlantic used to take several weeks, but now could be accomplished within one single week, which secured the wine lice a safe crossing, neatly tucked away in the American vines that were shipped to Provence as part of an experiment.

Thankfully, America was not only the source of the problem; the solution to the phylloxera-infestation would also come from there. The wine louse was probably the reason why imported European plants never really thrived in eastern America, while on the other hand, the American vines seemed unaffected; they had lived side by side with the lice for thousands of years, growing immune to the pest in much the same way they had the mildew. Granted, the lice do attack the American vines, but they can withstand the infestation and the plant defends itself by rejecting the infested leaves. This is how the American plants survive, and is after all also in the lice's interest, because without vines, there is no food.

The European vines on the other hand, had never been exposed to the phylloxera-louse and so they had no effective biological defence mechanism. And to top that, it was the roots that were affected first. A discoloured leaf does not mean the leaf itself is under attack, as is the case with American vines, it is simply because the roots no longer function. The vines' only defence is to rid itself of the root, but that also means that there is no supply of water or nourishment to the remaining part of the plant.

Finally, the solution chosen was grafting European vines onto American roots, thus combining the stamina of the American roots and the quality of the European vines. It is still the only way to combat the louse, which continues to be fairly widespread even today.

From Provence and Languedoc, the wine lice spread all over Europe, however, few other places suffered an infestation on a par with that in the South of France, where the vines were all but totally devoured before a solution to the problem was found.

For Provence, a region that had gambled all on the production of wine and its highly successful export to the rest of Europe and America, it meant financial ruin and the end of several vineyards. In the department of Var alone, production fell from 4 million hl to 600,000 hl during this period. Districts such as Cassis and Bandol have never managed to reach the same level of production as before the phylloxera-infestation and several sorts of grapes have completely vanished. The number of wine-carrying ships that would dock at Bandol harbour fell from 350 a year before the crisis to a total of 8 in 1910. This meant that the town lost a quarter of its inhabitants, who had to try and find work in Toulon instead.

Ironically, the infestation of wine lice led to an increase in the import of American vines as there was great demand for roots to graft, and thus the downy grape mildew (*Plasmopara viticola*) returned from America and infested the Provençal vineyards around 1880.

Unlike the powdery mildew, downy mildew will inevitably kill a vine if it is not treated. Fortunately though, the cure for this downy mildew was quickly found and it happened, as is the case with many great inventions, by accident. A wine grower who had a field that ran along a church path sprayed the outer edge of his field with a strong, blue-coloured copper-solution in a desperate attempt to keep the churchgoers from stealing his grapes. One day, Professor A. Millardet from the University of Bordeaux wandered past. He noticed that the

areas sprayed with this poisonous mixture were not only free from grape-thieves but they had not been attacked by the downy mildew either. Following this discovery, he and his colleges in Bordeaux developed the famous blue Bordeaux-mixture consisting of copper sulphate and slaked lime. The fungus has not yet been eradicated and this mixture is still in use.

Fortunately for Provençal wine growers, downy mildew doesn't like the dry, regional wind known as the *mistral*, so they were left less out of pocket than others.

Having solved the mystery of the mildew, the wine growers had to start from scratch again. The effect of the American pests had been enormous. For a number of years, France had to import wine, previously totally unheard of. In Marseilles, several wine merchants made lots of money by producing wine from raisins imported from Greece. So, even while Provence was in the process of re-establishing its vineyards around the year 1900, it became obvious that there was money to be made from producing as much wine as possible. Furthermore, the expansion of the railway system meant new opportunities for export to the north.

However, establishing quality vineyards demanded capital that was lacking in poorer Provence, unlike in the traditionally wealthier regions of Bordeaux and Burgundy. And so Provençal wine growers planted high-yielding but uninteresting grapes like Carignan, Aramon and various hybrids of American and European varieties. These hybrids are resistant to the phylloxera-louse, but unfortunately produce wine of poor quality. You can still find vineyards that use these vines, but they are being phased out.

This concentrated effort on quantity rather than quality cost Provence the good reputation it had built up over the preceding 200 years. In the Middle Ages, people moved with the vines up into the mountains, but now they began to plant vines in the fertile soil in the river valleys, which was better suited to growing vegetables and grain.

At first, this new approach appeared to pay off, but in time, production increased to such levels that the price of wine collapsed. This collapse was reinforced by the fact that Algeria, Languedoc and Roussillon were also producing huge amounts of wine. And, as if that was not enough, in 1914, the Great War broke out.

The First World War affected the French far worse than did the

Second World War. Thousands of young Provençal men were sent to the north of France to be poisoned by gas in the trenches on the Western Front. Meanwhile the vineyards were tended by the women and children left behind. And to make matters worse, the vines suffered massive attacks of mould fungus. The few healthy grapes that were ripe for picking were sent to the soldiers in the trenches who needed all the sustenance they could lay their hands on.

Only a few wine producers managed to take an interest in improving the quality of wine until after the end of the war, and by then there was an increased interest in heightening the quality of Provençal wines. But as the problem of erratic quality also affected the rest of the French wine production, it was decided to establish the INAO (*Institut National des Appellations d'Origine*) in 1935, an organisation in charge of creating specific rules for which grapes and methods of cultivation are applicable in each region and district as well as protecting the individual regional wines from being copied. It was also agreed that prime districts would be awarded an AOC (*Appellation d'Origine Contrôlée*).

Cassis was the first region within Provence to receive this distinction in 1936. Bandol, Bellet and Palette followed shortly after. Today all of the Provençal districts belong in the AOC category. They produce more than 1 million hl per year, which makes Provence one of the most important wine regions in all of France.

A decisive factor in the improvement of the quality of Provençal wine has been the co-operatives. Originally, the co-operatives would pay farmers according to weight but in time they decided to set the price according to the quality instead. And in this manner, the co-operatives have actually helped nourish an interest for cultivating vines of high quality. Today the co-operatives use professional oenological assistance and modern equipment to produce their highly affordable and splendid wines. In the department of Var alone, there are close to 100 co-operatives.

After the Second World War, waves of tourists started arriving in the seaside towns all along the coast. Few wines are better suited to be enjoyed on a hot summer day on the beach or in the square of some small Provençal village than the local rosé wine. The tourists proved a grateful audience and perfect consumers. The producers made their move and increased production and today rosé wines are

still dominant on the Provençal market. However, it was not only the tourists who helped shape the future of wine production in Provence. In 1956, Provence suffered from a particularly fierce winter frost that destroyed thousands of old olive trees. The indigenous pale green pines, *pins d'Alep*, also perished in great numbers. This meant that in many places, instead of re-establishing the old olive groves, more vines were planted. The surface of the Provençal landscape changed once again.

The mid-1960s brought about the start of yet another new era, with foreign wine producers settling all over Provence, bringing new life to the various districts. Some of these new settlers were from Algeria, the so-called *pieds-noirs*, like the Bunan family of Moulin des Costes and Mas de La Rouvière in Bandol. Georges Brunet arrived in Aix from Bordeaux, and went on to produce the Château Vignelaure as proof that Provence had the potential to produce absolutely top quality wines. Over time, the influx has continued, both from other parts of France as well as from abroad.

The common characteristics binding these newcomers together have been financial acumen, visionary strategy, and a willingness to experiment. They have been able to start from scratch and plant only the vines they felt were most suitable. And they have been able to afford to invest in the latest technology.

Many of the newcomers find that although the AOC-regulations help maintain the identity of a specific district, they also stifle innovation, which is why many new producers tend to pay less than complete attention to the rules governing the precise cultivation of the grapes. It's worth remembering that it's exactly this disregard for the status quo that has often proved the recipe for success in many emerging wine countries. The number of 'foreign' wine growers has accelerated over the last 25 years, and these are the people responsible for Provence often being spoken of as 'the new California'. Although most Provençal wine growers would wince at such a description, there might just be something in it. Provence is no longer recognised merely as the production site of everyday rosé wines; today it produces a wide range of quality wines of all colours.

LE TERROIR

The French believe that a local district can have vital influence on the quality of wine produced in it and they often invoke the notion of *le terroir*, which is the French expression for the physical factors encompassing the interaction of soil, general climate and microclimatic conditions. Based on these conditions, the wine farmer will chose his vines and methods of cultivation, and it is principally the *terroirs* that determine the regulations in all of French wine legislature.

The soil provides taste and quality, but it's the sun that produces energy and ripens the grapes, the wind that dries out the soil and the stones that reflect the sun and accumulate heat.

There are many areas of Provence, around Les Baux and Bandol by way of example, where vines grow on old seabeds, obtaining sustenance from calcium-rich fossils of primeval sea creatures. In other areas it can be the cool Mediterranean breeze or the relentless roar of the *mistral* that have the greatest influence.

Different vines adapt to different conditions, and this is where the ability of the wine grower is so important because within existing regulations, there will be certain vines that are particularly suited to grow on his specific fields.

The choice of production methods and the composition of grapes are also of crucial importance.

GRAPES

The choice of grape is not merely dependent on local conditions; it also depends on which sort of wine the producer is interested in producing. The range of grapes is as varied as that of apples.

Unlike most other wine regions in France, Provence is home to so many different kinds of grapes they could fill out a large botanical garden on their own. In all, 58 different grapes are allowed in this region.

The Greeks, the Romans and the Crusaders introduced many of the different grapes currently cultivated in Provence. Furthermore, the new and highly innovative producers have imported different sorts that do not traditionally belong in Provence. Most of the Provençal wines consist of a blend of grapes.

The black grapes primarily used to produce rosé and red wine are:

Grenache Noir. This vine originates in Spain and it thrives on dry slopes. It is the most dominant grape in Provence and it yields slightly aromatic wines that are big and full-bodied but quite pale.

Tibouren. The Romans originally introduced this Middle Eastern vine to Italy. Today it practically only exists in Provence, where it is only used to produce rosé wine. The grapes yield a fresh, fruity, big and quite pale wine.

Tibouren thrives close to the sea and used to be the preferred grape in the vineyards around Saint-Tropez. Many wine producers still make wonderful and aromatic rosé wines based on Tibouren and some choose to blend it with Cinsault, which can also produce excellent results.

Carignan Noir. This is a highly productive and robust vine of Spanish origin. It thrives in poor soil and heat, which is why it used to be quite common in Provence. Although the old vines or the strictly trimmed younger vines can yield grapes of very high quality, they are often exchanged for different sorts. On its own it produces wine of great colour but also slightly anonymous, but it can be useful in the production of rosé wine when blended with Grenache.

Mourvèdre. This vine originates in Spain and produces small and compact clusters of grapes. A good example is found in Bandol where proximity to the sea helps create this phenomenon. The grapes produce some of the best wines in Provence, indeed, all of France. They can be dark and spicy with a hint of pepper, however, the Mourvèdre wines are only at their very best when allowed to mature in oak casks.

Mourvèdre is a great antioxidant, which means that it has preservative properties. This not only ensures a longer life for Mourvèdre wines, it also means that Mourvèdre can be used to prolong the lives of other more perishable wines produced from grapes such as Grenache. Some producers even greatly reduce or completely avoid the use of sulphates by utilising the preservative properties of the Mourvèdre grape.

The Mourvèdre-vine has long been underestimated and ignored, but it is now experiencing a bit of a revival, even outside Provence.

Syrah. This black grape, which by all accounts was introduced to the South of France by the Romans, produces excellent, durable, full-bodied and colourful wines. Mixed with Grenache it produces great rosé wines, and with Mourvèdre and Cabernet Sauvignon it produces fine and durable red wines. This grape is becoming more and more widespread across Provence and it is often recognisable by its characteristic peppery taste.

Cabernet Sauvignon. The classic grape from Bordeaux is one of the most popular grapes in the world. Traditionally, it does not belong in Provence, but if grown on fields that are not too dry, it can produce excellent wines that improve when left to mature in casks. It is very well suited to complement the classic Provençal grapes, adding a bit of roundness as well as a soft hint of blackcurrant.

Cinsault. This is a vine that thrives on dry slopes. The grapes produce pale and fresh wines low on acidity. Cinsault can be used to produce good rosé wines when blended with Mourvèdre or Grenache. It can also be used to balance and soften Syrah wines.

Aramon/Ugni Noir. This vine is probably the most productive and it used to be a highly popular choice in the South of France following the infestation of wine lice. It produces rather dull wines though, and its popularity is rapidly diminishing. Aramon is called '*pisse-vin*' in Hyères, a district in the department of Var – an expression that it is fairly easy to understand, even if you don't speak French.

The white grapes primarily used for white wines are:

Rolle. The robust Rolle originates in Italy – in Sardinia it is called *Vermentino* – and it has long been considered a speciality in Italian-influenced Bellet. It has also been produced as an edible grape and dried to make sweet raisins.

These days, it is becoming more and more common within the region of Provence. Rolle produces lovely, aromatic, crisp and big wines. You will often get a good result when blending it with Ugni Blanc, which can add a little of the acidity that Rolle can sometimes lack.

Clairette Blanche. This vine, which can be highly productive even in poor soil, produces big, acidic wines with a flowery aroma.

Ugni Blanc. This is the most common green grape in all of France. It was probably introduced to Provence from Italy in the 1300s, when the popes resided in Avignon.

Ugni Blanc has been particularly popular because it is unusually productive. In Provence, it produces yellowish wine, low on alcohol but quite acidic. This acidity helps produce appealing and fresh wines, which it can otherwise be difficult to cultivate in hot climates. This is also why Ugni Blanc is suitable for blending in with more characteristic grapes that have problems obtaining sufficient acidity.

Sauvignon Blanc. The green grape of the Sancerre wines, which produces wines low in alcohol, with a delicate acidity and a bouquet of fresh green herbs.

Chardonnay. This classic green and highly aromatic grape from Burgundy is becoming more and more popular in Provence. It thrives in calcareous soil when not exposed to severe heat. The wines can be round, soft and buttery; they often have a green hue and they are well suited for maturing in casks.

Sémillon. This is a productive vine, and its grapes give off herbal aromas, which makes them well suited to supply structure to wines produced on the basis of Ugni Blanc.

Roussanne. This grape is common in both Rhône and Provence, where its late ripening poses no problems. The wines made from Roussanne have a refreshing herbal aroma. The grapes are often blended with Marsanne, because it adds the acidity and direct freshness that Marsanne lacks.

Marsanne. This is an exquisite grape of the white Rhône wines with a flowery bouquet. In Provence, you will only find it in Cassis. Wines based on Marsanne are low in acidity, which is why you get the best results when blended with Ugni Blanc and Roussanne that are higher in acidity.

Bourboulenc. An old Greek grape that is very common in the South of France. It ripens late, but its high level of acidity helps make it attractive when producing well-balanced wines. It is only rarely used on its own, but it is common in blended wines.

WINE PRODUCTION

Microscopic yeast fungi live on the skin of grapes (the greyish and wax-like film that covers the ripe grapes) and when they come into contact with the sugar inside the grapes in oxygen-free conditions, it turns into alcohol and carbon dioxide.

Carbon dioxide is a gas – when dissolved it is called carbonic acid. This will evaporate unless there is further fermentation after the wine has been bottled, as is the case with Champagne. Above a bubbling fermentation vat, there is a layer of carbon dioxide and this gas can cause the death of a wine worker if she or he is unlucky enough to fall into the vat.

When producing dry wines, the yeast cells are allowed to convert all the sugar content into alcohol, while sweet wines are produced by disrupting the fermentation process before using up all of the sugar. As the wine ferments, the sugar is used up in step with the rising percentage of alcohol, but at a certain stage, the yeast cells will die because the percentage of alcohol is too high.

There is not just one sort of yeast fungus on the grapes; there are several different species, each with their own alcohol tolerance level. Some of the fungi will die when the alcohol percentage rises to 4, however, when one fungus dies, others take over, and that is why wines can have an alcohol content as high as 14.5%. To be in total control of the fermentation process, many wine producers will choose to use only industrially processed yeast fungi. The alcohol content of the wine will then depend on how much sugar was contained within the grapes as well as which yeast strains have been used.

When the grapes are pressed, the must will contain oxygen, which the yeast fungi will use to multiply – something they are very good at. In just ten days, one single yeast fungus can create more than one million other fungi. When there is no more oxygen in the must, the serious alcohol production sets in.

The fermentation process can take place in practically any kind of vessel, from oak casks to steel vats, you only have to make sure that the carbon dioxide can escape, without letting oxygen in. Oak wood will add flavour and tannic acid, however, most producers will choose glass-lined steel or concrete vats for financial reasons.

The fermentation process generates heat, and if it gets too hot (over 38°C) the fermentation process is at grave risk of coming to a halt. So lengthy, cool fermentation processes make for the best results. Which is why cold storage plants are so important, not least in a rather hot region like Provence.

Once the initial fermentation process is completed and the must's sugar levels are down to approximately 2 g per litre, the yeast cells start dying. They explode and release flavourings, which help produce the wine's specific taste and aroma: its *bouquet*. However, the dead cells can also prove fertile ground for unwanted bacteria, which is why the wine is racked, i.e. the must is separated from the dead yeast cells by being poured into another vat.

This will allow for a new fermentation process to begin, should the wine producer so choose. This would be a so-called malolactic fermentation that takes place aided by bacteria, which turns the malic acid in the wine into carbon dioxide and lactic acid. Lactic acid is a little softer in taste, and furthermore, this fermentation prolongs the life of the wine. Malolactic fermentation is useful when making red wines, whereas it is not always preferable if you want fresh and fruity rosé or white wines for quick consumption. This is why many Provençal producers choose to block this fermentation process with sulphur.

After separating dead yeast cells and must, most producers will choose to clear and filter the wine. This can be done with egg white or modern filters; however, some producers find that filtering the wine also does away with some of its flavours, which is why they decide not to filter their wines (allowing the wine to form a harmless sediment).

At this point in the process producers can choose to leave the wine to mature, but in principle it is ready for bottling after which it may or may not be left to mature for a little longer. Sulphur will be added to preserve the wine.

RED WINE

The black grapes are pressed and left to ferment with the skins, which is what gives red wine its colouring, its tannin and its more robust taste. This is also why red wines are often more durable than white wines. Tannin is the component that can make wine seem aggressive and bitter, however over time the tannin will balance out and instead assist in creating full-bodied and soft wines.

While in the fermentation vats, the skins from the black grapes will almost form a lid: it is called putting a hat on the vat – a *chapeau de marc*. To stop this uneven distribution of grape skins and must they have to stir the vat several times a day. This is called *remontage*. The fermentation temperature for red wine (21–24°C) is often a little higher than for white wine.

After no more than 3–4 days, the skins can be discarded, but you will get the best result if you leave them for 2–3 weeks. Fermentation can be prolonged even further depending on whether or not the producer wants a wine that is ready for consumption right away. The longer the skins stay in the must, the longer it will take the wine to be ready for consumption. It is referred to as short or long *macération*.

Now the wine, which is called *vin de goutte*, is ready to be drained from the fermentation vat. The skins and wine left in the vat will then be pressed, which produces a wine high in tannin, which can then be carefully blended in with the initially drained-off wine.

As well as this classic process, a new method is gaining in popularity: *macération carbonique*, a process that originates in the Beaujolais region in which whole grapes are poured into a vat filled with carbon dioxide. This starts a fermentation process within the grapes without activating the yeast fungi. Eventually the grapes will explode due to the accumulation of carbon dioxide and the must will flow, after which it will be subjected to regular fermentation. This procedure makes for fresh and highly fruity wines; only they do not keep that well, because the skins release no noteworthy amount of tannin.

WHITE WINE

White wine can be made from both white and black grapes, as long as the must from the black grapes remains colourless. This is rare, and you never come across it in Provence, which is why Provençal white wines are made solely from white grapes.

When producing white wine, harvesting before it gets too hot is important – early in the morning is good. The grapes should be pressed without delay to stop the must fermenting with the skins, which happens when producing red wine.

Slow fermentation at temperatures no higher than 15–20°C (perhaps even lower) make for the best white wines.

Generally, Provençal wine producers are not interested in using the bacterial induced malolactic fermentation process, which can deprive the wines of their freshness. This is also why the grapes are picked quite early as it ensures that their acidity is preserved.

Usually, the white wines will be ready for consumption 6–8 months after the grapes are harvested. However, some producers also make wines that are more durable, and one way of doing that is called *macération pelliculaire*, where the must is allowed to draw more flavour from the grape skins.

ROSÉ WINE

Rosé wines can be pale or dark depending on which technique is used in the production process. Generally, rosé wines are made solely from black grapes that are either pressed rather quickly (*la presse directe*), or bled (*saignée*), which is the method most commonly used in Côtes de Provence.

When using *la presse directe* method, the grape skins are removed from the must and the grapes are pressed without delay, which results in a very pale rosé wine. When producing rosé wine in this fashion, the grape skins are only left in the must for a very short while. This is why it is imperative that the grapes are harvested at exactly the right time. They will only release their characteristics when fully ripe.

When using the *saignée* method, the initial procedure is the same as when producing red wine, but after 4–12 hours the must will contain enough alcohol for the skins to release colour and the must will have to ferment separately from then on. This method is also known as *vin d'une nuit* – wine in one night. *Saignée* means 'bleeding', a reference to the fact that you allow the black grapes to 'bleed'. Rosé wines can be very pale or a deep red colour depending on whether the grapes are left to bleed for 2 or more than 24 hours. The *saignée* rosé wines are often fruitier than *la presse directe* ones. Some producers also choose to combine the two methods to obtain structure while also maintaining the fruity quality.

All Provençal rosés are left to ferment until dry and, as the grapes often have a high sugar content, the percentage of alcohol will be quite high as well, up to 13.5%. Malolactic fermentation is rarely used, which helps keep the wines fresh and fruity. On average, a rosé wine will be ready for consumption six months after harvesting. Some producers will leave the wine to mature in casks or bottles for a while before selling it, which may reduce the wine's immediate freshness a little, but on the plus side, can add more complex flavourings.

Rosé wines can be rather difficult to produce and they demand constant attention – especially if you want to produce the modern, very pale varieties.

MARC DE PROVENCE

Marc is a spirit – a so-called *eau-de-vie* – and usually pronounced with a silent c, although many Provençal seem unaware of this rule.

Marc refers to the leftovers from the pressing of grapes – pips and skins – from which the spirit is produced, as opposed to spirits produced from wine such as Cognac and Armagnac.

The leftovers are immersed in water, which is then heated to produce the alcoholic marc.

For the production of marc, only grapes that are also used to produce wine are allowed, which is why marc is similarly influenced by local conditions.

The Provençal volume of marc production is around 2000 hl a year.

Eau de Vie de Marc

Cordelier

Vieux Marc de Provence

Eau-de-vie de Marc
originaire de Provence

Distilleries et Domaines
de Provence

D 45%Vol. 70cl

04300 Forcalquier / Produit de France

MATURING IN CASKS

The Greeks and Romans were most likely inspired by the Celts when they started maturing wine in casks rather than amphorae. The casks were easier to handle and the quality of wine improved greatly after maturing in wooden casks rather than in bags made from animal skins or unglazed amphorae. The oldest wine cask in the world was discovered in the excavations in the old Roman quarter of Fréjus, and has been dated all the way back to 25 BC.

Practically all wine producing regions use oak for their different casks because oak contains tannin, which wards off both fungi and insect infestations. New and smaller oak casks add a vanilla flavour to the wine whereas older casks merely function as containers; so the large Provençal *foudres* do not add much taste to the wine, but they are highly useful because they allow for a slow circulation of air, which ensures a well-balanced maturing of the wine.

Unfortunately, the casks are very expensive and the production of *foudres* is rapidly dwindling: there are only a few workshops left in France. In Provence, there is still one cooper's shop in La Londe-Les-Maures; *Tonnellerie Kennel*, the only workshop this side of Lyon.

Kennel's grandfather emigrated from Switzerland and set up shop in Provence. Kennel has specialised in rebuilding and converting old casks from local vineyards. Domaine du Jas d'Esclans, Châteu de l'Isolette and Domaine de Garbelle are among its customers. Kennel has also specialised in renovating German beer casks from Munich, transforming them into Provençal foudres and furthermore, the workshop collaborates with coopers in Bordeaux, who make the classic *barriques* (small casks that only contain 225 litres), however, Kennel also make their own, if they have the time. Nonetheless, many of the oak casks that we encounter at the different vineyards are imported from abroad, Eastern Europe in particular.

ORGANIC WINE

The upsurge in environmental awareness that has swept across Europe over the last 25 years has had a strong influence on Provençal wine producers.

Whereas biodynamic agriculture borders on lunacy, biological or organic agriculture is a serious science. The principles in this approach to wine growing are that you cultivate your fields in accordance with nature's rules, without artificial fertilisers or industrially produced pesticides. Furthermore, you reduce the amount of sulphur used during the process of turning grapes into wine, which is greatly helped by improving sanitation.

Although vines are not particularly demanding in terms of fertilisers, artificial fertilisers are still widely used in traditional wineries. It is, however, possible to substitute artificial fertiliser with sheep's manure, seaweed or green manure. Green manure consists of mustard or leguminous plants such as clovers, which you then place between the vine rows.

The leguminous plants have the ability to absorb nitrogen from the air and when plants then wither or are moved down, these vital nutrients are released. Many organic vineyards put this process to highly effective use.

In spring, they plant white clover underneath the vines, which also helps keep weeds down. The clover absorbs more nitrogen than it needs, and of course this is beneficial for the vines. At the height of summer, when the sun is really strong, the clover withers and stops competing for the sparse rain that falls at that time of year, allowing the vines to soak it all up.

Vines are highly susceptible to infestations of various kinds; which can be anything from snails, mites and beetles to scale insects, wasps and larva. The traditional way of protecting plants from this threat is to use chemical pesticides. However, there are other options and an increasing number of organic wineries make use of these alternatives. Traps with pheromones that attract insects are useful, as most insects actually use pheromones to attract the opposite sex. By chemically copying these pheromones and hanging traps, it is possible to gather hundreds of insects ready for mating, and thus keep the number of pests down. A simple, yet extremely effective process.

Fungus infections, however, are the organic wine grower's worst nightmare. The only way to combat these is to choose resilient vines, spraying them with sulphur powder and the Bordeaux-mixture when needed. The organic wine growers defend the use of sulphur and copper by claiming that they are natural components.

Although organic procedures can be fascinating and highly effective, it is practically impossible to produce 100% organic wine. They will never be able to avoid spraying for mould fungus and severe insect infestations. Furthermore, it will highly difficult to avoid the use of sulphur during the process of winemaking altogether.

There are several supervisory bodies that keep a keen eye on the organic wineries. By way of example, they regulate the frequency with which organic producers can spray their vines and still label their production organic, and they also decide the length of time soil must be free of pesticides before growing organic vines. If a wine meets these organic criteria, the label will often read *Agriculture Biologique* (AB).

THE CORK OAK

The little town of Gonfaron is surrounded by beautiful scenery at the foot of the forest-clad mountain range, Les Maures, and it used to be a large-scale-producer of corks, made from the bark on local cork oaks. Production almost ground to a complete halt, but recently, the oak forest has once again been alive with the buzzing voices of harvesters. The production of corks in the South of France is rather limited though; it is only a small contribution to the production worldwide. The main producers of corks are Portugal, Spain and Algeria.

The cork oak (*Quercus suber*) is a hardy, slow growing, evergreen tree, whose large roots help it overcome both strong winds and drought. Its thick bark is resistant to both heat and cold, enabling it to survive forest fires, which is why you'll often find a lone surviving cork oak in the wake of a forest fire.

The cork oak should be approximately 20 years old and 80 cm in circumference when subjected to the first harvest, *le démasclage*. This is during summer, between June 15 and August 15, when the bark is dry and easy to pry off the tree trunk. It is very important that the living cells behind the dead bark are left intact, because otherwise the tree will not survive.

Once the bark has been stripped from the trunk, it will be another 12 years before the next layer of cork is ready for harvesting. The quality of a first harvest is never great, and you only get the best cork after five or six harvests. An active cork oak can live to be approximately 150 years old.

After harvesting, the bark is left outside for close to two years, while it dries and shrinks. Then it is boiled and fungi-killing agents are added. The bark will swell up following this treatment and after drying again for a couple of weeks will be ready to be made into corks. You will get somewhere between 15 and 25 kg from 100 kg bark.

VINTAGE

The climate in Provence is quite stable with only few deviations and vintage is of much less importance here than for example in Bordeaux or Burgundy. Yet, wines from different years can still vary to some degree.

Frost in late spring, when the vines have fresh sprouts, or a hail-storm when they blossom can reduce the harvest significantly. This, however, does not necessarily diminish the quality of wine produced, quite the opposite in fact. It is much worse if late summer never arrives and the grapes fail to accumulate enough sugar, or if the rains set in during harvest season, which can cause the grapes to swell up, making the skin crack and leaving them open to fungal attacks.

When talking to Provençal wine farmers you have to be aware that many will refer to a sizable harvest as a good year, but it does not necessarily have any effect on the quality of wine. Above all else, you need sun-ripened grapes and a dry harvest to produce good wine.

With a few exceptions, the Provençal rosé and white wines should be consumed within a year or two, however, there are two kinds of red wine. The light, fruity wines without tannin should be consumed fairly quickly, while the more robust wines improve greatly if left to mature for at least 5–6 years – even longer if possible. Practically all districts produce both kinds of red wine, however the red Bandol and the wines from Palette will probably benefit most from matur-ing for a long time.

VINEYARDS
ALL YEAR ROUND

The wine harvest – *les vendanges* – begins in late September, and for wine farmers it is the climax of their year. Provence is only just waking up after a long hot summer but once the wine harvest sets in, every drowsy little village bustles with activity.

Many farmers harvest their grapes mechanically, as machines have the advantage of being able to harvest grapes at the exact right moment and quickly, which preserves the good quality of the wine. However, the mechanised harvest can also be quite hard on the vines as well as the grapes, which is why some of the best producers still avoid this method. They prefer to harvest grapes in the way it's been done for the last two thousand years – by hand. Other producers do not even have a choice. Their vines grow on steep mountainsides or terraces onto which they would never manage to get a harvesting machine.

There are many romantic notions of life as a grape picker, but in actual fact it is demanding work and very often terribly hard on your back. Although you may find it hard to believe, the Provençal autumn can be quite tricky and once the rains set in, walking up and down those steep slopes and slippery terraces is not much fun. Yet the grape pickers are often high-spirited and the little villages arrange numerous wine festivals during the harvest season.

Most wine farmers round up the family when it's time to harvest, with only larger vineyards employing workers from outside. Picking grapes can be a welcome way of making a little extra money, not least for young students.

During the harvest season, huge lorries drive through the towns, top-heavy with grapes to be delivered to the local, pleasantly hectic co-operative. Here the grapes are weighed and the sugar content sampled before including the grapes in the wine production – which is also how the farmer and co-operative settle the price. Once harvesting and pressing is over, you will see huge piles of grape skins outside the vineyards, which will either be used as fertiliser, fodder or sold to producers of *marc*, the French equivalent of the Italian *grappa*.

By the end of October, the soil in between the vines is ploughed to cover the roots and protect them against frost, and in some places the leftover grape skins will be used as fertiliser. In November, the beautiful red and yellow leaves start to fall, which means it is time for the farmers to start pruning the vines. This is extensive work and it continues all the way into February. The cut off branches are burnt and the ashes spread over the fields, allowing the nutrients in the branches to benefit the vines yet again. Nothing is wasted.

Pruning is how the wine farmer shapes his vines, ensuring optimal conditions for producing exactly the number and quality of grapes that he needs. If he wants quantity, he will not do much pruning, while the producer who is looking to harvest quality grapes full of

flavour will prune the vines quite severely. In Provence, vines are often pruned according to the *gobelet* method, which leaves the vine able to stand without the support of poles or steel wires. It has been used since Roman times and is particularly useful in fields that are subjected to the harsh winds of the *mistral*, because steel wires are more likely harm the vines in a howling gale.

In March, the fields are ploughed to aerate the soil around the vines and to keep the emerging new growths to a minimum while the vines 'weep' – juices drip from vines that have been pruned in winter. The vines have large buds at this time and, whereas they could easily withstand frost in winter, they are now highly sensitive to the cold.

In April, the buds start blossoming and they are prone to attacks

of mould fungus if not sprayed with sulphur. The weeds that grow between the vines can also be sprayed or manually removed. In Provence, the vines bloom in late May, depending on the variety. Even this late in the year, sudden hailstorms can have devastating effects on a crop.

After the vines have blossomed, farmers continue to spray against mould fungus, and depending on the weather, this can continue well into August. However, one month before harvesting, any kind of spray-

ing is banned. Preparations for harvesting and wine production are undertaken in early September, while farmers still keep a keen eye on the ripening process of the grapes. Some years, the harvest will start earlier than others; it is all a question of being out in the fields, constantly checking the sugar content of the grapes to determine when to start harvesting. For those farmers affiliated with a co-operative, it is the co-operative that decides when to harvest. When it is particularly wet, the harvest can continue right up until the end of October.

BELLET

Bellet is the best kept secret in Nice. Even in Nice, people will often give you a puzzled look if you ask for wines from Bellet, even though Bellet lies just to the north: approximately ten minutes by car along Promenade des Anglais or from Nice Airport. But then again, perhaps it's not so strange, because the area only covers 50 ha and the yearly production is never more than about 1000 hl, including red, white and rosé wine.

When you drive through the narrow, windy roads in this wine district, you have to be careful not to miss the little terraces covered with vines, because wine fields are not the dominant feature here. Greenhouses for growing carnations are, along with the modern villas that threaten to rob the area around Nice of its original charm. And in all honesty, one can hardly describe the district of Bellet as

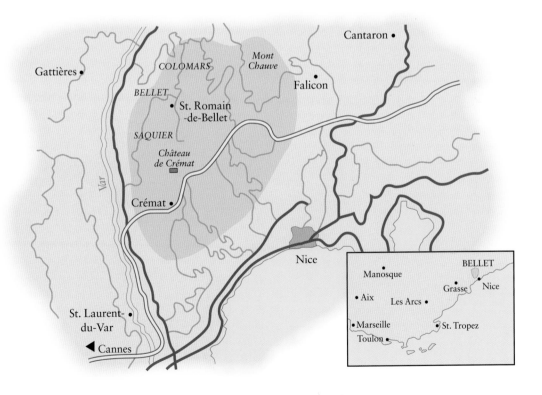

CHATEAU
DE
CREMAT

VIGNE
SAINT-JEAN

CAVES CAP...

Champagnes *Vins fins*

Villars
Bandol
Cassis
Palette
Cotes du Rhone
Hermitage
St.Joseph
Gigondas
Chateauneuf
du Pape

Beaune
Pommard
Volnay
Meursault

PIZZA
...zzarella   9.50€
...e   10.50€
...AISONS   11€
...ière   11€
...APENADE   12 €

charming; however, there are nice views over the river Var and the compact villages on the opposite side of the river.

Following the Great War, the quality of wine from this district was quite poor and Bellet wines all but disappeared, however the local farmers managed to turn things around, not least thanks to the owner of Château de Crémat, Jean Bagnis. The improved quality earned them an AOC in 1941.

Bellet is only home to a small handful of wine producers who bottle their own wine, and of these, Château de Crémat and Château de Bellet are the best, although Domaine de Font-Bellet and Clos Saint-Vincent also produce very attractive wines in all three colours.

Naturally, the indefatigable Romans also went to Bellet. *Via Julius Augustus*, the road that led to the *Trophee des Alpes* in La Turbie, passed Saint-Roman, and at Château de Crémat you can still find remains of old Roman buildings. The Romans had an outpost on the mountainside where they burned torches to show convoys which way to go. However, one evening the Roman legionaries were not paying attention and sparks from the torches set fire to the pinewood. The entire mountainside was scorched and thus Château de Crémat got its name (*crémat* means burnt).

Nice did not become part of France until 1860 and the whole area is still greatly influenced by Italy. Several of the grapes cultivated in Bellet originate in Italy and wines from this district are rather different from those from the rest of Provence. Bellet is particularly renowned for its characteristic and aromatic white wines, which are primarily based on Rolle. The result is formidable and it has inspired many other Provençal producers to use this grape more often. Ever since 1961, the Chardonnay grape has also been popular as it thrives in the calcareous soil on the high terraces that are not over exposed to the harsh sun. White wines from Bellet are some of most durable in all of Provence and they actually improve when allowed to mature for up to 10 years.

In Bellet they also produce pleasant rosé wines and excellent red wines based on Cinsault, Grenache, Braquet and Fuella grapes, the latter also known as Folle Noire. The red wines are highly characteristic and not at all like other red wines from Provence. They are warmer and have more of a burnt aroma; you would be better off looking for similar wines across the border in Italy.

The red wines from Château de Bellet are primarily based on Braquet with Folle Noir as a minor component. This is highly unusual, because Braquet is normally only used to make rosé wines. The red wines may appear quite light and pale but they are nonetheless good and quite racy. At Château de Crémat on the other hand, they use Folle Noire as their basic grape, which gives the wines more body, colour and they also last longer. Both châteaux leave their wines to mature in little casks made from fresh oak.

Apart from the *mistral* and the breeze from the Mediterranean, the most common wind in Bellet is *la Tramontane*; a cool, dry northerly wind that blows through the Var valley in the early hours of the morning. The wind and altitude put the average temperature in Bellet at 4–5°C below the temperature along the coastline, which is also why you will see grape pickers on the narrow terraces as late as October.

This is a highly prestigious district that produces great wines, but unfortunately they are also rather expensive. You have to be willing to fork out in order to become familiar with these exclusive little pearls form Nice. Hopefully, the high prices will ensure the survival of the vineyards, or it will not be long before housing developments will have ruined Bellet as well.

In Nice, the head chefs feel very deeply about these rare wines and they serve them with their finest menus. This is wise, because the white and rosé wines are exquisite as accompaniment to the famous regional specialties such as *salade Niçoise* and *pissaladière*. The majority of the wine production is enjoyed locally as well as in up-market hotels and top-class restaurants along the coast. Outside the Côte d'Azur consider yourself very lucky if you come across a wine from Bellet, although they are exported to enthusiasts all over the world – even Japan.

PRODUCERS IN BELLET

Château de Bellet
06200 Saint-Romain-de-Bellet
Phone: 0493 378157

Château de Crémat
06200 Chemin de Crémat
Phone: 0492 151215

Clos Dou Baille
06200 Saint-Roman-de-Bellet
Phone: 0493 298587

Clos Saint-Vincent
06200 Saint-Romain-de-Bellet
Phone: 0492 151269
www.clos-st-vincent.fr
contact@clos-st-vincent.fr

Collet de Bovis
06200 Nice
Phone: 0493 378252
spizzo.jean@wanadoo.fr

Domaine Augier
06200 Nice
Phone: 0493 378147

Domaine de Font-Bellet
06200 Nice
Phone: 0493 378283

Domaine de la Source
06200 Nice
Phone: 0493 298160
www.domainedelasource.fr
contact@domainedelasource.fr

Domaine de Toasc
06200 Nice
Phone: 0492 151400
www.domainedetoasc.com

Domaine de Vinceline
06440 L'Escarène
Phone: 0493 796744
vdauby@gmail.com

Les Coteaux de Bellet
06200 Saint-Roman-de-Bellet
Phone: 0493 299299

CÔTES DE PROVENCE

Côtes de Provence is a large and very varied region that spans three departments and 84 municipalities and it is possibly the best known of the Provençal wine districts. There are 68 wine producing municipalities in Var, 15 in Bouches-du-Rhône and one in Alpes-Maritimes. Côtes de Provence was awarded its status as a VDQS-district (*Vin Délimité de Qualité Supérieure*) in 1951. In 1977, the wine producers' hard work and dedication were rewarded with an AOC quality stamp. The yearly production is approximately 100 million bottles, which makes Côtes de Provence the sixth most productive area in all of France. Rosé wine makes up as much as 65% of the production, red wine 30% and white wine only 5%.

Côtes de Provence is primarily known for its huge production of rosé wines, many of which are inexpensive and a wonderful accompaniment on a hot summer's day.

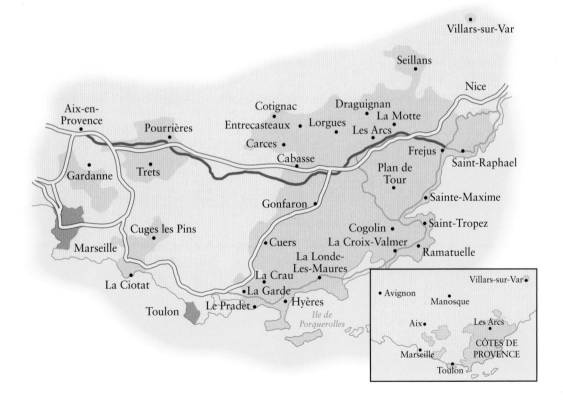

However it's the sheer volume of wine production that has made it very difficult for the producers of quality rosé wines to make an impact on the market, which is a shame because here some of the best rosé wines in the world are produced. Whereas regular rosé wines are pleasant to drink, the best of them are unique with a strong character as well as a fruity and expressive taste. They are simply world-class. And on top of that, they are still reasonably priced.

The Provençal themselves are very fond of rosé wine, not least because it is the wine that best complements their cuisine. It has an advantage over both red and white wines as it can be enjoyed with almost anything. Even something as delicate as artichoke is not a challenge for a rosé wine.

Although Côtes de Provence is best known for its rosé wines, the red wines produced in this district are also remarkable. Do not expect to come across a typical Côte de Provence red wine, because it does not exist, but there are many producers who make excellent red wines at highly affordable prices. These wines can be fresh with a fruity flavour or full-bodied with hints of raisin, sun and heat.

The introduction of Syrah and Cabernet Sauvignon grapes has proved highly beneficial to the area. A lot of the great red wines from Côtes de Provence often contain more of these grapes than recommended by the INAO. It's no secret, and no one is particularly bothered by it, because everyone knows that it is the non-regional grapes that have created little miracles in Côtes de Provence red wine production.

There isn't much of a tradition of white wine production in Côtes de Provence; white grapes are not supposed to take up more than 10% of the planted vineyards, however, the white wines can be surprisingly good. They are always dry but have a tendency to oxidize, so enjoy them straight away and don't leave the bottles to collect dust.

The improvement of white wines in Côtes de Provence is primarily due to the increased cultivation of the Rolle grape and the introduction of cold storage plants, as it's especially important to manage the temperature during the fermentation of white wines. The introduction to ways of controlling the temperature is not least thanks to the repatriated *pied noirs* from Algeria. They were used to struggling with scorching heat and well aware of the benefits of using cold storage plants.

The fact that so many foreign quality wine growers chose to settle here has proved highly beneficial for Côtes de Provence. But local Provençal have also contributed to the district's inclusion in the AOC, not least the Ott family with their two properties, Château de Selle and Clos Mireille, the Matton-Farnet family of the Château Minuty and the Rasque de Laval family who for decades were in charge of the production at Sainte-Roseline.

Rosé and red wines should be based on the Cinsault, Grenache, Tibouren and Mourvèdre grapes. In addition wine growers are allowed to include the following: Barbaroux, Cabernet Sauvignon, Syrah, Callitor and Carignan, as well as the white grapes: Rolle, Ugni Blanc, Sémillon and Clairette (which are the grapes most of the white wines in the region are made from).

The maximum crop yield is 50 hl per ha and all wines must be at least 11% proof after fermentation. *Saignée* is the traditional production method when making rosé wines, but they are also allowed to use *la presse directe*. However, at least 20% of all rosé wines must be produced using the *saignée* method, as it is considered the best method of production for rosé wines, at least if you are fond of fruitier wines.

In Côtes de Provence you will also come across wines with the classification *Cru Classé*, which is a label more commonly recognised in Bordeaux in the districts of Médoc, Sauternes, Graves and Saint-Émilion. Côtes de Provence is the only region outside Bordeaux where this prestigious appellation is granted. It was accepted by the INAO in 1955, exactly 100 years after it was first used in Bordeaux.

When Côtes de Provence was awarded VDSQ status in 1951, a group of ambitious wine growers led by Baron Henri de Laval from Château Sainte-Roseline were dissatisfied. They strove to refine the wines even further and thus 'borrowed' the classification *Cru Classé* from Bordeaux.

Originally, 23 properties were allowed to use the classification, because they where considered to be the best wineries at the time, however, the classification itself did not signify anything in particular.

Today there are many producers whom it would be only fair to include in this group, but due to pressure from wine producers in Bordeaux, the INAO have refused to allow new producers the use of the classification *Cru Classé*. It may appear a little strange that on the one hand INAO prohibits the acceptance of new producers of quality wines into this group, while at the same time allowing certain 'old producers' to continue using the appellation *Cru Classé*. And yet, it has to be said, that although there is a great deal of snobbery connected to these *Cru Classé* wines, and although they are quite often overpriced, the wines are generally of very high quality. Furthermore, the properties that have the use of the classification are unusually beautiful, and the architecture alone makes them worth a visit. The remaining 18 properties allowed to use the classification *Cru Classé* are:

Château Sainte-Roseline, Les Arcs
Domaine de Bregancon, Bormes
Domaine du Noyer, Bormes
Domaine de Saint-Maur, Cogolin
Domaine de la Croix, La Croix-Valmer
Château Minuty, Gassin
Domaine de la Clapière, Hyères
Domaine de l'Aumerade, Hyères
Domaine du Galoupet, La Londe
Clos Mireille, La Londe
Domaine de la Source Sainte-Marguerite, La Londe
Castel Roubine, Lorgues
Domaine du Jas d'Esclans, La Motte
Domaine de Rimauresq, Pignans
Clos Cibonne, Le Pradet
Domaine de Mauvanne, Les Salins d'Hyères
Château Saint-Martin, Taradeau
Château de Selle, Taradeau

Côtes de Provence is a rather large district to be awarded only one AOC. Considering the varied climatic and geological conditions, it is hard to understand why they haven't split the region into smaller areas, each with its own AOC. But perhaps they were just busy upgrading the entire Provençal wine production before countries like Portugal and Spain grabbed more of a stronghold within the EU?

Two good examples of the varying topography within the district of Côtes de Provence are the wine fields in Villars-sur-Var in the

Alpes-Maritimes and those on the island of Porquerolles off the coast of Carqueiranne in Var. In the former, which lies behind Nice and Bellet, there is only one winery, Clos Saint-Joseph. The last remaining vineyards were destroyed during the infestation of wine lice in the 20th century. The vines grow on terraces 250–300 m above sea level. In the Île de Porquerolles, on the other hand, vines grow in slate-containing fields that used to be covered by pine forests and *maquis*, which are constantly exposed to the breeze from the salty Mediterranean. The wine fields in these two areas have very little in common apart from the fact that they are allowed to grow the same grapes.

Because of its varying terrain, Côtes de Provence is split into climatic and geological sub-divisions. There are normally three: La Côte de Brise in between Toulon and Fréjus including les Maures, where the main influence is the Mediterranean breeze; La Gravette with La Motte, Les Arc, Flassans, Carces and Le Thoronet where it is limestone and the Alps that dominate; and finally La Sainte-Victoire by Aix, where it is the area's red soil that influences the wines.

This is a very rough sub-division, and it is not just the area's geographical differences that influence the wines; the producers' contribution is the decisive factor.

By following the coast between Toulon and Fréjus (La Côte de Brise), you'll pass through many famous coastal towns, including Saint-Tropez and Sainte-Maxime. The beauty of the landscape continues as far as Ramatuelle, Gassin, Le Lavandou and the outskirts of Hyères, but you shouldn't venture further than Toulon.

Many of these seaside towns have been spoiled by merciless building development, and their roads can be jammed in summer by solid traffic. But out of season, Saint-Tropez is still a charming seaside town, where the fishermen in their traditional wooden boats land fresh fish every morning.

Not only are wines from the coast quite different from those further inland, but because of the enormous influx of tourists in the summer season, life in seaside towns is much more hectic and very different from life in peaceful rural Provençe. Many foreigners have chosen to settle in these commonplace seaside towns, but here even the vegetation has changed to such an extent that it can no longer be termed truly Provençal. The gardens of the luxury villas are full

of botanical interlopers that have now spread into the wild. You'll find Australian mimosas and eucalyptus, Mexican agaves and cactus figs, African palms as well as Chinese lemon and mandarin trees.

Many old and historically interesting vineyards still exist in La Côte de Brise. A good example is the old Roman town of Fréjus, which was where Emperor Augustus allowed his legionaries to retire after completed service. He gave them land and money and, of course, they started cultivating wine. Today local producers can put 'Fréjus' on their wine labels in recognition of the unique character of the area. A little north of town, you find the infamous area that used to be a hide-out for highwaymen, which also gave the area its nickname *'Curebeasse'*, Provençal for the highly unwelcome phrase that greeted many a traveller, 'Empty your bag!'

Today there are no more highwaymen, and in between the tall, broad-crowned umbrella pines you'll find Domaine de Curebéasse. The soil here varies greatly. In many places it's volcanic – dry and poor, which is perfect for grapes such as Rolle and Ugni Blanc. With these, the winery produces striking, bright and aromatic white wines. Their rosé wine is made from Mourvèdre and Tibouren grapes and its lovely aroma and crisp taste are most certainly worth trying.

In Saint-Tropez there's a co-operative that sells very cheap wines, but, much more interesting are the wines from the towns and villages in the Saint-Tropez hinterland such as Cogolin, Ramatuelle, La Croix-Valmer and Gassin. A little west of Saint-Tropez is one of Provence's most successful co-operatives, Les Celliers des Vignerons de Ramatuelle. Here they produce a wonderfully refreshing rosé wine based on Tibouren, which is also sold *en vrac* – where you bring your own container.

The area around Ramatuelle is exclusive but very beautiful and it offers the occasional breath-taking sea view. If you drive down towards Gassin, you will pass the 18th century Château Minuty, which is one of the most beautiful châteaux in the region. This is where a distinctive and spicy red wine based on Grenache, Cinsault, Mourvèdre and Syrah is produced. The wine is subjected to a moderate *macération carbonique* and then left to mature for about a year, in Hungarian *foudres*. The family built a small chapel (*oratoire*) in memory of a son who was killed in the Franco-Prussian war (1870–71). This chapel now lends it name to the wine (*Cuvée de l'Oratoire*) and during each harvest season they have a Mass for the grape pickers. Minuty also produces an elegant and flowery rosé wine based on Tibouren, counted among the best wines in all of Côtes de Provence. The château's succulent and prestigious white wine is based on Rolle, Clairette and Viognier. The Viognier grape came from the north of the Rhône district and isn't really allowed in Côtes de Provence, which is why this exclusive wine can only be sold as a *Vin de Pays*. The Farnet family have produced wine at Minuty since 1936 and they also have a vineyard around Vidauban. The wines from this vineyard are called Domaine Farnet and they are not only very good, they are also less expensive. The wines from Château Minuty are a must on the wine lists in local restaurants – and always a good choice.

In Gassin you also find the exclusive co-operative Maîtres Vignerons de la Presque'Île de Saint-Tropez, established by a group of highly skilled wine makers who produce distinguished wines for many high-class restaurants and chefs along the coast. Some of their better wines are Château de Pampelonne and Saint-Roch les Vignes.

The town itself is a quiet, well-preserved medieval town with an astonishing view across the tiled roofs around the Bay of Saint-Tropez. During the turbulence of the Middle Ages, the town had a spectacular view of the sea and therefore of any uninvited guest that may be arriving, not least the Saracens who conquered the area in 850 AD.

In La Croix-Valmer the vineyards belonging to Domaine de la Croix are right next to where Constantine the Great camped with his army on his way from Arles to Italy to fight Maxentius in 312 AD. During the night, Constantine was woken by a startling vision: in the starry sky above him there was a burning cross followed by the words *in hoc signo vinces* (in this sign you will conquer). This convinced Constantine and his men that converting to Christianity was the right thing to do. The cross adorned their shields and banners, and united in faith they journeyed on towards victory. Today the cross adorns the labels on wines from Domaine de la Croix. A rosé made from the old Provençal grape Tibouren, which thrives so well in this coastal area, is among the winery's finest wines.

Further on towards Toulon, you pass La Londe-les-Maures, situated at the foot of Les Maures, which is covered in cork oaks, chestnut trees, some pine trees and masses of wild ivy. Many of the trees are several hundred years old. There is a particularly beautiful cork oak in the Pansard Valley, just outside the town – it is 18 m tall and more than 5 m in circumference. La Londe-les-Maures is a seaside town, but is fortunate in being surrounded by interesting vineyards. At Château de Galoupet the Tibouren grape is mostly cultivated, from which they produce striking and aromatic rosé wines. However, Domaine du Bastidon, Clos Mireille (a property belonging to the Ott family), Domaine de la Source Sainte-Marguerite and Domaine Saint-André de Figuiere are also worth a visit.

The old town of Hyères is well known for its production of palm trees that are exported to a number of Arabic countries. To adhere to the Koran they only use soil from the recipient country. However, if you leave the palm trees, the beaches and the windsurfers, you can visit a number of great wineries such as Domaine de la Jeanette, Domaine de la Grande Bastide and Domaine de Mauvanne.

You can also choose to sail the 15 km from Hyères to Île de Porquerolles and visit the vineyards there. The island is a natural gem and a protected National Park. The vineyards function as wide firebreaks, which is an elegant way to minimise the risk of forest fires on this forest-clad island. One vineyard, Domaine d'Île, sells decent everyday wines at very reasonable prices, and their rosé wine is a particularly good buy. Domaine de la Courtade was established in the early 1980s and uses its own technology as well as the classic, small oak casks that contain only 225 litres. The salty sea breeze and the soil, which you do not come across on the mainland unless you are 500–600 m above sea level, make for a unique *terroir*. Inspired by Bandol, whose vineyards flourish close to the sea, the Domaine adopted the Mourvèdre grape, and even though the vines are still young, has managed to secure superb results. By using 90% Mourvèdre grapes, a particularly delicious, full-bodied and long-lasting red wine has been achieved. Ingeniously, the grapes from the youngest vines in the fields (Mourvèdre, Grenache and Syrah) are used to produce a less prestigious but altogether lovely red wine called Alycastre. The wine's subtle and exotic aromas are achieved by using equal measures of Sémillon and Rolle grapes.

La Gravette is an area of Côtes de Provence that differs greatly from La Côte de Brise. In the countryside, vineyards are situated in unspoiled landscape and an air of tranquillity replaces the hectic

atmosphere of the coast. This rural backcountry seems able to accommodate both nature and people more easily. As soon as you turn towards the mountains, away from the coast, the houses change character. You can be 100% certain that the most colourful houses will be found close to the Mediterranean and the further you move away from the sea, the more primitive they become.

The area around La Motte and Le Muy is a good place to start your journey into the countryside. It is completely dominated by vineyards. La Motte was the first Provençal town to be liberated by American soldiers in 1944. A unit of paratroopers was dispatched over the fields one starry August night and greeted by lovely, ripe grapes. The Germans fled La Motte without putting up a fight; however, tougher battles had yet to be fought, as the American cemetery in Draguignan reminds us.

Each Sunday mid-morning there is a particularly bustling market in Le Muy, where everything from crisp grilled-chickens to multi-coloured Provençal fabrics is sold; it's one of the best in Provence, and people come from far and wide to sell as well as to buy.

Just outside town, you'll find Château du Rouët hidden in the middle of a forest of fully-grown umbrella pines, cork oaks and strong scented thyme. The vineyard's best wines go by the name of Cuvée Belle Poulle – Cuvée of the beautiful chicken. It's a very odd name for a wine, but of course there's a story to be told: *La Belle Poulle* was the name of the frigate that brought Napoleon's ashes from St Helena to France in 1840. When the ship was broken up, an uncle of the Savatier family at Château du Rouët made sure that the vineyard's chapel was equipped with a couple of oak doors from the frigate. The Chapel is not open to the public, but the aromatic rosé and white wines are well worth a visit.

Another important vineyard outside Le Muy is Château Rêva, which has just undergone extensive modernisation and also produces excellent rosé wines. On the road from Le Muy to Callas you will come across several charming and attractive vineyards. The whole terrain is elevated but also reasonably flat, which gives wonderful views across straight rows of vines and olive trees, while in some places, it's possible to catch a glimpse of the Mediterranean in the background. Visiting Château d'Esclans and Domaine du Jas d'Esclans, will give you a chance to witness how different wines can be when they're produced in almost identical geographical conditions – which is a common feature in the Côtes de Provence.

If you follow the River Argens further westwards, you will reach one of the key wine towns in Côtes de Provence, Les Arcs-sur-Argens. Les Arcs has a picturesque Old Town with a fabulous view of the town's many tiled roofs, but it is the local vineyards in particular that demand attention. This is because here you'll come across the Coopérative l'Arçoise, a dynamic co-operative that produces a number of great wines. They also sell grape-seed oil made from grapes left over from the wine production. The grape-seeds are pressed industrially in special mills, which yield 1 litre of oil from approximately 12 kg seeds. Grape-seed oil is less aromatic than olive oil, but can be heated to a higher temperature, which makes it suitable for frying. By producing wine, marc and grape-seed oil this co-operative use up close to 100% of the grapes.

From Les Arcs you can continue in any direction really. Just outside town is the Château Saint-Pierre, where vines have been cultivated for centuries. It doesn't look like much of a château from the outside, but its wines are delightful and very reasonably priced. The vineyard's prestige range is definitely worth a recommendation. It's a family run vineyard and in recent years, has won well-deserved acclaim.

Traditionally, the most important wine producer in Les Arcs is Château Sainte-Roseline. The Château is really an old monastery, which has housed many different orders. The wine fields are well kept with lots of old vines planted in the red-brown soil. Some of the vines are said to date back to the days when Pope John XXII ruled out of Avignon (1316–1334). The vineyard produces different types of wine, but all of very high quality. The most exciting wine, though, would be the red Cuvée Prieuré, which is made from Cabernet and Mourvèdre and left to mature for 12 months in small oak casks. This makes it round and full-bodied and it is claimed that it can be left to mature for up to another 15 years.

Château Sainte-Roseline was established in the Middle Ages and right next to the reception area, there is a beautiful chapel with the tiny Sainte-Roseline neatly embalmed in a glass case. Considering that she's more than 700 years old, she's really aged rather well.

Legend has it that one winter was particularly cold and the locals

were starving to death. The Château, however, was well stocked with food, but as a safeguard in case the Saracens decided to attack or besiege the town, it was decided not to distribute food among the town's starving families. The daughter of Marquis de Villeneuve, the lovely Roseline, could not stand idly by while the locals died, so every day she filled her basket with cheese, bread, sausage and wine and distributed the food amongst those most in need.

Her father was furious when he found out that his stock of food was dwindling and he ordered his guards to catch the thief. One morning, as Roseline was on her merry way with her basket full of supplies from her father's pantry, she was stopped at the gate by the guards. Roseline froze with fear and covered the basket with her apron. However, only when the guards looked, God had intervened and turned the food into a fragrant bouquet of roses.

Roseline never fully recovered from that experience, and later she joined a convent. When she died she was canonised and became Sainte Roseline. Roseline's chapel is very beautiful and Giacometti as well as Marc Chagall has decorated the walls – so it is an even more important landmark to visit.

In the vicinity of Les Arcs, you find Vidauban, which is yet another important wine town. The co-operative La Vidaubanaise was founded in 1912, which makes it one of oldest in Provence. Today its production is around 40,000 hl, which also makes it one of the biggest, and its wine is exported all over Europe.

The Château de Rasque in Taradeau is built on the foundations of an old Roman vineyard, but apart from that nothing here is old. Its location is absolutely lovely and they have spared no expense in terms of technical equipment or interior design. The Château's spicy wines are all of good quality, but they are also quite expensive. The fact that they mature in casks implies that they should be left to mature for 5–6 years after bottling, before being opened.

Close to Château de Rasque, is another vineyard belonging to one of the region's famous wine families. It is the Ott family's Château de Selle, and its wonderful wines can be found at the top end of the price range. The full-bodied wines from this vineyard are highly durable and will continue to develop for up to 20 years, which is rare for Côtes de Provence. The rosé wine is one of the very best in France, and is one of the Provençal wines you are most likely find on the wine lists in high-class restaurants, which is absolutely correct when you realise that it maintains its high quality year after year. Wine from Château de Selle is always a sure buy.

If you travel on from Vidauban, you come across several good wine producers. To the west, there's the Le Luc with Domaine de la Bernarde among others, and not far from there, seek out the Gonfaron, producers of Domaine de la Garnaude and Domaine du Val d'Anrieu.

In Le Thoronet there is a well-preserved monastery of the Order of Cistercians that dates all the way back to the 12th century. Today, however, it is no longer the monks who cultivate wine but the people at Domaine de l'Abbaye, which results in excellent, bright rosé wines and aromatic white wines. They also produce red wine based on Grenache, Syrah and Cabernet Sauvignon, subsequently left to mature in casks, which results in a spicy wine that will keep for up to 10 years.

In Carces, you find Domaine de Saint-Jean and in Correns, Domaine de Réal Martin. If you turn back towards Les Arcs, through Lorgues, you pass Castel Roubine, which was established by the Knights Templar in the Middle Ages, and for many years the Danes owned it. Well hidden in the mountains above Lorgues, you find one of the new and exiting vineyards, Château de la Berne. The property is 520 ha in all, of which 50 ha are planted with vines. Since 1985, a group of Englishmen have invested vast sums of money in the vineyard that includes a cellar with beautiful oak casks. Their attractive rosé wine is based on Cinsault, Syrah and Grenache, but their red wine is also worth noting. They rely on a great deal of Cabernet Sauvignon and Syrah to prop up the Provençal grapes and add a little more character to the wine. At Château de Berne they also host a number of different events and courses where guests can learn more about Provençal gastronomy.

If you are in the area anyway, a detour to Domaine de Matourne a little outside Flayosc is recommended.

The owner isn't that interested in promoting his wines, which is a pity, because this Domaine produces unusually fine wines based on Cabernet Sauvignon and Syrah. Flayosc is a pretty little Provençal village with narrow streets, stone houses with verdigris or brown shutters and an old moss-covered fountain in the square, between the cafés. It is one of those villages that has next to nothing, but

startlingly, there are a couple of really good restaurants, where hearty Provençal food is served.

The western part of Côtes de Provence, which is east of Aix and overlooked by Montagne Sainte-Victoire, is a very beautiful and exciting wine region. There are 17 vineyards and 5 co-operatives which have been allowed to print Sainte-Victoire on their labels, to distinguish them from the other wineries in Côtes de Provence. This is a clever way of indicating that your wines are distinctly different and you will quite likely see similar initiatives within other areas of the *appellation*. In Sainte-Victoire they have decided to use mainly Grenache, Syrah and Cinsault, however, you also find quite a few Cabernet Sauvignon grapes in the fields. Approximately 80% of the production is rosé wine, the remaining 20% red wine. The white wines have not yet been accepted in this new *appellation*.

One of the most important wine villages in the area is Trets with Mas de Cadenet, where the vines grow in the deeply red soil, sheltered by a huge white mountain. Only the *saignée* method is used to turn Cinsault and Grenache into wine, which produces attractive and succulent rosé wines. Another characteristic type of rosé wine can be achieved by allowing the wine to mature in casks, which makes for wines that are not fruity but voluptuous. At Mas de Cadenet they follow nature and use no artificial fertilisers but rather droppings from the sheep that graze on the fields surrounding the vineyard.

The German-owned Domaine Richeaume in Puyloubier is a modern vineyard a little north of Trets. They strive to cultivate their wine organically, and the red wine left to mature for 12–14 months in oak casks is a great example of what Cabernet Sauvignon and Syrah grapes can achieve in Provence.

Naturally, there are many more places of interest in Côtes de Provence and many more wines worthy of our attention. Do not forget to include the red wines because there is no doubt that in time, the red wines in particular will be able to make Côtes de Provence as well known as it is for producing rosé wines.

At Maison des Vins in Les Arcs you can taste all the well-known wines from Côtes de Provence, but they won't always give you the same dedicated service or in depth knowledge that you will always receive when buying wine directly from the producers.

PRODUCERS IN CÔTES DE PROVENCE

Bastide de Bertrands
83340 Le Cannet-des-Maures
Phone: 0494 730294

Cave des Vignerons de Cogolin
83310 Cogolin
Phone: 0494 544054
vin-1@wanadoo.fr

Cellier des Archers
83460 Les-Arcs-sur-Argens
Phone: 0494 733029
www.cellierdesarchers.fr
celliersdesarchers@free.fr

Cellier Saint-Bernard
83340 Flassans-sur-Issole
Phone: 0494 697101
cellier.st-bernard@orange.fr

Celliers des Vignerons de Ramatuelle
83350 Ramatuelle
Phone: 0494 792360

Château La Chapelle de Sainte-Roseline
83460 Les Arcs-sur-Argens
Phone: 0494 995030
www.sainte-roseline.com
contact@sainte-roseline.com

Château d'Astros
83550 Vidauban
Phone: 0494 997300
www.astros.fr
contact@astros.fr

Château d'Esclans
83920 La Motte
Phone: 0494 604040
www.chateaudesclans.com
chateaudesclans@sachalichine.com

Château de Berne
83510 Lorgues
Phone: 0494 604352
www.chateauberne.com
vins@chateauberne.com

Château de Brégançon
83230 Bormes-les-Mimosas
Phone: 0494 648073
www.chateau-de-bregancon.fr
chateaubregancon@wanadoo.fr

Château de Cabran
83480 Puget-sur-Argens
Phone: 0494 408032
www.chateaudecabran.com
cabran@wanadoo.fr

Château de Garcinières
83310 Cogolin
Phone: 0494 560285
www.chateau-garcinieres.com
garcinieres@wanadoo.fr

Château de Jasson
83250 La Londe-les-Maures
Phone: 0494 052484
www.chateaujasson.com
chateau.de.jasson@wanadoo.fr

Château de Léoube
83230 Bormes-les-Mimosas
Phone: 0494 648003

Château de Maravenne
83510 Lorgues
www.maravenne.com
contact@maravenne.com

Château de Mentonne
83510 Saint-Antonin-du-Var
Phone: 0494 044200

Château de Mesclances
83260 La Crau
Phone: 0494 667507
www.proprieteviticolevar.com
mesclances@yahoo.fr

Château de Miraval
83570 Correns
Phone: 0494 863933
www.miraval.com

Château de Pampelonne
86350 Ramatuelle
Phone: 0494 563204
info@mavigne.com

Château de Rasque
83460 Taradeau
Phone: 0494 995220
www.chateaurasque.com
acceuil@chateaurasque.com

Château de Selle
83460 Taradeau
Phone: 0494 475757

Château de l'Aumerade
83390 Pierre-du-Var
Phone: 0494 282031
www.aumerade.com

Château de Saint-Martin
83460 Taradeau
Phone: 0494 997676
www.chateaudesaintmartin.com
info@chateaudesaintmartin.com

Château du Galoupet
83250 La Londe-les-Maures
Phone: 0494 664007
www.galoupet.com
galoupet@club-internet.fr

Château du Rouët
83490 Le Muy
Phone: 0494 992110
www.chateau-du-rouet.com

Château les Crostes
83510 Lorgues
Phone: 0494 739840
www.chateau-les-crostes.eu
chateau.les.crostes@wanadoo.fr

Château Barbanau
13830 Roquefort-la-Bédoule
Phone: 0442 731460
www.chateau-barbanau.com
barbanau@wanadoo.fr

Château Barbeiranne
83790 Pignans
Phone: 0494 488446
www.chateau-barbeiranne.com
barbeiranne@wanadoo.fr

Château Barbeyrolles
83990 Saint-Tropez
Phone: 0494 563358

Château Baron-Georges
13114 Puyloubier
Phone: 0442 663138

Château Boise
13350 Trets
Phone: 0442 292295
www.grandboise.com
contact@grandboise.com

Château Clarettes
83460 Les Arcs
Phone: 0494 474505
crocespinellivin@aol.com

Château Deffends
83660 Carnoules
Phone: 0494 283312
www.chateaudeffends.com
verges.xavier@wanadoo.fr

Château Ferry Lacombe
13530 Trets-en-Provence
Phone: 0442 294004
www.ferrylacombe.com
info@ferrylacombe.com

Château l'Afrique
83390 Cuers
Phone: 0442 612000
sumeire@sumeire.com

Château l'Arnaude
83510 Lorgues
Phone: 0494 737067
www.chateaularnaude.com
info@chateaularnaude.com

Château La Font du Broc
83460 Les Arcs-sur-Argens
Phone: 0494 474820
www.chateau-fontdubroc.com
caveau@chateau-fontdubroc.com

Château La Tour de l'Évêque
83390 Pierrefeu-du-Var
Phone: 0494 282017
www.toureveque.com
regine.sumeire@toureveque.com

Château la Martinette
83510 Lorgues
Phone: 0494 738493
www.chateaumartinette.com
info@chateaulamartinette.com

Château Minuty
83580 Gassin
Phone: 0494 561209
www.chateauminuty.com
informinuty@orange.fr

Château Pas du Cerf
83250 La Londes-les-Maures
Phone: 0494 004881

www.pasducerf.com
info@pasducerf.com

Château Réal-Martin
83143 Le Val
Phone: 0494 864090

Château Réal d'Or
83590 Gonfaron
Phone: 0494 600056
realdor.free.fr
realdor@free.fr

Château Reillanne
83340 Le Cannet-de-Maures
Phone: 0494 501170

Château Rêva
83920 La Motte
Phone: 0494 702457
www.chateaureva.fr
chateaureva@wanadoo.fr

Château Roubine
83510 Lorgues
Phone: 0494 859494
www.chateauroubine.com
riboud@chateauroubine.com

Château Saint-Julien d'Aille
83550 Vidauban
Phone: 0494 730289
www.saintjuliendaille.com
contact@saintjuliendaille.com

Château Saint-Pierre
83460 Les Arcs-sur-Argens
Phone: 0494 474147
www.chateausaintpierre.fr
contact@chateausaintpierre.fr

Château Sainte-Béatrice
83510 Lorgues
Phone: 0494 676236
stebeatrice@wanadoo.fr

Château Sainte-Marguerite
83250 La Londes-les-Maures
Phone: 0494 004444
www.chateausaintemarguerite.com
info@chateausaintemarguerite.com

Château Thuerry
83690 Villecroze
Phone: 0494 706302
www.chateauthuerry.com
thuerry@chateauthuerry.com

Clos Gautier
83570 Carcès
Phone: 0494 800505
clos.gautier@free.fr

Clos Mireille
83250 La Londes-les-Maures
Phone: 0494 668026

Clos Saint-Joseph
06710 Villars-sur-Var
Phone: 0493 057329
www.leclossaintjoseph.com
a.sassi@wanadoo.fr

Coopérative l'Arçoise
83460 Les Arcs-sur-Argens
Phone: 0494 733029

Coopérative Vinicole la
Vidaubanaise
83550 Vidauban
Phone: 0494 730012

Cuvée des Abbes
83340 Le Cannet-des-Maures
Phone: 0494 500594
Guilde-vignerons@wanadoo.fr

Domaine de Curebéasse
83600 Fréjus
Phone: 0494 408790
www.curebeasse.com
courier@curebeasse.com

Domaine de Féraud
83550 Vidauban
Phone: 0494 730312

Domaine de Grandpré
83390 Pouget-Ville
Phone: 0494 234286
vvr@domainedegrandpre.fr

Domaine de Matourne
83780 Flayosc
Phone: 0494 704347
www.domainematourne-
vinwinewein.com
jurgen.spaethe@wanadoo.fr

Domaine de Marchandise
83520 Roquebrune-sur-Argens
Phone: 0494 454291

Domaine de Mauvan
13114 Puyloubier
Phone: 0442 293833
mauvan@wanadoo.fr

Domaine de Mont Redon
83260 La Grau
Phone: 0494 578212
www.chateaumontredon.fr
contact@chateaumontredon.fr

Domaine de Peigros
83390 Pierefeu
Phone: 0494 481261

Domaine de Planes
83520 Roquebrune-sur-Argens
Phone: 0494 829003

Domaine de Saint-Baillon
83340 Flassans
Phone: 0494 697460

Domaine de Siouvette
83310 La Môle
Phone: 0494 495713
www.vins-siouvette.com
sylvaine.sauron@wanadoo.fr

Domaine de l'Abbaye
83340 Le Thoronet
Phone: 0494 738736
Domaine.de.labbaye@wanadoo.fr

Domaine de l'Amaurigue
83340 Le Luc-en-Provence
Phone: 0494 501720
Domaine-l-amaurigue@wanadoo.fr

Domaine de l'Île
83400 Porquerolles
Phone: 0494 583160

Domaine de la Courtade
83400 Île de Porquerolles, Hyères
Phone: 0494 583144
www.lacourtade.com
domaine@lacourtade.com

Domaine de la Croix
83420 La Croix-Valmer
Phone: 0494 797349
www.domainedelacroix.com
basidecroix@orange.fr

Domaine de la Jeanette
83400 Hyères
Phone: 0494 656830

Domaine de la Lauzade
83340 Le Luc
Phone: 0494 607251
www.lauzade.com
julia@lauzade.com

Domaine de la Madrague
83420 La Croix-Valmer
www.domainedelamadrague.com
info.lamadrague@orange.fr

Domaine de la Mascaronne
83340 Le Luc
Phone: 0494 607132

Domaine de la Rouvière
83390 Pierrefeu-du-Var
Phone: 0494 481313
domain-de-la-rouviere@wanadoo.fr

Domaine de la Source Sainte-
Marguerite
83250 La Londe-les-Maures
Phone: 0494 668146

Domaine des Aspras
83570 Correns
Phone: 0494 595970
www.aspras.com
mlatz@aspras.com

Domaine des Diables
13114 Puyloubier
Phone: 0681 439462
laissezvoustenter@orange.fr

Domaine des Escaravatiers
83480 Puget-sur-Argens
Phone: 0494 455180

Domaine des Grands Esclans
83920 La Motte
Phone: 0494 702608
www.domaine-esclans.com
Domaine.grands.escalns@orange.fr

Domaine des Myrtes
83250 La Londe-les-Maures
Phone: 0494 668300

Domaine des Pierecèdes
83390 Cuers
Phone: 0494 486715
www.domainedespierecedes.com
alainbaccino@free.fr

Domaine des Thermes
83340 Le Cannet-des-Maures
Phone: 0494 607315
www.domaine-des-thermes.com
info@domaine-des-thermes.com

Domaine du Dragon
83300 Draguignan
Phone: 0498 102300
www.domainedudragon.com
domainedragon@wanadoo.fr

Domaine du Jas d'Esclans
83920 La Motte
Phone: 0494 102929
www.jasdesclans.fr
mdewulf@terre-net.fr

Domaine du Val d'Anrieu
83590 Gonfaron
Phone: 0494 783093

Domaine la Bernarde
83340 Le Luc
Phone: 0494 607131

Domaine La Tourraque
83350 Ramatuelle
Phone: 0494 792595
www.latourraque.fr
latourraque@wanadoo.fr

Domaine Gavoty
83340 Flassans
www.gavoty.com
domaine.gavoty@wanadoo.fr

Domaine Rabiega
83300 Draguignan
Phone: 0494 684422

Domaine Richeaume
13114 Puyloubier
Phone: 0442 663127
www.domaine-richeaume.com
info@domaine-richeaume.com

Domaine de Rimauresq
83790 Pignans
Phone: 0494 488045
www.rimauresq.fr
rimauresq@wanadoo.fr

Domaine Saint-André de Figuiere
83250 La Londe-les-Maures
Phone: 0494 004470
www.figuiere-provence.com
figuiere@figuiere-provence.com

Domaine Saint-Martin
83340 Le Luc-en-Provence
Phone: 0494 607025
Vignerons-du-luc@wanadoo.fr

Domaine Sainte-Lucie
13114 Puyloubier
Phone: 0668 653322
www.saintelucie-provence.com
saintelucie-provence@orange.fr

Domaine Sorin
83270 Saint-Cyr-sur-Mer
Phone: 0494 266228
www.domainesorin.com
luc.sorin@wanadoo.fr

Domaines Farnet
83990 Saint-Tropez
Phone: 0494 561209

Domaines Ott
Clos Mirelle
83250 La Londe-les-Maures
Phone: 0494 015350
www.domaines-ott.com
closmirelle@domaines-ott.com

Estandon
83460 Les Arcs
Phone: 0494 475654

Hermitage Saint-Martin
83250 La Londe-des-Maures
Phone: 0494 004444
www.chateauhermitagesaintmartin.com
enzo@chateauhermitagesaintmartin.com

La Commanderie de Peyrassol Le Luc
83340 Flassans-sur-Issole
Phone: 0494 697102
www.peyrassol.com
contact@peyrasol.com

Les Vignerons de Gonfaron
83590 Gonfaron
Phone: 0494 783002
www.vignerons.gonfaron.org
m.vignerons.gonfaron@wanadoo.fr

Les Vignerons de Mont Sainte-Victoire
13114 Puyloubier
Phone: 0442 663221
Vignerons-msv@wanadoo.fr

Les Vignerons du Luc
83340 Le Luc
Phone: 0494 607025

Maîtres Vignerons de la
Presque'Île de Saint-Tropez
83580 Gassin
Phone: 0494 563204

Mas de Cadenet
13530 Trets
Phone: 0442 292159
www.masdecadenet.fr
guy.negrel@masdecadenet.fr

Mas de Victoire
83350 Ramatuelle
Phone: 0494 591240

Vignoble Kennel
83390 Pierrefeu-du-Var
Phone: 0494 282039
www.vignoble-kennel.com
info@vignoble-kennel.com

Val d'Iris
83440 Seillans
Phone: 0494 769766
www.valdiris.com
info@valdiris.com

COTEAUX VAROIS

Coteaux Varois was awarded an AOC in 1992. The district consists of 28 municipalities in Var, bordering both Côtes de Provence and Coteaux d'Aix. It is a rather large and quite varied district with Brignoles as its centre. The annual production is around 100,000 hl.

Brignoles was in its prime in the middle ages, when the Counts of Provence resided here in summer. Both soil and climate vary greatly within this *appellation*, which is also why you encounter very different wines. The red wines, which are the most important, are primarily based on Grenache, Syrah and Mourvèdre. The second most frequently used grapes are Carignan, Cinsault and Cabernet Sauvignon. These wines should preferably be enjoyed while young; however, there are producers who make wines that gain from maturing for 3–5 years.

The district's rosé wines are primarily based on Grenache and Cinsault, with Syrah, Mourvèdre, Carignan and Tibouren as the second most frequently used grapes. The white wines are based on Grenache

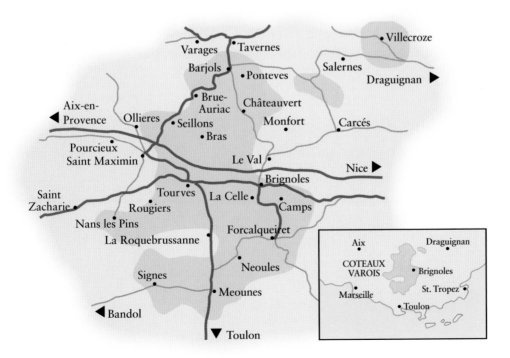

Blanc, Sémillon, Ugni Blanc, Clairette and Rolle. The dissemination of the aromatic Rolle grape is strengthened at the expense of the slightly more anonymous Ugni Blanc.

Within this district, you should be aware that the best wines are not necessarily AOC-wines: *Vins de Pays du Var* certainly deserve a closer look because producers here experiment with 'banned' grapes or produce wines based on one single grape, and these can only be sold as *Vin de Pays*. These wines are not necessarily cheaper than AOC-wines, although they may appear of lower value on paper. They are often very exciting acquaintances.

The soil here consists primarily of limestone, but it can also be quite rich in clay and in many places, the soil is very rich in iron, which colours it red. Furthermore, there are also occasional occurrences of the mineral bauxite, rich in aluminium, which used to be mined around Tavernes, among other places. Ever since the old days, soil rich in clay from Coteaux Varois has been used to produce the beautiful *tomettes*: the red, hexagonal tiles found on the floors of so many old Provençal houses. However these days, Salernes would be the place to go for inspiration when planning the renovation of floors, kitchens or bathrooms in Provençal houses, as it is primarily there that you find producers of tiles and pots.

The landscape in Coteaux Varois is typically Provençal: dotted with little, old villages, large pinewoods and vineyards set against the red soil. The population used to be quite dependent on the forests, as they used to extract resin from the pine trees, which was used as perfume and for turpentine.

At Domaine Saint-Jean-de-Villecroze, situated 350 m above sea level, they have cultivated wine since the days of the Templars and cellars have been dug into the rock. This is a traditional way of building within the area, because Villecroze means 'the hollow town' and several caves used to be inhabited. The cellars at Saint-Jean all have state-of-the-art equipment and the temperature is closely controlled; it is where the old and the modern world of wine producing meet and the results are quite remarkable. The wines ferment in steel vats and then they are left to mature in small oak casks that are placed in a damp, cool environment, supplied by the fresh spring that runs through the cellar.

At the winery, they strive to grown their vines according to the principles of organic cultivation, without the use of pesticides, and apart from producing regular Coteaux Varois wines, they also produce wines solely based on Syrah or Cabernet Sauvignon. These so-called *vins de cépages* are undeniably a product of a strong Californian influence and when left to mature for a while, they surpass other Coteaux Varois-wines effortlessly. They cannot be sold as AOC-wines because they do not adhere to the regulations, so instead they are sold as *Vin de Pays du Var*. The vineyard also produces a smaller number of equally lovely wines that fall under Côtes de Provence.

At neighbouring Domaine de Saint-Jean, you find a similarly idyllic and exiting property, the Château Thuerry. It is 300 ha in size, of which 50 ha are used for growing wine and the château produces both Côtes de Provence and Coteaux Varois wines.

In Le Val you find the beautiful Domaine de Fontainebleau that dates all the way back to the 1750s. This is a place to splash out a little on their Cuvée Speciale red wine. It is one of the best wines in the district. Around Brignoles you also find Domaine de l'Escarelle among others, where they produce great red wine. Domaine de Ramatuelle, might be a little more interesting, and apart from decent red wines, they also produce a lovely bright, rosé with a flowery aroma, which is sold at reasonable prices.

In Garéoult you find Domaine de Garbelle, which is a classic Provençal vineyard built with local stone, featuring with brown shutters and a slightly sloping roof with old tiles that remind one of withering autumn leaves. Not ostentatious, but simple and beautiful. The vineyards are shielded from the easterly winds by the pinewood Bonne Garde and from the western winds by La Montagne de la Loube. To the south, the vines grow in red, calcareous soil. Since 1988, the Gambini family have produced their own wine rather than handing over their crop to the local co-operative, which has proved highly successful. The best of their wines are the rosé and red wines. The rosé is based on Grenache and Cinsault and produced by the *saignée* method. The red wine is base on Syrah and Grenache and left to mature for 5–6 months in casks to improve its body and expand its aroma. Once bottled, it can successfully be left to mature for another three years. The Gambini family have also tried to grow Mourvèdre vines, but they do not ripen easily in these parts, sometimes not until October, and although the strong Mourvèdre would possibly help improve the red wines, they are on the brink of giving up. On the other hand, they have succeeded in producing very attractive white wines with Rolle.

Domaine du Loou is close to La Roquebrussanne and the owner, Daniel di Placido, is Italian and chairman of the *appellation*. It is very much to his credit that Coteaux Varois has been able to go from being a VDQS to an AOC-district in just eight years. At Domaine Du Loou he has created a model vineyard that produces particularly great rosé and white wines.

Another important wine village in Coteaux Varois is Saint-Maximin-la-Sainte-Baume and just outside the village is another of the numerous great wineries in this AOC-district, namely Domaine du Deffends, and its *rosé d'une nuit*, based on Grenache and Cinsault, is elegantly bright and aromatic. It is a perfect example of a modern rosé wine. Its red wine, Clos de la Truffière, is made from Cabernet Sauvignon and Syrah and then left to mature in oak casks. It is durable and tasty. The Lanversin family, who manage the vineyard, are of the opinion that the area's microclimate is responsible for the production of great wines – 'no more than 10% is down to the farmer', they claim.

The old Domaine des Annibals, on the way to Bras, stands out from the rest of the district's wineries, as their best product is in fact a white wine. If you continue towards Brue-Auriac and Château Saint-Estève, you find yet another great wine producer, who will give you great value for your money.

These days, Coteaux Varois is developing fast and it is most definitely one of the lesser-known districts of Provence worth keeping an eye on in the future – and their wines are still very affordable.

A living wine museum has been established in connection with La Maison des Coteaux Varois in La Celle. The idea is to collect all the old Provençal vines in a sort of botanical garden. However, locating some of the old varieties has proved hard work as, while they have great cultural value, they are no longer popular. Various places including Château Simone in Palette have helped, and they have contributed several rare vines such as Majorquin and Barbaroux. Today there are approximately 90 types of vines in the museum's small vineyard and the museum might very well become important for future wine growers, as it is far from unthinkable that old vines may have qualities that can be useful in the future. And so the museum becomes a kind of Noah's Ark for Provençal vines.

Producers in Varois

Bergerie d'Aquino
83170 Tourves
Phone: 0494 864680
www.aquino.fr
info@aquino.fr

Château de l'Escarelle
83170 La Celle
Phone: 0494 690998
contact@escarelle.fr

Château de Margillière
83170 Brignoles
Phone: 0494 690534
www.chateau-margilliere.fr
contact@chateau-margilliere.fr

Château la Calisse
83170 Tourves
Phone: 0494 772471
www.chateau-la-calisse.fr
contact@chateau-la-calisse.fr

Château la Martine
83860 Nans-les-Pins
Phone: 0494 789052
stovna@orange.fr

Château Margüi
83670 Chateauvert
Phone: 0617 725717
www.chateaumargui.com
philguillanton@yahoo.fr

Château Miraval
83570 Correns
Phone: 0494 863933
www.miraval.com
miraval@club-internet.fr

Château Saint-Estève
83119 Brue-Auriac
Phone: 0494 721470
www.chateau-saint-esteve.com

Château Thuerry
83690 Villecroze
Phone: 0494 706302
www.chateauthuerry.com
thuerry@chateauthuerry.com

Château Trians
83136 Néoules
Phone: 0494 040822
www.trians.com
trians@wanadoo.fr

Domaine de Clapiers
83149 Bras
Phone: 0494 699546

Domaine de Fontainebleau
83143 Le Val
Phone: 0494 595909

Domaine de Garbelle
83136 Garéoult
Phone: 0494 048603
www.domaine-de-garbelle.com
contact@domaine-de-garbelle.com

Domaine de Ramatuelle
83170 Brignoles
Phone: 0494 691061
www.domaine-ramatuelle.com
ramatuelle2@wanadoo.fr

Domaine de Valcolombe
83690 Villecroze
Phone: 0494 675716
www.valcolombe.com
valcolombe@wanadoo.fr

Domaine des Annibals
83170 Brignoles
Phone: 0494 693036
www.annibals.fr
dom.annibal@orange.fr

Domaine des Chaberts
SCI Dom. de Chaberts
83136 Garéoult
Phone: 0494 049205
www.chaberts.com
chaberts@wanadoo.fr

Domaine du Deffends
83470 Saint Maximin
Phone: 0494 780391
www.deffends.com
domaine@deffends.com

Domaine du Loou
83136 La Roquebrussanne
Phone: 0494 869497
domaine-du-loou@wanadoo.fr

Domaine La Rose des Vents
83136 La Roquebrussanne
Phone: 0494 869928
larosedesventss073@orange.fr

Domaine Saint-Jean de Villecroze
83930 Villecroze
Phone: 0494 706307
www.domaine-saint-jean.com
contact@domaine-saint-jean.com

Domaine Saint-Jean-le-Vieux
83470 Saint-Maximin-la-Sainte-Baume
Phone: 0494 597759
www.saintjeanlevieux.com
domaine@saintjeanlevieux.com

BANDOL

In 1941, Bandol, situated between Marseilles and Toulon, was awarded the AOC-*appellation*. The district covers six municipalities across 1,600 ha, and they produce approximately 60,000 hl wine per year including numerous unique wines. Bandol is primarily known for its red wines, but wineries here also produce delicate rosé and white wines.

Although most of the vineyards are located inland, it is Bandol the seaport from which the wines of the district are named. Bandol's natural harbour and its proximity to the sea have been very important for wine production, and wine has been exported from here since ancient times, which is also why it is not unusual for local fishermen to catch well-preserved Roman amphora in their nets, when fishing just outside the harbour.

Cargo ships can dock at the harbour in Bandol regardless of the weather, and especially during the 20th century, wines bound for Italy, North America, Brazil and the West Indies were shipped out

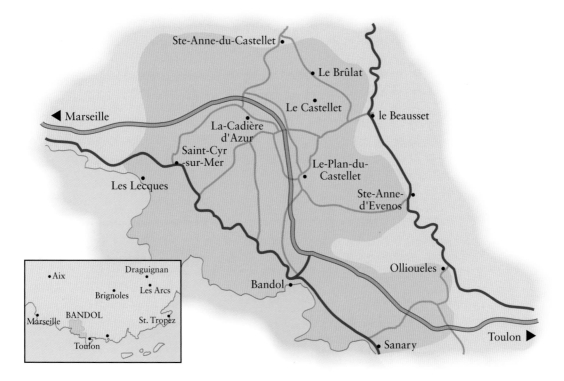

from here. The wines from Bandol were most likely popular because they withstood the long journey at sea quite well. In much the same way as Madeira, some even claimed that Bandol wines improved when journeying overseas, which would have been quite important at a time when wine's durability was rather poor. While other wines quickly turned to vinegar, wines from Bandol only really came into their own after a troublesome journey across the sea, which made it an ideal wine to ship out to faraway colonies. The demand for wine from Bandol was so great that casks were marked with a huge 'B', leaving the customers in no doubt about the wine's authenticity.

As the harbour was not deep enough to allow the ships to moor directly at the quay, the wine-filled casks were thrown into water and then hauled on board from there. Loading the ships in this manner must have been extremely laborious and it is quite remarkable that the wine actually survived such rough treatment. Nonetheless, loading continued in this manner right up until the end of the 18th century. Most of the casks were locally produced, and this line of work was just one of the many side-businesses that followed in the wake of the wine export. And, although Bandol also suffered greatly because of wine lice, they were back in business well before many of the other Provençal districts.

Today, Bandol is no longer an important port in terms of exporting wine; the harbour is now a state-of-the-art marina and in summer it is buzzing with lots of tourists and enormous yachts. There are also numerous cafés and restaurants, and although many of the old stone houses along the seafront are gone, the place still exudes a very pleasant and lively atmosphere – and it still possible both to taste and buy Bandol wines here.

At bit further inland, however, you find one of the most exquisite wine areas in all of Provence. If new building developments have left Bandol a little scarred, that's far from the case up here. Lovely, winding roads take you past the vineyards located on steep hills and mountainsides nestled in between little villages. It is almost like a big amphitheatre. Only the vineyards on the mountainsides are included in the AOC-*appellation* though, while wine produced in the valleys is sold as *Vins de Pays de Mont Caume*.

The vineyards in Bandol are located in the area along the Riviera that benefits most from the sun, but come July-September when the sun is scorchingly hot, the vines are kept cool by the soft Mediterranean breeze. To protect the meagre, pebbly soil from eroding, the local wine growers have built terraces supported by stone walls, and it is these sunny *restanques* that supply the grapes for indisputably one of the best wines from Provence, the red Bandol. This wine should be left to mature in oak casks for at least 18 months before being bottled and at the earliest it should be enjoyed after another 5–8 years. Most will improve even more if left to mature for longer, and a 20-year old red Bandol is very likely not past its prime. It is a wine that demands patience.

The climate in Bandol fluctuates relatively little, which ensures a very stable wine production of high quality, although variations do occur.

As well as the obligatory 18 months in oak casks, many producers choose to leave the wine to mature for another couple of years after being bottled before putting it on the market, and it is quite common to find several vintages on offer at the same time. Choosing the youngest (and therefore cheapest) wine and then just patiently leaving it to mature further is a very sensible approach to buying wines from Bandol as prices are generally high. In terms of quality though, you cannot argue about the price.

Most of the great French wines are based on one or just a few different grapes. This is true of Burgundy where they use Pinot Noir and Bordeaux where they use Cabernet Sauvignon and Merlot. In Bandol it is the Mourvèdre grape that supplies the characteristic taste and it is exactly because of this grape that the wine must be left to mature before it is ready for sale, because wines based on Mourvèdre can be unpleasantly aggressive and sharp when young. However, when left to mature it will be just as round and velvety soft in old age as it is disagreeably tannic in youth. In other words, the compulsory 18 months in casks is not supposed to add flavour, but it allows the wine to become soft and rounded. Only very few wine producers use new casks, as the flavourings from fresh oak will often be too penetrating.

In Bandol there is a saying that the Mourvèdre grape needs heat as well as a sea view to thrive, and if truth be told, it does indeed rarely thrive outside the area of Bandol. The grapes seldom reach maturity when moved too far inland. However, the famous red wines from Palette do include Mourvèdre as one of the primary grapes, not least

Châteauneuf-du-Pape. The Mourvèdre grape is a great preservative, which is most likely why wines from Bandol are so durable, and undoubtedly helped them survive the long sea journeys.

Apart from Mourvèdre, the wine producers in Bandol use Cinsault, Grenache, Carignan, Syrah, Tibouren and Calitor, however, at least 50% of the wine must be based on the Mourvèdre grape, and in some instances it can be as much as 90 or even 100%. The maximum yield per ha is 40 hl, but most producers keep it as low as 30–35 hl.

In Bandol, they observe the old French saying, 'Plus le cépage est vieux – plus le vin est bon' (the older the vine, the better the wine), and vines that are less than eight years old cannot be used to produce AOC red wines, only Vin de Pays or Vin de Table. These unusually harsh regulations make it thoroughly worthwhile to take a closer look at the Vin de Pays wines. And, in all fairness, the regulations do ensure high quality, because just as the wines should be of a certain age to be fully enjoyed, it is not until the vines are close to 30 years old that they are at their best.

The white wines based on Clairette, Ugni Blanc and Bourboulenc as well as Sauvignon are also of good quality. The rosé wines are for the most part produced by using the *presse directe* method, and as they contain Mourvèdre they do not necessarily have to be enjoyed while young, they can actually improve when left to mature, which is quite unique for a rosé wine.

In Bandol there are a couple of leading wine producing families. The Ott family is one with their Château de Romassan in Le Plan-du-Castellet, a beautiful château especially renowned for its exquisite, but also very expensive, rosé wine: the spicy and almost salmon col-oured Cœur de Grain, based on Mourvèdre, Cinsault and Grenache. It matures in oak casks and is then bottled in the Ott family's char-acteristic bottle. They also sell a wonderful Vieux Marc de Rosé, left to mature in oak casks for eight years.

Another important wine producing family is the Bunan family, who migrated from Algeria to Bandol in the early 1960s. Today, the Bunan brothers manage three different properties and they produce some of the best wines in the district. Furthermore, they distil their own marc and they sell both homemade honey and olive oil. Their cellars are equipped with the latest technology, which enables the family to produce many different kinds of wine, which is quite unusual in these parts. The Bunan brothers not only produce traditionally round and soft wines from Moulin des Costes, they also produce an attractively rounded wine based solely on Mourvèdre from Château la Rouvière. And again, patience is a virtue, as the wine should be left to mature for quite a while, at least 8–10 years. The beautiful headquarters of the Bunan family is in La Cadière-d'Azur, home to the 16th century Domaine de Salettes as well.

The Romans used to cultivate both vines and olive trees in Domaine de Salettes' fields, and since 1602, the vineyard has belonged to the Boyers family – in other words, 16 generations of wine growers – quite a record.

Château de Pibarnon in La Cadière-d'Azur is the highest situated vineyard in Bandol and it boasts views of both vineyards and the sea. The vines are cultivated on terraces as high as 270 m above sea level and nurtured by calcareous soil. Their red wine is based on 90% Mourvèdre and 10% Grenache. It is left to mature in casks for years and should be left for at least another 6–8 years after bottling, by then it will also have developed a velvety character with a hint of vanilla, leather and tobacco. You get hints of even more flavours if you leave the wine for twice as long. Many consider the red wine from Pibarnon to be the best in Bandol. It is most certainly one of them. Pibarnon's excellent rosé and white wines are produced by malolactic fermentation, which is not that common in warmer areas.

In Beausset, you find the beautiful Domaine Tempier, which like Domaine de Frégate sports an old sailing ship on its pretty label, probably loaded with wine from Bandol. Domaine Tempier is one of the most historically important vineyards in Bandol and their wines are nothing short of outstanding. For centuries, the Peyraud family have fought to re-establish Bandol's former reputation as a district producing wine of high quality. Their vines are organically grown and they utilise the anti-oxidant properties of Mourvèdre in the production, which means that they need hardly add sulphur to the Tempier rosé wine – a healthy way of preserving wine.

There are several other great vineyards in Bandol and the district is absolutely worth a visit in its own right – not least if you like dark, rustic red wines, and if you are not frightened off by the raw youngsters that you will most certainly also come across at tastings.

PRODUCERS IN BANDOL

Château de Pibarnon
83740 La Cadière-d'Azur
Phone: 0494 901273
www.pibarnon.com
contact@pibarnon.com

Château de Romassan
83330 Le Castellet
Phone: 0494 987191

Château des Baumelles
83330 Sainte-Anne du Castellet
Phone: 0494 326320
Earl.bronzo@wanadoo.fr

Château la Rouvière/Moulin des
Costes
83740 La Cadière-d'Azur
Phone: 0494 985898
bunan@bunan.com

Château Pradeaux
83270 Saint-Cyr-sur-Mer
Phone: 0494 321021

Château Sainte-Anne
83330 Sainte-Anne-d'Évenos
Phone: 0494 903540
chateaustanne@free.fr

Château Vannières
83740 La Cadière-d'Azur
Phone: 0494 900808
www.chateauvannieres.com
info@chateauvannieres.com

Domaine de Font-Vive
83330 Le Beausset
Phone: 0494 986006
Barthesph2@wanadoo.fr

Domaine de Frégate
83270 Saint-Cyr-sur-Mer
Phone: 0494 325757
www.domainedefregate.com

Domaine de Lafran-Veyrolles
83740 La Cadière-d'Azur
Phone: 0494 901337
www.lafran-veyrolles.com
contact@lafran-veyrolles.com

Domaine de Salettes
83740 La Cadière-d'Azur
Phone: 0494 900606
www.salettes.com
salettes@salettes.com

Domaine de Souviou
83330 Le Beausset
Phone: 0494 905763
www.souviou.net
contact@souviou.net

Domaine de Terrebrune
83190 Ollioules
Phone: 0494 740130
www.vin-bandol-terrebrune.fr
delille@terrebrune.com

Domaine de Val d'Arenc
83330 Le Beausset
Phone: 0494 987189

Domaine de la Bastide Blanche
83330 Sainte-Anne-du-Castellet
Phone: 0494 326320
www.bastide-blanche.fr
contact@bastide-blanche.fr

Domaine de la Bégude
83330 Le Plan-du-Castellet
Phone: 0442 089234
www.domainedelabegude.fr
contact@domainedelabegude.fr

Domaine de la Garenne
83740 La Cadière-d'Azur
Phone: 0494 900301
www.domainedelagarenne.net
contact@domainedelagarenne.net

Domaine de la Laidière
83330 Sainte-Anne-d'Évenos
Phone: 0494 036575
www.laidiere.com
info@laidiere.com

Domaine de la Noblesse
83740 La Cadière-d'Azur
Phone: 0494 987554

Domaine de la Tour du Bon
83330 Le Brulat-du-Castellet
Phone: 0494 326162

Domaine de la Vivonne
83330 Le Castellet
Phone: 0494 987009
www.vivonne.com
info@vivonne.com

Domaine de l'Hermitage
83330 Le Beausset
Phone: 0494 987131
www.domainelhermitage.com
contact@domainelhermitage.com

Domaine de l'Olivette
83330 Le Castellet
Phone: 0494 985885
www.domaine-olivette.com
contact@domaine-olivette.com

Domaine des Baguiers
83330 Le Plan-du-Castellet
Phone: 0494 904187
www.domainedesbaguiers.com
jourdan@domainedesbaguiers.com

Domaine du Cagueloup
83270 Saint-Cyr-sur-Mer
Phone: 0494 261570
jcastell@wanadoo.fr

Domaine du Pey-Neuf
83740 La Cadière-d'Azur
Phone: 0494 901455
domaine.peyneuf@wanadoo.fr

Domaine du Dupuy de Lôme
83330 Évenos
Phone: 0494 052299
www.dupuydelome.com
contact@dupuydelome.com

Domaine du Val-d'Arenc
83330 Le Beausset
Phone: 0494 987189

Domaine la Suffrène
83740 La Cadière-d'Azur
Phone: 0494 900923
www.domaine-la-suffrene.com
contact@domaine-la-suffrene.com

Domaine le Galantin
83330 Le-Plan-du-Castellet
Phone: 0494 987594
domaine-legalantin@wanadoo.fr

Domaine les Luquettes
83740 La Cadière-d'Azur
Phone: 0494 900259
www.les-luquettes.com
info@les-luquettes.com

Domaine Ray-Jane
83330 Le Plan-du-Castellet
Phone: 0494 986408

Domaine Sorin
83270 Saint-Cyr-sur-Mer
Phone: 0494 266228
www.domainesorin.com
luc.sorin@wanadoo.fr

Domaine Tempier
83330 Le Beausset
Phone: 0494 987021

Les Vignerons de la Cadiérenne
83740 La Cadière-d'Azur
Phone: 0494 901106
www.cadierenne.net
cadierenne@wanadoo.fr

CASSIS

The town of Cassis is often confused with the blackcurrant liqueur from Burgundy, which is rather unfortunate, because spelling aside, they have absolutely nothing in common. This little wine district, situated in the department of Bouches-du-Rhône, is proud to be one of the first districts to be awarded an AOC as far back as 1936. The little seaport Cassis, situated between La Ciotat and Marseilles, gives its name to the district, which consists of only one municipality with 16 wine-producing properties. The wine fields cover 200 ha and the yearly production is around 7,700 hl.

The 416 m tall cliffs of Cap Canaille rise above Cassis, boasting wonderful views of the town and the Mediterranean Sea. If you cross these cliffs from La Ciotat, you will experience magnificent landscapes with fabulous views both inland, all the way to Massif de La Sainte-Baume, and across the Mediterranean before ascending to Cassis through the sea-facing vineyards.

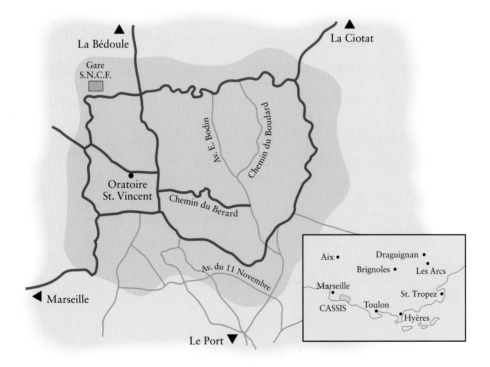

It is easy to like the old fishing village of Cassis if you visit at any time other than the extremely busy summer season. September or October is a good time to visit, although even then you might think that half of Marseilles has decided to visit at weekends. Nonetheless, we should not forget that these visitors are also part and parcel of the pleasant and joyful atmosphere of the seaside; after all, you go there to have a nice time. Unlike many seaports along the Mediterranean, Cassis has miraculously managed to avoid the onslaught of modern buildings. In the harbour you find the little white and blue fishing boats, which remind you that in the old days, Cassis was first and foremost a fishing village that provided the restaurants in Marseilles with fresh sardines and anchovies.

The harbour also offers boat trips to *les Calanques*, the bright white rocks located between Cassis and Marseilles that create a number of fjords with rock-caves and little beaches that can be reached on foot and also enjoyed visually from the sea. A boat trip will give you an exceptional experience of the Azure blue Mediterranean.

Along the town's old and narrow streets the air is filled with the magnificent and penetrating smell of fish soup emanating from the numerous great restaurants that all serve a 'genuine' *bouillabaisse* or the lesser-known *bourride*. Above the town itself, you find terraced vineyards that also help protect the town from erosion during the heavy spring or autumn rains. From these fields you get the truly sublime accompaniment to the *bouillabaisse*, the seafood and the grilled fish – the white Cassis.

The white Cassis is a lovely wine, and is not even expensive. It is a conservative wine, which can be beautifully straw-coloured and extremely dry with a strongly perfumed bouquet that allows the wine to penetrate the spicy fish soups. The worst thing to be said about is that it is really difficult not to drink too much of it.

The Provençal literary Nobel Laureate, Frédéric Mistral mused in his writings about how he could taste the rosemary and the heather as well as the myrtle in the wine, and although the Provençal are generally prone to using plenty of romantic imagery when communicating, Frédéric Mistral was not far off.

In Cassis, they also produce rosé and red wines based on Cinsault, Grenache, Carignan, Barbaraux and Mourvèdre. The rosé wines are often charming, and although only a very limited number of red

wines are produced, these too can be quite exciting. There is really no contest though; the white wines are the main attraction. They are primarily based on Marsanne, Ugni Blanc, Clairette, Grenache Blanc and Sauvignon, and these grapes make up approximately two thirds of the entire production, not not least because of the demand for white wines to go with the seafood at local restaurants.

Most of the brilliant white wines produced in Cassis do not keep well and they should be enjoyed as young as possible. The best way to do this is on a hot summer day by the harbour accompanied by a plate of *fruit de mer*. What more could you possibly want?

Cassis is one of the older wine districts in France and it was renowned as far back as the 12th century; however, wine cultivation can be traced all the way back to 600 BC, possibly on account of its proximity to the sea, which after all used to be vital for the export of wine. A local anecdote tells how 20 sailors from Cassis were ransomed from a warship with a load of the town's valuable wine.

The terrible infestation of wine lice in the late 19th century completely destroyed the local vineyards, and production has never reached its former levels. The disaster almost caused the loss of one type of wine altogether: a greatly appreciated type of Muscat about which Frédéric Mistral wrote, 'Bees cannot produce honey more sweet than this sparkling diamond.' The wine was known as *vin paia* or *vin paillé* because the grapes were left to dry on straw matts (*paille* means straw) before being pressed. Once the grapes had been harvested they were left in the sun, which hardened the skins and made the grapes less susceptible to rot. Afterwards, the grape-bunches would be hung under the ceiling to dry even more.

The grapes would be ready for pressing around Christmas, after which they were poured into a vat that had been smeared with Mourvèdre in appreciation of its preservative properties. Then the wine would be left to mature for up to three years before it was ready to be enjoyed. This procedure resulted in golden, concentrated sweet wine, which is in short supply today.

The soil in Cassis is meagre and hard, consisting mainly of chalk and clay, and both the *mistral* and the sea breezes can be quite hard on the vines, fortunately though, they are capable of surviving in places that would be utterly unsuitable for the cultivation of any other crop.

PRODUCERS IN CASSIS

Bodin
13260 Cassis
Phone: 0442 010011
chateau-fontblanche@terre-net.fr

Château Barbanau
13830 Roquefort-la-Bédoule
Phone: 0442 731745
www.chateau-barbanau.com
barbanau@wanadoo.fr

Château de Fontblanche
13260 Cassis
Phone: 0442 010011
chateau-fontblanche@terre-net.fr

Château de Fontcreuse
13260 Cassis
Phone: 0442 017109
www.fontcreuse.com

Clos d'Albizzi
13260 Cassis
Phone: 0442 011143
www.albizzi.fr
contact@albizzi.fr

Clos Saint-Michel
13260 Cassis
Phone: 0442 010033

Clos Sainte-Magdeleine
13260 Cassis
Phone: 0442 017028
www.clossaintemagdeleine.fr
clos.sainte.magdeleine@gmail.com

Clos Val Bruyère
Hameau de Roquefort
13830 Roquefort-la-Bédoule
Phone: 0442 731460
www.chateau-barbanau.com
barbanau@wanadoo.fr

Domaine Caillot
13260 Cassis
Phone: 0442 010535

Domaine Couronne de Charlemagne
13260 Cassis
Phone: 0442 011583
www.couronnedecharlemagne.com
bp@couronnedecharlemagne.com

Domaine de la Ferme Blanche
13260 Cassis
Phone: 0442 010074
fermeblanche@wanadoo.fr

Domaine des Quatre-Vents
13260 Cassis
Phone: 0442 018810
alain.demontillet@wanadoo.fr

Domaine du Bagnol
13260 Cassis
Phone: 0442 731460

Domaine du Paternel
13260 Cassis
Phone: 0442 017703
www.domainedupaternel.com
domaine.paternel@wanadoo.fr

La Badiane
83100 Toulon
Phone: 0607 879805
www.labadiane.fr
contact@labadiane.com

Mas de Boudard
13260 Cassis
Phone: 0442 017266

PALETTE
APPELLATION PALETTE CONTROLÉE

PRODUCE OF FRANCE

Château
Simone

Nº 4818

12%vol

75cl

Mis en bouteille au château
ROUGIER, PROPRIÉTAIRE, MEYREUIL (B.-du-R.) - FRANCE

G 20193

PALETTE

The Romans were very fond of bathing in the hot springs in Aix-en-Provence. They named the town *Aquae Sextiae* after the Roman consul, Sextius, who enjoyed the healing baths around 120 BC. Today the hot and slightly radioactive springs still supply the town's beautiful moss-covered fountains with water.

Aix-en-Provence is considered the spiritual capital of Provence. It is also one of the most beautiful towns in France with is baroque mansions, numerous students and innumerable cafés shaded by the plane trees along the famous main street, the Cours Mirabeau.

Not far from here, you will find one of the smallest but also one of the most interesting wine districts in all of Provence, Palette. It lies just east of Aix and includes the municipalities of Meyreuil and Le Tholonet as well as a small share of Aix. The most striking feature in the area is the white mountain, la Montagne Sainte-Victorie, which

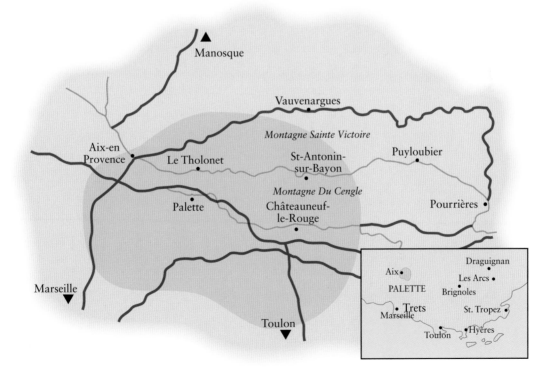

rises more than 1000 m above sea level and which Cézanne tried to capture in many of his paintings.

Palette was awarded an AOC in 1948 and is one of the smallest *appellations* in all of France, with only approximately 50 ha and a yearly production of 1800 hl. The district's vineyards were established by the Carmelite Friars and Good King René approximately 500 years ago. The beautiful Château Simone in Meyreuil still displays traces from that time; King René's (1409–1480) hunting lodge is one example, still located up in the pinewood behind the château. It was here that he used to entertain his hunting guests by serving the wild boars that had been killed in the day's hunt. The wine accompanying the food would of course be King René's own highly esteemed rosé wine, produced from vines cultivated in the fields below the woods. It was this rosé that made René known as the 'Wine King'. He introduced both the Muscat grape and silkworms to Provence and there is a statue of him holding a bunch of grapes at the end of Cours Mirabeau. You often come across his name, because although he was no great warrior, the Provençal consider his abilities as a mathematician, poet and wine grower deserving both of respect and recognition.

Château Simone looks more like a fairy-tale palace than a Provençal vineyard; however, the wines from here are still quintessentially Provençal. The owners themselves, the Rougier family, state that, 'He who has not tasted a wine from Château Simone will not understand the Provençal soul.' Which might be a slight exaggeration, but it is true that the wines from this property taste of Provence.

All three types of wine are based on old Provençal grapes that you will not find in many other places because the family is keen on tradition and feels no need to compete with the popular Burgundy-style wines. The château faces due north and its cellars are cool, which is why they have been spared the expense of investing in costly technological equipment – why bother when nature does it for you? And it is impossible to ignore their results: the wines from Château Simone are right up there with the best from anywhere in France. For those who truly appreciate Provençal wine, there is no getting around Château Simone.

However, which of the château's wines are the best? Winston Churchill, who was a great fan of the Simone-wines, was partial to their white wines. When young they are very fruity but left to mature a little they develop a characteristic bouquet of honey, pine and lime. They will keep for up to 7–8 years, which also makes them quite unique in Provence. Churchill may be right in his appraisal of wines from Palette; though the red wines are equally brilliant, full-bodied and opulent. As youngsters they can be quite aggressive and coarse, but after maturing for approximately 7–8 years they obtain a lovely softness that continues to develop for years to come. The cellars at Château Simone contain wines that go as far back as the 1920s, although it is commonly agreed that they peak after 10–12 years, and a 10-year-old Château Simone is indisputably a great wine experience. The vintages may differ slightly, but they always strive to produce wines that vary as little as possible from year to year.

The fields face north and the grapes attain maturity at a slow pace, so harvesting does not start until October, a couple of weeks after the neighbouring areas of Côtes de Provence and Coteaux d'Aix. The soil is calcareous and full of fossils from long extinct animals. One of these animals has been named after the Rougieri family, who have been in charge of the wine production at Château Simone for six generations. The combination of cool climate and calcareous soil is probably the main reason for their successful production of highly attractive white wines.

Seventeen ha are planted with vines at Château Simone and their yearly production yields around 80,000 bottles, which is roughly 80% of the entire production in Palette.

In terms of rosé and red wines, their primary grapes are Mourvèdre, Grenache and Cinsault. They also use Castes, Terret Gris, Durif, Brun-fourca and Manosquin, Muscat Noir, Syrah, Petit Brun, Tibouren, Cabernet Sauvignon and Carignan.

The grapes used for white wines can also be used in red wines, but they must not make up more than 15% of the must. Their red wines must mature in casks for 18 months before being sold, however, at Château Simone they leave the wines for even longer. The rosé wines are also left to mature for a couple of years before they are ready to be put on the market, which is quite unusual. These wines are dark and powerful with a hint of sundried herbs.

White wines are based on Clairette as the prominent grape, followed by Grenache Blanc, Muscat Blanc, Terret-Bourret, Pique-Poul,

Ugni Blanc, Ugni Rosé, Pascal, Aragnan, Colombard and a local Tokay, and they too are left to mature in oak casks.

Paul Cézanne was a family friend of the Rougier's and the landscape around Château Simone has featured in many of his paintings. When he mentions 'lovely Provençal wine' in his letters, he is most likely referring to wines from Château Simone. Several of Cézanne's paintings could easily have been painted on the château's terrace, from where you have a magnificent view over la Montagne Sainte-Victoire. Whether or not this was the case, his paintings from the turn of the century, of voluptuous girls bathing, were certainly painted by a small stone bridge, *Le Pont des Trois Sautets*, which still exists and is located quite close to the château's main entrance.

Everything about this vineyard appears beautiful and romantic, but alas, it is not perfect: the A8 motorway runs close by, which does rather ruin the idyllic setting. If you drive along the motorway from Aix to Nice, you can actually catch a glimpse of Château Simone. If you look really closely, up on the right hand side, it is possible to get a clear view of the château and its two towers as well as the neatly shaped trees in the park.

Even though Château Simone is the most important vineyard in Palette, one should not disregard Château Crémade in Le Tholonet. Unfortunately this vineyard tends to be overlooked because of Château Simone's distinguished history, which is not at all fair, because their wines are also of high quality. Comparing wines from the two châteaux can be a little difficult though, because they are so very different. Château Crémade was established approximately 50 years ago. Their production is based entirely on recommended grapes, but they use modern equipment and, whereas Château Simone uses old casks, at Château Crémade they only use small casks of fresh oak that they purchase in Cognac and then sell on after use. Their cellar is equipped with the latest cooling facilities and technology. Their vineyards face west and the climate is slightly warmer than at Château Simone, and, with an average age of 40 years, their vines are also a little younger.

After visiting Château Crémade, taking the road towards Pourrières along Saint-Victoire is a good idea. It is part of the *route de Cézanne*, which runs through breathtakingly beautiful scenery. In early summer, the broom stands vividly yellow against the naked white rock in the background. For the remaining part of the year, the equally modest and continuously blossoming thyme provides the colour. In 102 BC, this area witnessed a bloody battle, in which the Roman General, Gaius Marius, mercilessly obliterated several Germanic tribes, and the mountain was named after his victory (*Victoire*). It is also claimed that the town Pourrières was named after the stench of dead bodies – *pourrir* means rotting decay – which is not at all unlikely, because the Romans were ruthless and they killed more than 100,000 men, who were just left on the battlefield under a scorching sun.

The wines from Palette must be at least 11% proof, and the vineyards are not allowed to produce more than 40 hl per ha. Unfortunately, you rarely come across these wines outside the district itself, but within Provence you can get lucky and find wines from here in well-stocked wine shops in some of the larger towns. Furthermore, you can find wines from Palette on the wine lists in choice restaurants in Aix and in some of the famed restaurants along the coast.

In the old days in Provence, they used to produce the so-called *vin cuit* and Palette was particularly celebrated for its version of the wine, which gets many a mention in Provençal literature. These concentrated, liqueur-like Muscat wines were especially enjoyed on festive occasions: for example at Christmas as accompaniment to the thirteen desserts. The famous writer of cookbooks, J-E Reboul described the making of *vin cuit* as follows:

'Take 10 litres of must from ripe and sweet grapes and leave to simmer over low heat until frothy. Once the must is reduced to approximately 6–7 litres, pour into a cask and leave to cool. Once cold, it is ready for bottling. To give it intoxicating properties, add 100 ml of schnapps for every litre of must. The schnapps should not be added until the wine has cooled down considerably, just before bottling. After a month the wine is decanted and bottled in fresh bottles, and it is now ready for the cellar'.

This type of wine can occasionally be found at vineyards around Aix or in the local *pâtissiers*. Each Christmas, '*Distilleries et Domaines de Provence*' send their version of *vin cuit* onto the market.

PRODUCERS IN PALETTE

Château Crémade
13100 Le Tholonet
Phone: 0442 667680
www.chateaucremade.com
chateaucremade@yahoo.fr

Châeteau de Meyreuil
13590 Meyreuil
Phone: 0442 580396

Château Henri Bonnaud
13100 Le Tholonet
Phone: 0442 668628
www.chateau-henri-bonnaud.fr
contact@chateau-henri-bonnaud.fr

Château Simone
13590 Meyreuil
Phone: 0442 669258

VIN ROUGE
PRODUIT DE FRANCE

RED WINE
PRODUCT OF FRANCE

SANS LE SOLEIL , JE NE SUIS RIEN

CHATEAU VIGNELAURE

2001

COTEAUX D'AIX EN PROVENCE

13 % alc./vol.

APPELLATION COTEAUX D'AIX EN PROVENCE CONTRÔLÉE

750 ml

MIS EN BOUTEILLE AU CHATEAU
PAR VIGNELAURE S.A. PROPRIÉTAIRE A 83560 RIANS (FRANCE)

Château Vignelaure a sélectionné dans la récolte 2001
199.500 Bouteilles et 608 Magnums de ce grand vin
Cette bouteille porte le N° 18245

www.vignelaure.com

COTEAUX D'AIX-EN-PROVENCE

Coteaux d'Aix is a large and varied wine district, located almost exclusively in Bouches-du-Rhône. Vines take up around 5000 ha of land and their yearly wine production comes to around 200,000 hl. This area encompasses traditional Provençal scenery with quiet villages and several areas full of *maquis*, a kind of vegetation that has evolved because of the over-exploitation of the evergreen oak woods. The vegetation is 2–4 metres in height, dense and almost impassable. Many of the plants are unpleasantly thorny and it is quite a feat if you are able to move outside the regular paths without being cut, something the Resistance took advantage of during the Second World War. The Resistance actually named itself after this vegetation, *le maquis*.

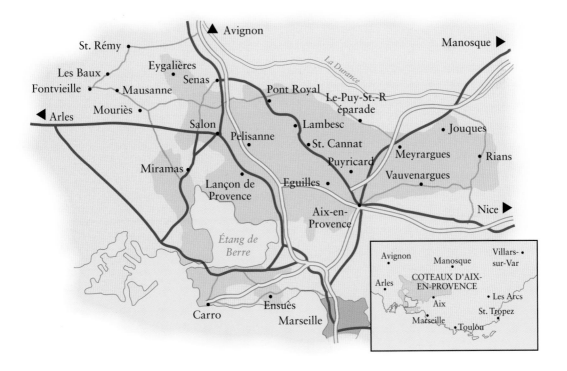

Once the maquis is destroyed by fire or by high numbers of grazing sheep and goats, it transforms into another kind of vegetation known as *garrique*. It is a little like heather and formerly it was only found on dry and very stony land, but now it is far more widespread than the *maquis*. The scenery is impressive and amongst the more typical plants you also find lavender, rue, thyme, rosemary, bay leaf, myrtle, elderberry and the evergreen kermes oak, locally known as *Garoulia*, from which we also get aforementioned *garrique*. The wildlife is also quite varied, and if you are particularly persistent, besides the indefatigable cicadas, you will also encounter colourful ladybirds, praying mantises and scorpions, as well as numerous birds. A great part of this AOC-district is covered by *garrique*, however, once removed, vines can grow here with ease.

Rosé and red wines from this district are primarily based on Cabernet Sauvignon, Carignan, Cinsault, Counoise, Grenache, Mourvèdre and Syrah. Generally, price and quality are well matched and legislation is proposed to reduce the use of less interesting grapes, especially Carignan. They would also like to reduce the use of the 'foreign' Cabernet Sauvignon, although this grape produces fine and durable wines. However, the locals are afraid of creating a mini-Burgundy and thus destroying the district's specifically Provençal characteristics, which is a pity really, as the district does not have a long track record of producing quality wines. On the contrary, they used to go for the high-yielding and wine lice-resistant hybrid.

The vineyards are situated around Aix, bordering on Côtes de Provence. Furthermore, Coteaux d'Aix-en-Provence is separated from Coteaux de Pierrevert to the north by the Durance. It is a rather large area that stretches all the way down to the salt-lake *Étang de Berre*, where among others, Château Calissanne has 120 ha from which they produce a number of fine wines. However, Château Calissanne is also the last stop before the refineries, where the air turns yellow and horribly polluted.

Château de Beaupré, located in Saint Cannat, was established by Baron Émile Doublon in 1890 and the family still manage the property. The main building dates back to 1739 and it is a beautiful specimen of a Provençal *bastide*, surrounded by plane trees and trickling fountains. A *bastide* is usually a large, beautiful country house with an unornamented and even façade. The house is often a little

secluded and surrounded by a park-like garden, suitably distanced from the various farm buildings. After all, one did not leave the smelly gutters in town, only to end up with other harsh scents up one's nose. The *bastide* has several floors and you usually enter through a main hall with a majestic staircase leading up to the numerous rooms on the first floor, while the ground floor comprises the different salons, dining room and kitchen. Emphasis is on elegance and refinement.

At Beaupré they produce a red wine using the method of *macération carbonique*, with close to equal parts of Grenache and Syrah. The result is a fresh and ready-to-drink wine. The black current scented red wine with 90% Cabernet Sauvignon and 10% Syrah is also commendable, especially if left to mature for 8–10 years. This wine is yet another example of how well Cabernet Sauvignon thrives with its roots implanted in soil rich in chalk and clay. The vineyard's rosé wine is made from a mixture of Grenache, Cinsault and Cabernet. It is produced using the *saignée* method and with a lovely fruity taste, it is a great representative of the district.

Château du Seuil is located in the forest above Puyricard and some of the buildings date back to the 13th century. Traditionally, they grow vines, olives and almonds here. Almonds cultivated around Aix are used for the sweet Callisons d'Aix, the town's pride and joy and sold in every self-respecting patisserie. Today they grow vines on 56 ha of the château's sloping grounds and their best wine is a red wine based on Grenache, Syrah and Cabernet Sauvignon. It matures for 12 months in new oak casks and is called *le Grand Seuil*. The regular red wine made from the same grapes but not left to mature for as long, is also good. Furthermore, they produce some of the district's rare but great white wines, based on Grenache Blanc and Sauvignon Blanc.

For years, they have produced excellent red wines at Château Vignelaure in Jouques using Cabernet Sauvignon as the wines' backbone; the official directive to reduce the use of this grape is most likely not highly appreciated here. The red wines from Château Vignelaure are often compared with various wines from Burgundy, but the vineyard is very much unique and certainly one of the more remarkable ones within the district.

Georges Brunet, who originally came from the famous Château la Lagune in Burgundy, established this vineyard because he wanted to prove that it was indeed possible to produce wines of high quality in Provence. He succeeded, and for a number of years the château has been one the most highly acclaimed Provençal vineyards. Today, Vignelaure is owned by Swedes, but that has in no way impaired the château's standards.

The sympathetic German, Peter Fischer, who manages the beautiful Château Revelette, also in Jouques, is also struggling with the AOC regulations. Fischer comes from an extremely rich family and as a young man he ran away to the Napa Valley in California, where they taught him the wine trade. Greatly inspired by the Americans, he returned to Europe and bought the vineyard in Jouques. It is a *bastide* from the 17th century, surrounded by shade-giving plane trees and numerous statues. A little creek, filled with trout, runs through the grounds. On his labels, he has chosen the rather romantic title of *vigneron* – wine farmer. Peter Fischer is a skilful oenologist (connoisseur) and very fond of experimenting. For instance, he produces excellent red wines by letting half the must ferment using the *macération carbonique* technique, while leaving the other half to ferment in a traditional manner. Furthermore, he also produces delicate wines based only on Cabernet Sauvignon or Chardonnay; however, these wines have to be sold as Vin de Pays-des-Bouches-du-Rhône.

The white wines from Coteaux d'Aix are generally speaking the least interesting, but you can get lucky. They are based on Bourboulenc, Clairette, Grenache, Sauvignon, Sémillon, Ugni Blanc and Rolle. Wine producers in this district are allowed to harvest 60 hl per ha, which is actually the highest allowance in all of Provence. In practice though, the serious producers harvest far less.

Producers in Coteaux-d'Aix-en-Provence

Cellier des Quatre Tours
13770 Venelles
Phone: 0442 547111

Château Barbebelle
13840 Rognes
Phone: 0442 502212
www.barbebelle.com
contact@barbebelle.com

Château Bas
13116 Vernegues
Phone: 0490 591316
www.chateaubas.com
contact@chateaubas.com

Château de Beaulieu
13840 Rognes
Phone: 0442 502407

Château de Beaupré
13760 Saint Cannat
Phone: 0442 573359
www.beaupre.fr
contact@beaupre.fr

Château de Calissanne
13680 Lançon-de-Provence
Phone: 0490 426303
www.calissanne.fr
contact@calissanne.fr

Château de Fonscolombe
13610 Le-Puy-Sainte-Réparade
Phone: 0442 617000
chateaudefonscolombe@wanadoo.fr

Château de Vauclaire
13650 Meyrargues
Phone: 0442 575014

Château du Seuil
13540 Puyricard
Phone: 0442 921599
www.chateauduseuil.fr
contact@chateauduseuil.fr

Château la Coste
13610 Le-Puy-Sainte-Réparade
Phone: 0442 618998
www.chateau-la-coste.com
matthieu.cosse@gmail.com

Château Pigoudet
83560 Rians
Phone: 0494 803178

Château Revelette
13490 Jouques
Phone: 0442 637543
www.revelette.fr
contact@revelette.fr

Château Saint-Jean
13620 Carry-le-Rouët
Phone: 0442 447014

Château Vignelaure
83560 Rians
Phone: 0494 372110

Commanderie de la Bargemone
13760 Saint-Cannat
Phone: 0442 572244
www.bargemone.com
contact@bargemone.com

Domaine de la Vallongue
13810 Eygalières
Phone: 0490 959170
vallongue@wanadoo.fr

Domaine de Pont-Royal
13370 Mallemort
Phone: 0490 574015

Domaine de Valdition
13660 Orgon
Phone: 0490 730812
www.valdition.com
contact@valdition.com

Domaine la Cadenière
13680 Lançon-de-Provence
la-cadeniere@wanadoo.fr

Domaine Les Bastides
13610 Le-Puy-Sainte-Réparade
Phone: 0442 919766

Domaine Les Béates
13410 Lambesc
Phone: 0442 570758
www.lesbeates.com
contact@domaine-les-beates.com

Domaine Valcaire
13840 Rognes
Phone: 0679 712893
rgreynier@aol.com

Le Séouve
13490 Jauques
Phone: 0442 676087

Les Vignerons du Roi René
13410 Lambesc
Phone: 0442 570020

Mas de Sainte-Berthe
13520 Les-Beaux-de-Provence
Phone: 0490 543901
www.mas-sainte-berthe.com
info@mas-sainte-berthe.com

LES BAUX-DE-PROVENCE

Only a handful of the producers within the seven municipalities at the foot of the Alpilles mountains, surrounding the medieval town of Les Baux, are allowed to put Les Baux-de-Provence on their labels. The area covers 325 ha and the yearly production is around 7,000 hl. Previously, these producers had to accept belonging to the Coteaux d'Aix district, but in 1995 they were granted an independent *appellation*. Or, to be precise, the rosé and red wines were as the white wines are still sold as Coteaux d'Aix – the rules can be rather illogical at times, and you have to keep your eyes peeled. However, there is no doubt that the red wines from this district differ greatly from those of Coteaux d'Aix.

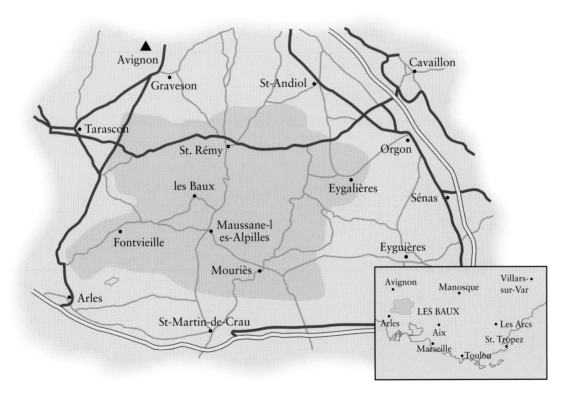

The wines from Les Beaux are closer to those from the southern Rhône, and it is beyond dispute that both soil and climate are much more homogenous in Coteaux des Baux than in Coteaux d'Aix.

Whereas neighbouring Coteaux d'Aix producers have achieved good results by using Cabernet Sauvignon, the producers in Les Beaux primarily use Grenache and Syrah, often supplemented with a few Mourvèdre grapes. They produce less than their neighbours and combining *maceration carbonique* with traditional wine production is widespread here. This gives fruity, fresh red wines with good colour and structure. But, as is often the case in Provence, the wines of the individual producers vary greatly – even the individual vineyard can sometimes offer a variety of quite different wines.

In the valley below Les Baux, you find Mas Sainte-Berthe where you can buy light, fruity red wines produced using the *maceration carbonique* technique, as well as full-bodied, round wines that can be left to mature for up to 8 years. The deeply red Cuvée Louis David, by some considered one of the best red wines in Les Baux, is based on almost equal measures of Grenache, Syrah and Cabernet and can be wonderfully luscious. They also produce the harmonious, dark rosé wine Cuvée Passe Rose, named after one of the beautiful princesses who lived at the fort situated above the fields. In medieval times, pilgrims would come to Mas Sainte-Berthe in great numbers to drink the water from the healing spring. Today, however, it is safe to encourage the wine tourists to go for the wine instead.

Wine growers in Les Baux take a great interest in organic cultivation and try to avoid using both pesticides and artificial fertilisers. Domaine de La Vallongue is a good example of a vineyard that takes a very keen interest in organic cultivation. The beautiful property is situated right in the heart of Les Alpilles, close to the little town of Eygalières. It is surrounded by huge rock formations that help shelter it against the *mistral*, which can be quite fierce around here. By contrast, the vineyards are completely exposed to the cold northern winds, but fortunately this actually helps reduce the risk of attacks by mould fungi.

Domaine de la Vallongue was nothing more than a peaceful sheep farm 40 years ago and there was not a single vine to be found on the dusty land, but when Philippe Paul-Cavallier bought the property, he quickly exchanged the sheep for vines. He turned 38 ha of garrique

into vineyards and started to take an interest in organic wine growing. The vineyard's flagship Cuvée Murielle is a rustic and luscious wine of high quality that can easily be left to mature for 5–6 years. At Vallongue they also produce a delicious red wine that is sold in bulk (bring your own container) as well as great olive oil.

Another important producer in Les Baux is Mas de la Dame. It was painted by Van Gogh in 1889, and one understands his fascination as it is a unique and magnificent property, surrounded by delightful almond trees, slender cypresses, vineyards and olive groves.

You also find great wines at Domaine de Terres Blanches in Saint Rémy and Domaine de Trévallon in Saint-Étienne-du-Grès, one of the more famous vineyards. It was established in 1973 by the Parisian architect Eloi Dürbach, who, among other things, has experimented with organic cultivation of Cabernet Sauvignon and Grenache as well maturing wine in new oak casks. He also produces lovely white wines based on Marsanne, Roussanne and Chardonnay. He is considered one of the true pioneers in Provence, and his wines are counted among the very best in all of France. That the American wine-guru Robert Parker has lavished great praise on Trévallon, maintaining that the vines produced here are among his greatest finds ever, has undoubtedly boosted sales, however, his interest has also rendered wines from Trévallon extremely expensive.

Right from the outset, Dürbach chose to disregard the current rules and regulations within the district, and Cabernet Sauvignon has been one of his favourite grapes, so you cannot really say that Trévallon wines are representative of the district.

The price of wines from Les Baux has gone up in recent years, although they are still worth every penny, and only rarely will you end up disappointed. The wines are produced in extremely beautiful surroundings with Les Alpilles almost surrounded like an island by the flat riverbeds of the Rhône. The white rocks are covered in pine forests, *maquis* or *garrigue*, inhabited by wild rabbits and several rare birds of pray.

Geologically the area is interesting because it is full of calcareous fossils and as the fortress in Les Baux is built from local stones, you can actually find numerous fossils of mussels that are millions of years old embedded in the walls. The entire fortress blends in so well with the surroundings that it can be quite difficult to distinguish the building from the rocks. Les Baux itself has given its name to bauxite, a mineral rich in aluminium, which was discovered here in 1812 and used to be mined in this area.

In its hey-day Les Baux hosted a rich cultural existence with a court and troubadours who would sing romantic love songs, but unfortunately the Counts of Les Baux snubbed the French Court and when, on top of everything else, they converted to Protestant-ism, Louis XII ordered Cardinal Richelieu to destroy the fortress, an order carried out to the letter in 1632. Following the destruction of the fortress, the town was desolate for centuries, but these days it is a popular tourist attraction.

From the fortress itself, you get an unrivalled view of the dry, flat valley, covered with vineyards, almond trees and well-groomed olive groves. Many of the vineyards are sheltered by cypresses to prevent the *mistral* from sweeping through at full speed. On the positive side, the *mistral*, a frequent visitor to this area, ensures clear blue skies, which makes for a great colour-combination with the milk-white mountains and silvery olive groves.

Another charming town in this area is Saint-Rémy-de-Provence, where the famous doctor and astrologer Nostradamus was born in 1503 – and his predictions still spark hefty discussions. Van Gogh spent a year in Saint-Rémy from May 8th 1889 to May 16th 1890, when he admitted himself to an insane asylum under the care of Dr Peyron. In that year, he painted 150 paintings of the town itself or its surroundings – not least his famous blue irises, as well as a number of his best landscapes and self-portraits.

mas de la dame

Coin Caché

rouge

2007

PRODUCERS IN LES BAUX-DE-PROVENCE

Château d'Estoublon
13990 Fontvielle
Phone: 0490 546400

Château Romanin
13210 Saint-Rémy-de-Provence
Phone: 0490 924587
www.romanin.com
contact@romanin.com

Domaine de la Vallongue
13810 Eygalières
Phone: 0490 959170
vallongue@wanadoo.fr

Domaine de Terres Blanches
13210 Saint-Rémy-de-Provence
Phone: 0490 959166
terres.blanches@wanadoo.fr

Domaine de Trévallon
13150 Saint-Étienne-du-Grès
Phone: 0490 490600

Domaine Hauvette
13210 Saint-Rémy-de-Provence
Phone: 0490 920390

Mas d'Auge
13990 Fontvielle
Phone: 0490 546295

Mas de la Dame
13520 Les Baux-de-Provence
Phone: 0490 543224
www.masdeladame.com
masdeladame@masdeladame.com

Mas de Gourgonnier
13890 Mouriès
Phone: 0490 475045

Mas Sainte-Berthe
13250 Les Baux-de-Provence
Phone: 0490 543901
www.mas-sainte-berthe.com
info@mas-sainte-berthe.com

CÔTES DU LUBÉRON

All the vineyards in Côtes du Lubéron are located in the department of Vaucluse, which consists of 36 municipalities east of Avignon, spread across 3,200 ha. It was awarded a VDQS in 1951 but had to wait until 1988 before being awarded the AOC.

The area surrounds the slopes on both sides of Montagne de Lubéron and it encompasses charming little villages like Cavaillon, Bonnieux, Oppède, Mirabeau and Cucuron. Most of the towns are situated up high – and often in the vicinity of an old fortress or castle, which emphasises the glorious past of the area. To the east, Côtes du Lubéron borders on Coteaux de Pierrevert, to the north you have Côtes du Ventoux, while to the south the area is separated from Coteaux d'Aix-en-Provence by the Durance.

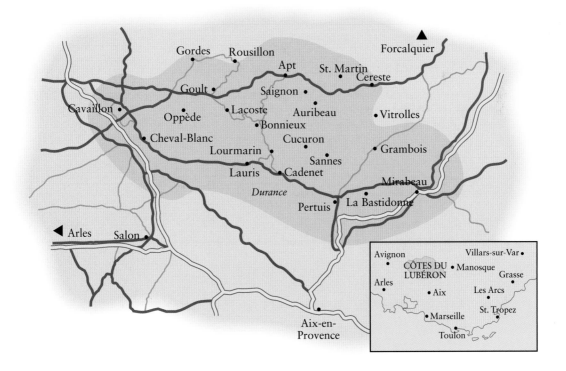

A nature reserve has been established in Montagne de Lubéron with plenty of forested areas, and is most definitely worth a visit. Côtes du Lubéron is one of the loveliest and most tranquil areas in all of Provence, which has also made numerous writers and artists settle here. Albert Camus is now a permanent resident – in the cemetery in Lourmarin.

Here, tourism seems to have a slightly more al fresco character than throughout the rest of Provence. Lubéron is simply a great place for enjoying nature, whether by car or foot.

The wines from Côtes du Lubéron, like the wines from Côtes du Ventoux, are somewhere in between Rhône wines and genuine Provençal wines. The climate is somewhat cooler than in the Rhône, which is also why they harvest later. The soil here is calcareous, but it can also contain lots of clay or sand. They produce white, red and rosé wines, and they must all be at least 11% proof. They can produce no more than 50 hl per ha, and the yearly production amounts to approximately 135,000 hl.

Unlike most of the other Provençal districts, Côtes du Lubéron is not traditionally considered a wine producing area, and the improved quality of wine is quite recent. Whereas they used to plant vines in the fat, flat stretches of land, and fruit trees on the mountainsides, these days, they have fortunately changed it around, which has improved the result greatly.

You get the best wines at private vineyards; however, the co-operatives actually produce 90% of the wines in this district. Their red and rosé wines are primarily based on Mourvèdre, Cinsault, Grenache, Syrah and Carignan and they are allowed to add the following: Counoise, Picpoul, Gamay and Pinot Noir – it is the only place in Provence that the two well known Burgundy-grapes, Gamay and Pinot Noir, are allowed, which signifies that this area is indeed a little different from the other districts.

The white wines are frequently also the best wines and they are based on Clairette, Grenache Blanc, Ugni Blanc, Rolle and Bourboulenc, however they also use Rousanne Blanc and Marsanne. These wines are light and fruity and with only a few exceptions, they should be enjoyed when young. However, as with all rules, there are important exceptions: only a few kilometres outside Bonnieux, you find Château de la Canorgue, where they produce one of the *appellation*'s

best cask-matured red wines based on Syrah. It is a robust wine that must be left to mature for some years before it will reveal all of its many qualities.

At Château de la Canorgue they strive to grow their vines organically, though they are not afraid to use modern technology. This vineyard was made famous when the film director Ridley Scott shot 'A Good Year' here in 2006. From the front of the property, beneath the mighty chestnut trees, there is a fantastic view of the ruins of Château de Lacoste, where the Marquis de Sade settled in 1771. The Marquis' excesses with prostitutes from Marseilles did not go down well with the Provençal Parliament, who condemned him to death. He did however manage to escape to Italy, only to return to Lacoste again. His torment – so to speak – was far from over and he was once again forced to leave his beloved château.

Château de l'Isolette is quite close to Château de la Canorgue and

they also produce excellent red wines matured in oak wood – again it is Syrah that provides the great results and in the fields around Isolette you find gnarled Syrah-vines that go as far back as 1916. The cellars at Isolette are filled with oak casks and it is an impressive sight to behold.

The district also offers many charming towns, of which Gordes is the best known, but Bonnieux is most certainly also worth a stopover or two for a wine tourist. It is a picturesque mountain village with narrow streets, pressing itself up against a very steep mountainside. From here you have an amazing view of the surrounding orchards, olive groves and vineyards and you can just glimpse Mount Ventoux in the far horizon. From Bonnieux, you can explore the nature reserve or cross to the south of the mountain range. The most beautiful area is to the north of Montagne de Lubéron. And don't forget, there is a bustling Saturday market in Apt, a village close to Bonnieux.

Producers in Côtes du Lubéron

Château de l'Isolette
84400 Apt
Phone: 0490 741670
pinatel@chateau-isolette.com

Château de Clapier
84120 Mirabeau
Phone: 0490 770103
www.chateau-de-clapier.com
chateau-de-clapier@wanadoo.fr

Château de Constantin-Chevalier
84160 Lourmarin
Phone: 0490 683899
allen.chevalier@wanadoo.fr

Château de Mille
84400 Apt
Phone: 0490 741194

Château la Canorgue
84480 Bonnieux
Phone: 0490 758101
j.pierremargan@wanadoo.fr

Château la Dorgonne
84240 La Tour d'Aigues
Phone: 0490 075018
www-chateauladorgonne.com
info@chateauladorgonne.com

Château la Sable
84160 Cucuron
Phone: 0490 772533

Château la Verrerie
84360 Puget-sur-Durance
Phone: 0490 083298
www.chateau-la-verrerie.fr
contact@chateau-la-verrerie.fr

Château Val-Joanis
84120 Pertuis
Phone: 0490 792077
www.val-joanis.com
info@val-joanis.com

Château de Marrenon
84240 La Tour d'Aigues
Phone: 0490774065

Clos de Baumelles
84120 Pertuis
Phone: 0490 292077
info@val-joanis.com

Clos Mirabeau
84120 Mirabeau
Phone: 0490 770026

Domaine Chasson
84220 Rousillon
Phone: 0490 056456
chateaublanc-chasson@wanadoo.fr

Domaine de Fontenille
84360 Lauris
Phone: 0490 082336
www.domaine-fontenille.com
domaine.fontenille@wanadoo.fr

Domaine de la Cavale
84160 Curcuron
Phone: 0490 772296
www.domaine-la-cavale.com
domaine-cavale@wanadoo.fr

Domaine de la Citadelle
84560 Ménerbes
Phone: 0490 724158
www.domaine-citadelle.com
contact@domaine-citadelle.com

Domaine de la Garelle
84580 Oppède
Phone: 0490 723120
www.lagarelle.fr
Christophe@lagarelle.fr

Domaine de Mayol
84440 Apt
Phone: 0490 741280
domaine.mayol@free.fr

Domaine de Régusse
04860 Pierrevert
Phone: 0492 723044

L'Excellence d'Amédée
84240 La Tour d'Aigues
Phone: 0490 074065
marrenon@marrenon.com

VENTOUX

Ventoux, also known as Côtes du Ventoux, is a large district, located in between Vaison-la-Romaine to the north and Apt to the south, covering approximately 7,000 ha. To the west you have Gigondas and several more of the well-known towns in the Rhône. To the south the district borders on Côtes du Lubéron. The vineyards are at the foot of the 1912 m high mountain, *Mont Ventoux*, which has given its name to the *appellation*. The yearly production amounts to 230,000 hl. The north side of the mountain is steep and covered with trees, scrub and lavender, while most of the vineyards are situated on the smoother, warmer south side, which is also notably easier to access.

The climate is cooler than in the Rhône because of the cold, gushing winds that blow down the mountain – *Mont Ventoux* simply means the wind-swept mountain. The most important of these winds is the *mistral*, which blows 130 days a year and it reaches speeds as high as 200 km per hour. Because of the cold winds, spring arrives later and autumn earlier than in the neighbouring districts.

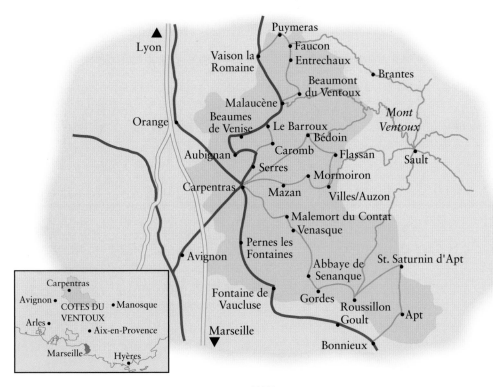

You can trek to the top of Mont Ventoux from several places and experience the amazing difference in climate and vegetation as you climb higher and higher. The trek starts in traditional Mediterranean vegetation, i.e. pine or oak woods, thyme and rosemary, but then many hours later, when you reach the naked mountaintop you find plants such as the yellow arctic poppy. Up here, you can also feel the strength of the gusting winds, and when it really blows a gale, the top of the mountain is practically inaccessible. It is most definitely cold at the top.

Cycling fanatics of all ages want to ride up the mountain; only they do not necessarily look as if they enjoy the ride. Perhaps they fail to remember that the British cyclist, Tom Simpson, dropped dead on his way up Ventoux in 1967 when Tour de France decided to include the mountain in the route (in which case they will be reminded as they pass his memorial stone on the way up).

Needless to say, the most comfortable way to get up the mountain is by car or to take your time exploring the area with all its gorges, rock formations, springs, plateaus and pretty villages when trekking. *Gorges de la Nesque* cuts through the rocks to the southeast and makes for a dramatic excursion with ravines dropping 300 m straight down in some places.

Malaucène, Bédoin, Brantes and Sault are charming and lovely villages that are all useful as a base for your trek up Mont Ventoux. They are quiet and not at all touristy. You feel far removed from the hustle and bustle of life in the seaside towns and it is a great place to wind down.

The mountain seems oddly disconnected from any other mountain ranges, although technically, it is part of the Alps. It rises in lonely majesty towards the sky and from its top, you have an absolutely amazing view of the local surroundings, the River Rhône and the Alps. In clear weather, you can almost see the Mediterranean. The top of Mont Ventoux is white and it looks as if it is covered in snow all year round. In winter, and in fact until late spring, there is indeed much snow, which affords you the opportunity to go skiing. However, in summer it is the loose, white limestone that plays tricks on the eye. At the turn of the 19th century, there were hardly any trees left, and it is only thanks to successful forestry that the mountainsides are once again covered in trees wherever they manage to take root. Many of the trees have been imported from abroad, for instance you will find lots

of evergreen cedars from the Atlas Mountains in North Africa. The forests are home to a highly diverse plant and animal life, which the locals take great advantage of – for one thing, the oak woods supply the Friday market in Carpentras with truffles all winter. There are so many truffles here that the market in Carpentras accounts for half the truffles sold in the whole of France.

Vaucluse, and especially the areas around Sault to the southeast of Mont Ventoux, is where you find the greatest concentration of lavender fields in France: they account for approximately 40% of the country's entire production. It is too cold to grow vines, but lavender thrives here, which is also why the surrounding landscape looks more or less blue all summer. The farmers around Sault have specialised in growing the rare grain, lesser spelt, which is used in soups among other things. Producing honey is another important line of work in this area and you will find numerous beehives along the edge of every lavender field.

On the mountain's north side, there are plenty of lime trees and tea is made from the flowers that are harvested in early July. This is also the time for the *fêtes de tilleul* in Buis-les-Baronnies.

Wine growing has become increasingly important to Ventoux, where their most important crops used to be cherries, grapes for eating (Muscat), apricots, asparagus, tomatoes and melons. They were awarded an AOC in 1973, which meant serious business for the district. The 16 co-operatives in the area have approximately 4,000 members and they produce 90% of the wine. Their main product is red wine, but they do produce a fair amount of rosé and a few white wines. The yearly production is around 315,000 hl. The red and rosé wines are primarily based on Grenache, Syrah, Cinsault, Mourvèdre and Carignan. They are also allowed to use Picpoul Noir, Counoise, Clairette, Bourboulenc, Grenache Blanc and Roussanne. For the white wines they use Clairette, Bourboulenc, Grenache Blanc and a little Roussanne. The co-operatives mostly produce light, bright, fresh and fruity red wines, which should be enjoyed within a year or two. This is a fairly obvious choice because the climate rarely allows the grapes to ripen sufficiently to give the wines the power and level of alcohol they would otherwise need. The wines are produced *en café* – leaving skins and must to ferment for no more than 48 hours – after which they are bottled and ready for consumption. These are uncomplicated wines, highly suitable to be enjoyed in a local café on a hot summer evening, slightly chilled, but it has to be said, they do not posses much of a personality. On the other hand, the 70 or so privately owned vineyards produce several remarkable wines. The red wines from the best vineyards are left to macerate longer than others, which is how they obtain the deeply red colour and sweetness that you also find in the better wines from neighbouring districts. This especially holds true for wines from the western part of Ventoux, around Carpentras, while wines from the eastern part will often be somewhat lighter. The full-bodied red wines will often benefit from being left to mature for 3–4 years or sometimes even longer. The white wines will often be sympathetic, crisp and display some of the freshness that other Provençal white wines often lack. You can also find nice and attractive rosé wines. In fact, generally speaking, if you make an effort, you can find lots of excellent wines at very reasonable prices in Ventoux.

Many of the vineyards are situated quite high up, some over 400 m above sea level, which makes it almost impossible for the grapes to ripen fully. Many of the fields consist of dry and not particularly great soil, some of them look red due to a high presence of ochre, or they will appear gravelly and calcareous.

Only a handful of the privately owned vineyards really stand out from the rest and the best vineyard is perhaps Château Pesquie in Mormoiron, which used to belong to the family of the famous Provençal writer, Alphonse Daudet. The Château's fields are situated between 250 and 350 m above sea level. Its cellars were renovated and modernised in 1990 and now they contain lots of new equipment, including stainless steel vats, and there is room for 300 *barriques* (small oak casks). All their wines are excellent. One of their particularly delicious and attractive white wines is based on Viognier. Their red wines are primarily based on Grenache and Syrah, with Syrah as the increasingly dominant grape as you work you way through the cuvees. Their flagship is called Quintessence and consists of 80% Syrah and 20% Grenache. It is a dark wine with a lovely sweetness, a hint of oak and dried herbs and of course the Syrah's characteristically peppery tones. Left to mature for a few years, this wine truly exemplifies exactly how much can be achieved in Ventoux. Increasing the proportion of Syrah grapes seems to be a general tendency at most of the better vineyards.

Producers in Ventoux

Cave de Lumières
84220 Goult
Phone: 0490 722004
www.cavedelumieres.com
info@cavedelumieres.com

Cave Saint-Marc
84330 Caromb
Phone: 0490 624024
www.cave-saint-marc.fr
contact@cave-saint-marc.fr

Château Blanc
84220 Roussillon
Phone: 0490 056456
www.chasson-chateaublanc.fr
chateaublanc-chasson@wanadoo.fr

Château Juvenal
84190 Beaumes-de-Venise
Phone: 0490 769001
vignerons@beaumes-de-venise.com

Château Pesquie
84570 Mormoiron
Phone: 0490 619408
www.chateaupesquie.com
contact@chateaupesquie.com

Château Valcombe
84330 Saint-Pierre-de-Vassols
Phone: 0490 625129

Domaine Aymard
84200 Carpentras
Phone: 0490 633532
jeanmarie.aymard@free.fr

Domaine de Bérane
84570 Mormoiron
Phone: 0490 617732
domainedeberane@wanadoo.fr

Domaine de Champ-Long
84340 Entrechaux
Phone: 0490 460158
www.champlong.com
domaine@champlong.fr

Domaine de Chantegrillet
84220 Roussillon
Phone: 0490 057483
guiton.eric@orange.fr

Domaine de Chaumard
84330 Caromb
Phone: 0490 624338

Domaine de Fenouillet
84190 Beaumes-de-Venise
Phone: 0490 629561
www.domaine-fenouillet.fr
contact@domaine-fenouillet.fr

Domaine de Fondrèche
84380 Mazan
Phone: 0490 696142
www.fondreche.com
contact@fondreche.com

Domaine de Font Alba
84400 Apt
Phone: 0490 744812
fontalba@tiscali.fr

Domaine de la Bastidonne
84220 Cabrières-d'Avignon
Phone: 0490 767000
www.vin-bastidonne.com
domaine.bastidonne@orange.fr

Domaine de la Massane
84410 Bédoin
Phone: 0490 656081

Domaine de la Verrière
84220 Goult
Phone: 0490 722088
laverriere2@wanadoo.fr

Domaine de Marotte
84200 Carpentras
Phone: 0490 634327
www.marottevins.fr
marotte@wanadoo.fr

Domaine de Repaire du Géant
84380 Mazan
Phone: 0490 698193
www.repairedugeant.com
contact@repairedugeant.com

Domaine de Solence
84380 Mazan
Phone: 0490 605531
www.solence.fr
domaine@terres-de-solence.com

Domaine de Tara
84220 Roussillon
Phone: 0490 057328
www.domainedetara.com
domainedetara@orange.fr

Domaine des Anges
84570 Mormoiron
Phone: 0490 618878

Domaine du Coulet Rouge
84602 Valréas
Phone: 0490 419142
france@enclavedespapes.fr

Domaine du Grand Jacquet
84380 Mazan
Phone: 0490 632487
www.domaine-grandjacquet.com
contact@domaine-grandjacquet.com

Domaine la Coquillade
84400 Gargas
Phone: 0490 745467

Domaine Pelisson
84220 Gordes
Phone: 0490 722849

La Courtoise
84210 Saint-Didier
Phone: 0490 660115
cave.la.courtoise@wanadoo.fr

La Ferme Saint Pierre
84410 Flassan
Phone: 0490 618095

La Vieille Ferme
84100 Orange
Phone: 0490 111200
www.lavieilleferme.com
mperrin@vinsperrin.com

Les Roches Blanches
84570 Mormoiron
Phone: 0490 618007

Les Vignerons de Canteperdrix
84380 Mazan
Phone: 0490 697031
oenologue@cotes-du-ventoux.com

Martinelle
84190 Lafare
Phone: 0490 650556
www.martinelle.com
info@martinelle.com

Saint Auspice
84405 Apt
Phone: 0490 749584
sylla@sylla.fr

Terra Ventoux
84570 Villes-sur-Auzon
Phone: 0490 618007
www.terraventoux.fr
a.fournier@cave-terraventoux.com

Vieux Clocher
84190 Vacqueyras
Phone: 0490 658418
info@arnoux-vins-com

COTEAUX DE PIERREVERT

This district sits in one of the most elevated locations in all of France. It belongs to the department of Alpes-de-Haute-Provence and covers approximately 210 ha and 42 municipalities. In reality though, only 10 municipalities produce wine.

Haute-Provence is a thinly populated and highly picturesque district. Both landscape and climate are very different from what you would expect in Provence, in winter for instance, there can be quite severe frost. This is why you encounter fewer olive trees here, and in many places they grow grain, corn, apples, pears and vegetables, rather than vines. Here you find huge and dense oak woods, occasionally interrupted by grey-violet lavender, yellow broom and wild flowers.

You also get outstanding lamb and delicate goat's cheeses from the mountain villages, and every spring, sheep and goats are herded through the towns up to the lush, dark-green pastures on the mountainsides.

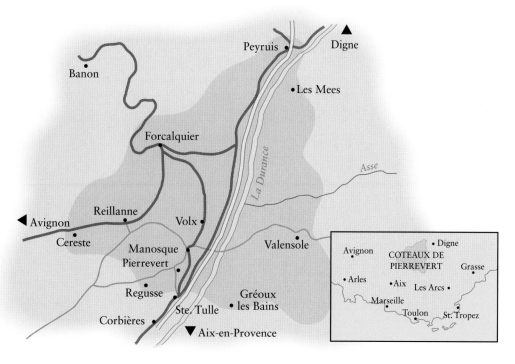

The vineyards are mainly situated around the sleepy little town of Pierrevert, also home to the co-operative, which for a number of years was the only producer in the area. The yearly production is around 60,000 hl and they produce red, white, rosé and sparkling wine. Coteaux de Pierrevert was awarded a VDSQ in 1959 and it was not until 1998 that they became members of the coveted AOC club. The majority of wines come from left bank of the Durance (Corbières, Pierrevert, Manosque, Sainte-Tulle and Les Mées).

The mountain wines are fresh and low in alcohol, and they are highly affordable. The wine growers are not allowed to produce more than 50 hl per ha and the wines must be at least 11% proof. The white wines are based on Clairette, Ugni Blanc and Marsanne, while the red are based on Grenache, Carignan, Cinsault, Mourvèdre, Terret Noir, Oeillade and Syrah.

The district's largest town, Manosque, is just a stone's throw from Pierrevert and even in winter it is a lively, charming place. Furthermore, it is an excellent base if you want to explore another of the pretty villages in Haute-Provence, Forcalquier, or the bright blue mountain lake, *Lac de Sainte-Croix*, situated by the dramatically steep *Grand Canyon du Verdon*. Manosque was also home to the famous Provençal author Jean Giono, who lived here all his life while writing stories about the modest lifestyle in highland Provence.

PRODUCERS IN PIERREVERT

Cave des Vignerons de Manosque
04100 Manosque
Phone: 0492 720146

Cave des Vignerons de Pierrevert
04860 Pierrevert
Phone: 0492 721906
www.cave-pierrevert.com
cave.pierrevert@wanadoo.fr

Château de Rousset
04800 Gréoux-les-Bains
Phone: 0492 726249

Domaine de Régusse
04860 Pierrevert
Phone: 0492 723044
www.domaine-de-regusse.com
contact@domaine-de-regusse.com

Domaine la Blaque
04860 Pierrevert
Phone: 0492 723971
www.domainelablaque.fr
domaine.lablaque@wanadoo.fr

DEFINITIONS OF TERMS

AOC: *Appellation d'Origine Contrôlé* is a geographical guarantee of origin. The best French wines belong to this category, but foodstuffs can also be awarded an AOC as many cheeses and the olive oil from Nyons bear witness.

Alpes-de-Haute-Provence: Provençal department.

Alpes-Maritimes: Provençal department.

Bandol: Independent AOC-district within the department of Var.

Barrique: Oak casks that hold 225 litres.

Bellet: Independent AOC-district within the department of Alpes-Maritimes.

Brut: *Appellation* used for dry sparkling wines

Cassis: Independent AOC-district within the department of Bouches-du-Rhône.

Cave: Wine cellar.

Celts: An Indo-European people who used to inhabit most of France, but today they live only in Brittany.

Cépage: Type of grape.

Co-operative: A union of wine producers.

Coteaux d'Aix-en-Provence: Independent AOC-district within the departments of Bouches-du-Rhône and Var.

Coteaux de Pierrevert: Independent AOC-district within the department of Haute-Alpes.

Coteaux Varois: Independent AOC-district within the department of Var.

Coteaux: Small hills or slopes.

Côtes du Lubéron: Independent AOC-district within the department of Vaucluse.

Côtes de Provence: Independent AOC-district within the departments of Var, Alpes-Maritimes and Bouches-du-Rhône.

Côtes: Cliffs or slopes.

Cuve: Container for the fermentation of wine.

Cuvée: The contents of a cuve.

Dégustation: Tasting.

Eau-de-vie: Schnapps.

Foudres: Large oak casks used to store wine, a Provençal speciality.

Garrigue: Type of vegetation found in the Mediterranean, a low, dense, soft-leaved, evergreen bush affected by the grazing of both sheep and goats.

Grafting: The splicing of two different plants that will be able to grow together.

Gris de gris: Bright rosé wine based on grapes with the addition of 'gris', in the shape of Grenache Gris or Cinsault Gris, by way of example.

Ha: Hectare, square measure of 10,000 m².

Hautes-Alpes: Provençal department.

Herbicide: Pesticide.

Hl: Hectolitre, cubic measure of 100 litres.

Hybrid: A cross of two different species of vines. No longer permissible in France.

INAO: *Institut National des Appellations d'Origine.* The official organization in charge of the AOC and VDQS *appellations*.

Les Baux-de-Provence: Independent AOC-district within the department of Bouches-du-Rhône.

Macération Carbonique: A specific method for producing wine whereby the fermentation process is initiated inside the grapes. It produces fruity wines low in tannins.

Maquis: Evergreen Mediterranean vegetation consisting of bushes that grow as high as 2–4 m or little trees and together they form dense scrubs. The most common types are kermes oak, holm oak, strawberry tree, *Erica arborea* and myrtle. The dense *maquis* is rich in wildlife but houses only few different plants. In clearings though, you might find a rich supply of spring-blossoming bulbous plants or herbs. *Maquis* is predominately found in coastal areas and those areas have usually been subjected to severe felling, burning or grazing.

Midi-area: Normally would include the entire area south of Lyon, but among wine connoisseurs it usually only refers to the western part of the French Mediterranean including the vineyards in Languedoc and Roussillon.

Microclimate: A very local climate, sometimes dependent on the structure of the soil or the angle of sunlight.

Mise en bouteille au Domaine/Château: The wine is bottled at the site of production.

Mistral: Cold, dry and very strong wind that comes from the north and sweeps through the Rhône Valley. It usually lasts for 1,3,6 or 9 consecutive days.

Négociant: Wine merchant, who buys up wine from the vineyards or co-operatives.

Oenology: Knowledge of wine and how it is produced.

Oidium tuckeri: American mould fungus that made its way to France through England in the mid-20th century.

Organic wine: Wine produced without the use of artificial fertilisers and pesticides. In practise though, you can only strive to cultivate wines in strict adherence to these principles.

Oxidising: Most commonly used about flat and dull white or rosé wines when they have been exposed to oxygen.

Palette: Independent AOC-district on the perimeter of Aix-en-Provence.

Pétillant: Slightly sparkling.

Phoenicians: Ancient Semitic civilisation known as great tradesmen.

Phylloxera vastatrix: American wine louse that ravaged the European vineyards in the late 19th century.

Pichet: Jug used to serve wine in restaurants and cafés.

Pieds-Noirs: Blackfeet. Expression used to describe the Frenchmen who repatriated from Algeria after independence.

Plasmopara viticola: Mould fungus from America.

Racking: After the initial fermentation, the wine is poured into other vats, which gets rid of old yeast cells.

Récolte: Wine harvest.

Restanques: Terraces supported by stone structures. They help prevent erosion and enable wine growers to cultivate wine on steep mountainsides.

Saignée: (Bleeding) a Provençal method of producing rosé wine, where the skins of black grapes are left in the must for 4–24 hours, which is how rosé wine achieves its colouring.

Souche: The foot of the vine.

Sulphur: A disinfectant used against fungus attacks in the fields and added to wine as sulphuric acid.

Tannic acid: Primarily found in the pips and skin of the grapes, it help preserve wine. Young wines with a high content of tannins can appear a little coarse while older wines with rounded tannins are soft and pleasant.

Var: Provençal department.

Vaucluse: Provençal department.

VDQS: *Vin Délimité de Qualité Supérieur.* A guarantee of origin that is easier to obtain than an AOC.

Vendanges: Wine harvest.

Ventoux: Independent AOC-district within the department of Vaucluse.

Vieilles vignes: Old vines. Often they yield a smaller quantity, but the grapes are often of a very high quality.

Vignes: vines.

Vigneron: Wine farmer.

Vin cuit: Wine that is quite like a liqueur made by concentrating the must by boiling.

Vin de cépage: Wine made from a single grape.

Vin de Pays: A guarantee of origin. Awarded to wines produced within a limited area, easier to obtain than a VDQS.

Vin de Table Francais: The lowest category of French wines.

Vrac: Wines that are not bottled but sold in bulk.

Yeast cells: Yeast fungi are one-celled organisms and also known as yeast cells.

BIBLIOGRAPHY

Attenborough, David: *The First Eden*. Little Brown and Company, 1987.

Beauchamp, Philippe: *Côte d'Azur – Mer & Montagne*. Editions Gilletta, 2005.

Biehn, Michel: *Les Meilleures Recettes de Provence*. Flammarion, 2002.

Boesgaard, Lars: *Provence*, Gyldendal 2006.

Bousquet-Duquesne, Elisabeth: *L'Âme des Maisons Provençales*. Editions Ouest-France, 2004.

Brennan, Georgeanne: *Savoring France*. Oxmoor House, 1999.

Brown, Erica: *Gastronomisk Rejse i Provence*. Gads Forlag, 1996.

Carrier, Robert: *Feasts of Provence*. Weidenfeld and Nicholson, 1992.

Conseil Géneral du Var: *Carnets du Patrimoine 1-4*, 2005.

Courtot, Roland et Rinaudo, Yves: *Le Guide du Var*. Editions La Manufacture, 1992.

Cros, Phillippe: *Painters of Provence*. Flammarion, 2000.

Domenge, Georges: *Cuisine de Tradition du Var et des Alpes du Sud*. Edisud, 1993.

Duck, Nöelle: *La Maison Provençale*. Flammarion, 2001.

Duplessy, Bernard: *Poteries et Faiences de Provence*. Aubanel, 2002.

Fabiani, Gilbert: *Mémoires de la Lavande*. Equinoxe, 2002.

Fauque, Claude: *Couleurs & Étoffes – une Passion Provençale*. Aubanel. 2005.

Ferniot, Christine: *Provence en Objets*. Aubanel, 2003.

Forbes, Leslie: *A Table in Provence*. Penguin Books, 1990.

Fortuné, Nadège: *Les Cuisines de la Provence*. Editions Campanile, 1998.

George, Rosemary: *French Country Wines*. Faber and Faber, 1990.

Girard-Lagorce, Sylvie: *Traditions Provençales*. Flammarion, 2001.

Grégoire, Fabian: *Habitat Traditionel en Provence*. Editions Equinoxe, 2005.

Guide Bleu: *Provence, Alpes, Côte d'Azur*. Hachette, 1987.

Jouanin, Francie: *A Taste of Provence*. Könemann, 2005

Le Foll, Nathalie: *Le Sel*. Editions du Chêne, 1997.

Le Guide Hachette des Vins de France. Hachette, 1989–2012.

Le Guide Vert Côte d'Azur og Provence. Michelin, 2000.

Livingstone-Learmonth, John: *The Wines of the Rhône*. Faber & Faber, 1992.

Lorgues, Christiane et René: *Provence de la Vigne et des Vins*. Editions Serre, 1990.

Lorgues, René: *Côtes de Provence, Vins et Vignerons*. Editions Serre, 1993.

Luret, Nicolas: *Guide des Vins de Provence*. Editions Jeanne Lafitte, 1994.

Maureau, Andrée: *Recettes en Provence*. Edisud, 1992.

Mayle, Peter: *Provence A–Z*. Alfred A. Knopf, 2006.

Olney, Richard: *The Beautiful Cookbook*. Harper Collins 1999.

Parker, Robert: *Wines of the Rhône Valley*. Dorling Kindersley, 1997.

Pouzadoux, Fabien: *Sur la Route des Côtes de Provence*. Editions CF, 1990.

Robinson, Jancis: *The Oxford Companion to Wine*. 2nd and 3rd editions, Oxford University Press, 1999 and 2006

Saint George, Amelia: *Provence – the Tradition of Craft and Design*. Conran Octopus, 2000.

Scheibli, Isabelle: *Faiences et Poteries Provençales*. A. Scheibli Editions, 1996.

Silvester, Hans: *Provence, Terre de Lavande*. Aubanel, 2004.

Silvioni, Marie: *Le Var*. Editions Gilletta, 2005.

Van Gogh, Vincent: *Breve fra Provence*. Gyldendal, 1995.

Venture, Rémi: *Provence*. Editions Hazan, 2001.

INDEX

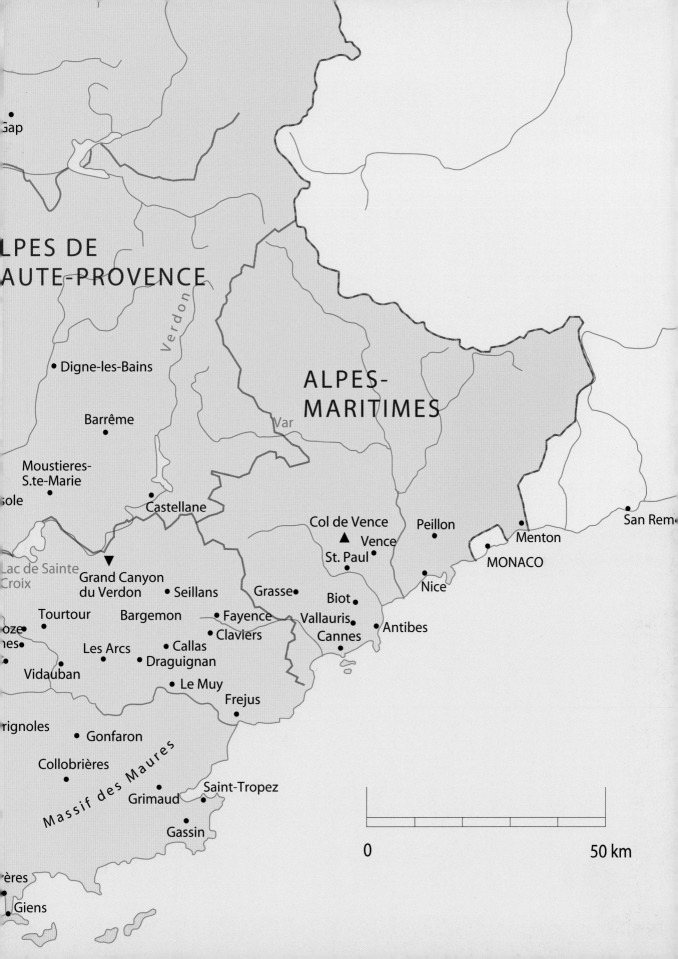

PROVENCE

Published in the UK in 2013 by Clearview Books
11 Grosvenor Crescent, London SW1X 7EE

© 2011 Lars Boesgaard
© 2013 English language text Clearview Books
© Photography Lars Boesgaard

Tine Duch photographed the finished dishes on pages: 25, 34, 47, 79,
102 (below left), 106, 117 (below right), 124, 136 (below left), 140 (below left),
161, 166 (below right), 190 (above left and below right), 224 (below),
249 (above right), 274 (left), 276 (right), 278 (middle) and 286

First published in Danish by Gyldendal A/S, Copenhagen in 2011

A CIP record for ths book is available from the British Library.
ISBN 978 1 908337 160

English translation: Iben Philipsen
Production: Simonne Waud
Editor: Catharine Snow
Copy Editor: Lucy King

Printed in China